Evangelical Lutheran Ministerium

Jubilee Memorial Volume of the Danville Conference

of the Evangelical Lutheran Ministerium of Pennsylvania and Adjacent States

Evangelical Lutheran Ministerium

Jubilee Memorial Volume of the Danville Conference
of the Evangelical Lutheran Ministerium of Pennsylvania and Adjacent States

ISBN/EAN: 9783337103781

Printed in Europe, USA, Canada, Australia, Japan

Cover: Foto ©ninafisch / pixelio.de

More available books at **www.hansebooks.com**

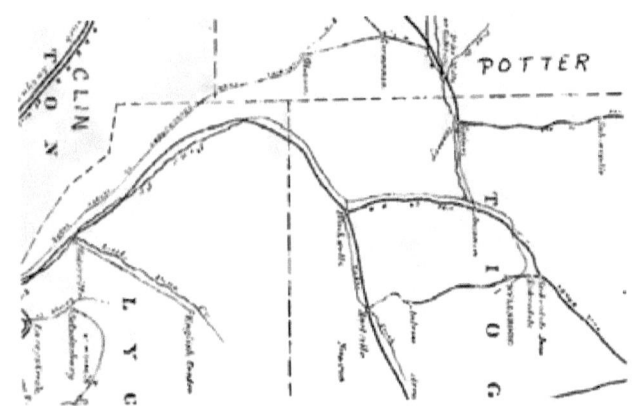

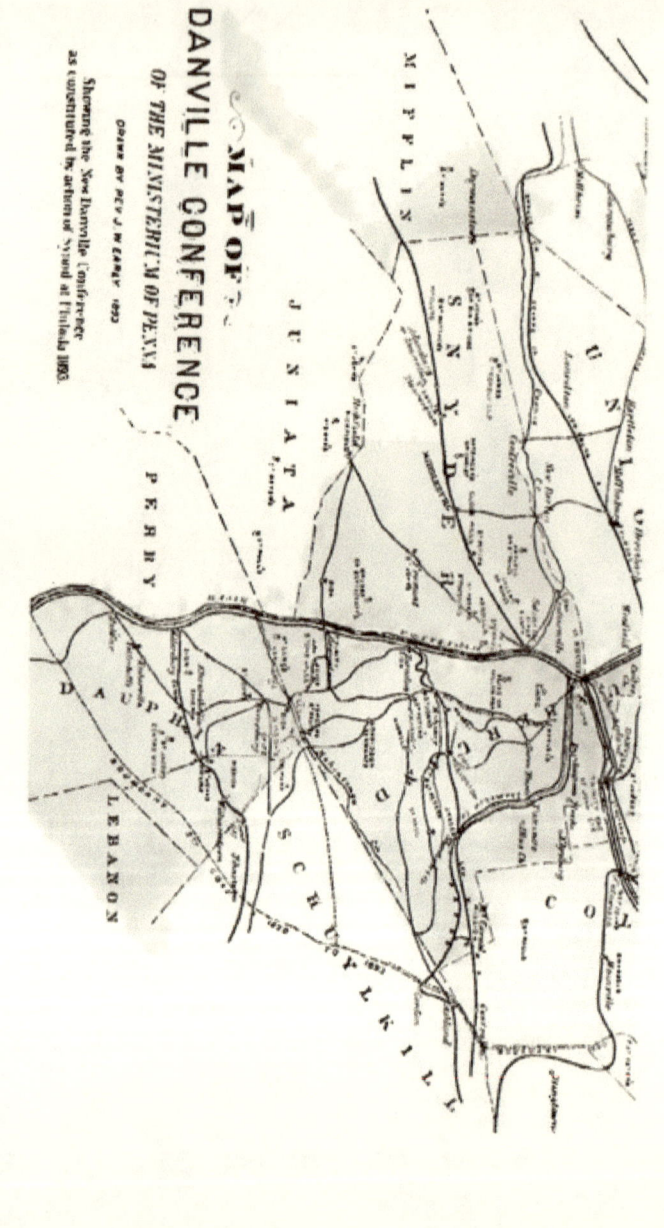

JUBILEE MEMORIAL VOLUME

OF THE

DANVILLE CONFERENCE

OF THE

EVANGELICAL LUTHERAN MINISTERIUM OF PENNSYLVANIA

AND ADJACENT STATES

EDITED BY
REV. S. E. OCHSENFORD, D.D.,
AND
REV. O. E. PFLUEGER, A.M.

PUBLISHED BY THE
DANVILLE CONFERENCE.
1898.

REMEMBER THE DAYS OF OLD, CONSIDER THE YEARS OF MANY GENERATIONS.—Deut. 32 : 7.

PREFACE.

AT THE CONVENTION of the Danville Conference, held at Jersey Shore, Pa., May 4-5, 1897, action was taken looking to a proper participation in the Jubilee Celebration of Synod, which action was in part:

"That this Conference elect a committee of three which shall be known as the 'Jubilee Committee of the Danville Conference,' and shall continue in office until the $9,000 apportioned by Synod to this Conference towards the Jubilee Fund shall have been raised, or until Conference shall otherwise discharge the same."

Amongst other duties this Committee was "charged with the publication of a History of the Danville Conference and its Congregations, together with biographical sketches of some of the early pastors who labored on the territory of the Conference, and a brief account of the Jubilee Celebration of 1898."

The Revs. O. E. Pflueger, S. E. Ochsenford, D.D., and E. L. Reed were elected this Committee. The Rev. Reed having resigned from the Committee, October, 1897, the work has since been carried on by the other two members.

After months of painstaking labor, it affords special pleasure to the Committee now to present to Conference and the Church, this "Jubilee Memorial Volume of the Danville Conference." The department of Biography was modified so as to include brief sketches of *all* pastors who have labored on the territory of this Conference, as well as of the pastors and present students of theology who hail from the same. Instead of the "brief account of the Jubilee Celebration," as was at first contemplated, we present to the readers a *full* account, with each address delivered complete.

The Committee makes grateful acknowledgment of the helpfulness of the Muhlenberg College Book and the Pennsylvania College Book, in the preparation of some of the biographical sketches, of material furnished by the Rev. J. W. Early, and incorporated in other sketches than those which bear his signature, and of the use of the portrait cuts as they appear in the account of the Jubilee Celebration, through the kindness of the Central Jubilee Committee.

May this Volume find a place in each Lutheran home on the territory of this Conference. May it serve to instruct and edify the believers and do honor and glory to God.

THE COMMITTEE.

CONTENTS.

I. CONFERENCE HISTORY.

	PAGE.
Introductory Statement	11-15
Sixth Conference	16-17
Fifth Conference	18-21
Danville Conference	22-24
Table of Conventions and Officers	25-28

II. CONGREGATIONAL HISTORIES.

Beavertown Parish	31-38
Berwick Parish	39-51
Catawissa, St. John's	52-56
Cogan Station, St. Michael's	57-59
Danville, Trinity	60-64
Danville, German Parish	65-71
Dushore Parish	72-77
Freeburg Parish	78-88
Jersey Shore, Zion	89-90
Lykens, St. John's	91-94
Lykens Valley Parish	95-106
Mahanoy Parish	107-117
Mainville Parish	118-124
Numidia Parish	125-132
Richfield Parish	133-135
St. John's, Lykens Valley	136-142
St. Peter's, Mahanoy	143-145
Salem, Snyder County	146-150
Selinsgrove Parish	151-160
Shamokin Parish	161-167
Stone Valley Parish	168-175
Sunbury, St. Luke's	176-179

Trevorton Parish.................................... 180-187
Turbotville Parish................................... 188-192
Williamsport, St. Mark's............................. 193-198
Williamsport, South, Christ.......................... 199-200

III. BIOGRAPHIES.

Alphabetical Arrangement............................. 201-290

IV. JUBILEE CELEBRATION.

Inception and Preparation............................ 293-296
German Jubilee Service: Jubilee Address.............   296
    Greeting from New York Ministerium..........   310
English Jubilee Service: Jubilee Address............   317
Open Air Service: The Ministerium...................   333
    Greeting from General Council...............   342
    The College of the Ministerium..............   346
    The Theological Seminary of the Ministerium.   357

PORTRAITS.

Conference Map, Frontispiece.

	PLATE.	PAGE.		PLATE.	PAGE.
Albert, J. J.,	I.	29	Pflueger, O. E.,	X.	243
Altpeter, P.,	XI.	249	Raker, J. H.,	XII.	263
Anspach, J. M.,	VI.	125	Reber, O.,	IX.	201
Bahl, Isaiah,	I.	29	Reed, D. E.,	V.	107
Barr, W. P.,	XIII.	283	Reed, E. L.,	VI.	125
Bayer, J. F.,	III.	57	Renninger, J. S.,	V.	107
Bergner, A.,	II.	39	Rick, W. F.,	XII.	263
Bruning, H. H.,	IV.	95	Rickert, W. H.,	VI.	125
Clymer, H. T.,	VIII.	161	Ritter, J. H.,	IX.	201
Cornman, W. O.,	V.	107	Roney, W. E.,	X.	243
Druckenmiller, G. D.,	XI.	249	Sander, J.,	VII.	151
Drumheller, C. K.,	VIII.	161	Schaeffer, G. J.,	X.	243
Dry, C. F.,	VIII.	161	Scheffer, N.,	IX.	201
Early, J. W.,	IV.	95	Scheirer, O. S.,	X.	243
Eggers, L. G.,	II.	39	Schindel, Jer.,	II.	39
Erle, C. L.,	I.	29	Schindel, J. P., Jr.,	II.	39
Erlenmeyer, C. G.,	II.	39	Schindel, J. P., Sr.,	I.	29
Eyer, W. J.,	I.	29	Snable, H. G.,	XI.	249
Fogelman, D. L.,	X.	243	Steck, T.,	III.	57
Geiger, W. H.,	VIII.	161	Stetler, D. M.,	VI.	125
German, J. P.,	VII.	151	Stetler, E.,	XII.	263
Groff, J. R.,	IV.	95	Stetler, I. H.,	XII.	263
Hemping, J. N.,	I.	29	Strauss, A. M.,	IV.	95
Henkel, D. M.,	III.	57	Stupp, S. B.,	IX.	201
Henry, S. S.,	V.	107	Uhrich, J. M.,	VII.	151
Hillpot, Jos.,	V.	107	Ulrich, L. D.,	XIII.	283
Horne, A. R.,	IV.	95	Ulrich, W. S.,	XIII.	283
Klingler, J. W.,	IX.	201	Wagner, R. S.,	III.	57
Kopenhaver, W. M.,	XIII.	283	Wahrmann, H. E. C.,	XI.	249
Kunkle, G. G.,	VII.	151	Walz, F.,	III.	57
Laitzle, W. G.,	II.	39	Wampole, J. F.,	IV.	95
Lenker, M. B.,	V.	107	Weicksel, F. A.,	XI.	249
Lentz, A. P.,	XIII.	283	Weicksel, H.,	III.	57
Lindenstruth, L.,	VIII.	161	Weicksel, W.,	X.	243
Meyer, H.,	XII.	263	Wenrich, S.,	VI.	125
Miller, H. P.,	XIII.	283	Wetzler, J. N.,	VIII.	161
Neiman, J. H.,	VI.	125	Yount, A. L.,	VII.	151
Ochsenford, S. E.,	IX.	201	Zuber, T.,	XII.	263
Pflueger, A. P.,	VII.	151	Zweier, C. D.,	XI.	249

JUBILEE PORTRAITS.

Synodical group 291

A. Spaeth 298
G. C. F. Haas........... 311
J. A. Seiss.............. 316
J. Fry.................. 332
F. J. F. Schantz......... 336
E. F. Moldehnke........ 344
T. L. Seip.............. 348
H. E. Jacobs........... 356

I. Conference History.

HISTORY

OF THE

DANVILLE CONFERENCE

OF THE

Ministerium of Pennsylvania.

BY THE REV. S. E. OCHSENFORD, D.D.

THE Evangelical Lutheran Ministerium of Pennsylvania and Adjacent States was organized in St. Michael's church, Philadelphia, August 26 (N. S.), 1748, as "The Evangelical Lutheran Ministerium of North America." Prior to this time, pastoral conferences had been held, from time to time, as occasion required; but this was the first meeting of pastors and lay delegates at which a permanent organization was effected. At this first meeting there were present Pastors Henry Melchior Muhlenberg, Peter Brunnholtz and John Fr. Handschuh, and John Nicolaus Kurtz, who was ordained at this meeting; the Rev. John Sandin, provost of the Swedish churches, and the Rev. John Christian Hartwig, pastor of Lutheran congregations in the Province of New York, and lay representatives from ten congregations in Pennsylvania, together with Peter Kock, trustee of the Swedish church in Philadelphia. Although Sandin and Hartwig did not formally unite with the new Synod, they took an active part in the organization and in the proceedings of the first convention, and in so far represented the congregations under their pastoral and official care. The proceedings of this convention constitute an important chapter of Lutheran history, since we find in them the foundation principles of the Church, and the beginning of that which has become one of the strongest factors in its working machinery in this country. The Synod is the source whence have emanated the most far-reaching movements of church work in every department of activity, in the doctrine, worship and life of the congregations, and in the educational, missionary and benevolent operations of the same. It is the bond that unites all the congregations into one body, and gives force and proves helpful to the operations of the individual congregations.

At the time of the organization of the Ministerium, seventy-three Lutheran congregations existed in this country; but they were widely scattered from upper New York to Georgia, and could not be represented at this convention. Those uniting in the organization of the Ministerium were located in the Province of Pennsylvania, in what are now Philadelphia, Montgomery, Berks and Lancaster counties. It may prove of interest, in this connection, to mention the places from which delegates were sent to this meeting. These came from the congregations at Philadelphia, Germantown, Providence (Trappe), New Hanover, Upper Milford, Saccum, Tulpehocken, Northkill, Lancaster and Earltown (New Holland). In the course of a few years the number of congregations began to increase, and before many years had passed the territory of the Ministerium embraced Pennsylvania, New York, New Jersey, Maryland, Virginia, North Carolina and Ohio; and it was to all intents and purposes a general synodical body for all the Lutheran churches throughout the country.

From the statement made with reference to the first

meeting of the Ministerium, it will readily be seen that the territory, now embraced by the Danville Conference, was not represented. As early as 1748, it appears that no Lutherans had settled in sufficient numbers in this part of the Province to bring about the organization of congregations. Our people had, no doubt, begun to settle on this territory early in the century, as they generally were the van-guard of civilization in nearly all the earliest settlements in Pennsylvania. We know that German settlements all along the Susquehanna, in Central Pennsylvania, antedate the Revolutionary War; but we have no evidence of the presence of Lutheran ministers on this territory until the year 1775, when the Rev. John Michael Enderline began his occasional visits from Lykens Valley, and organized Lutheran congregations on the west side of the river, in the present Snyder county. These lines are written within two miles of the locality where one of the first congregations was organized, in 1775. Accordingly, more than a quarter of a century had elapsed after the organization of the Synod, before the territory of our Conference was represented in its annual conventions.

In the early history of the Ministerium, Conferences were held, and Conference districts were arranged; but it is only in later years that the Conferences have been permanently organized. Prior to the middle of the present century, Conference districts had been established, within whose bounds the pastors, later the pastors with their lay delegates, were expected to meet, as occasion might require, or as the Ministerium might determine from time to time, or at the call of the president of the Ministerium, or whenever requested by individual pastors or congregations. There were no fixed regulations for the meetings and no fixed duties assigned. In the course of time, however, they seem to have been called upon to act as special committees of the Ministerium, in the adjustment of difficulties among pastors, between pastors and congregations, and within congregations. Their chief aim, originally, was for devotional purposes and fraternal encouragement, and it was intended that they should be held four times a year.

It is probable that the first division of the Ministerium into Conference districts was made in the year 1771, when five of these districts were constituted, as follows: York, Lancaster, Macungie, Philadelphia and New York districts. In the minutes of the Ministerium, of the year 1783, twenty different localities are mentioned as being embraced in these districts. Of course, the territory of our Conference is not included in this division, as there were at that time no Lutheran congregations in existence in this portion of the Province, though in 1766 a tract of land, was granted for church purposes, to Lutherans at Salem, in Snyder county, but the congregation was not organized until the year 1775.

This arrangement of Conference districts continued for about twenty years, when, owing, no doubt, to the extension of the synodical territory, seven Conference districts were constituted. Although this new arrangement of seven districts is given in the minutes of the Ministerium for 1801, yet the Virginia district held meetings as early as 1793, which would seem to indicate that it was then already a separate district. Following is the arrangement of 1801: 1. Philadelphia. Germantown, New Hanover, Pottsgrove (Pottstown), Vincent, Old and New Goshenhoppen, and neighboring congregations. 2. Easton, Macungie, Saccum, Whitehall, Missillum, Kutztown, Weissenburg and neighboring congregations. 3. Lancaster, New Holland, Manheim, Lebanon, Reading, Tulpehocken, Harrisburg, Jonestown, Sunbury, Lykens Valley, etc. 4. York, McAllisters (Hanover), Taneytown, Carlisle, Paradise, etc. 5. Baltimore, Frederick, Hagerstown, Greencastle, Chambersburg, etc. 6. Western district, embracing the territory west of the Allegheny Mountains. 7. The congregations in Virginia, etc. In this division our Conference territory was represented in the third district, and there is no doubt that at that time, quite a number of congregations were in existence on this territory besides those at Sunbury and in Lykens Valley.

In the year 1786 the New York district, the fifth in the former arrangement, was constituted a separate Synod, —the New York Ministerium—with representation, with right of debate and vote, in the parent body. In 1803 the North Carolina Synod was organized; in 1818 the Synod of Ohio was organized out of the sixth district of the arrangement just mentioned; in 1820 the Synod of Maryland and Virginia Synod was organized out of the fifth and seventh districts; and in 1825 the West Pennsylvania Synod was organized out of the sixth district; so that in the course of twenty-five years this second arrangement had undergone so many changes that a new division was found to be necessary.

In 1832 the Conferences were redistricted, with the following result, by counties: 1. Philadelphia, Chester, Montgomery and Bucks. 2. Lehigh, Northampton, Pike and Wayne. 3. Berks and Schuylkill. 4. Lancaster. 5. Lebanon and Dauphin. 6. Northumberland, Columbia, Luzerne, Lycoming, Susquehanna, Bradford and Tioga. In this arrangement, our Conference held the sixth place and embraced the same territory, now occupied, with the exception of Luzerne and Bradford counties; whilst Snyder and Union counties did not exist as separate counties, but were embraced in Northumberland county.

This arrangement continued in force, with some modifications, until 1870. The changes made necessary were brought about by the inroads made by the East Pennsylvania Synod, organized in 1842 out of material belonging to the fourth and fifth districts, and the consequent weakening of those districts, to such an extent that some rearrangement was deemed advisable. In the Synodical Constitution of 1863, we find the fifth district classified with the third, and the district formerly numbered six, numbering five. Later, Lancaster, Lebanon and Dauphin counties were combined to make the fourth district, ours being the fifth. In the readjustment in 1871, it retained its place as the Fifth Conference, and this continued until the last rearrangement in 1893, when the old Fifth Conference, with its territorial boundaries almost entirely unchanged, became known as the Danville Conference, one of the nine Conferences into which the territory of the Ministerium was divided.

In 1832, when the territory of the Ministerium was divided into six Conference districts, the sixth district embraced Northumberland, Columbia, Luzerne, Lycoming, Susquehanna, Bradford and Tioga counties, and consisted of seven pastors, 39 congregations and 3,322 communicant members. This arrangement virtually embraced the present territory, except that Luzerne county (now Luzerne and Lackawanna counties) was transferred, at the request of several pastors, to the second district. New counties were formed by the division of the old and larger counties, so that the enumeration of the counties, in 1832, does not fully and correctly designate the territory of the Sixth Conference, according to the present arrangement of counties; for the territory on the west side of the Susquehanna river, now embraced in

Snyder and Union counties, was then included in Northumberland county.

The Conference may, therefore, be said to date its organization, as a separate Conference, from the year 1832, with seven pastors and thirty-nine congregations, and occupying the sixth place in the list of District Conferences. In comparison with the other five districts, it was not the smallest, and in extent of territory, then, as now, the most extensive of them all, embracing the northern part of the State. from the southern extremity of Northumberland county to the New York State line, on both sides of the Susquehanna river and its branches. The statistics of the Ministerium of the year 1832, according to Conferences, were as follows:

Conference.	Pastors.	Congregations.	Communicants.
I.	9	25	5,248
II.	8	28	3,950
III.	6	21	2,300
IV	6	20	1,988
V.	8	33	4,043
VI.	7	39	3,322
Unassigned	4	4	329
	48	170	21,180

The recorded minutes of the Conference, now in the archives of the Ministerium at Mount Airy, Philadelphia, begin with the year 1838, when Conference met at Turbotville, in St. John's church, with Rev. Schindel as president, and Rev. Schulze, secretary. At first, the meetings were not held very regularly; for the meeting in the following year was omitted on account of the sickness of the pastor at Selinsgrove, where the meeting was to have been held. There were two meetings in 1840, one during the following year, two in 1842, and then no record of meetings until the year 1846.

In the Synodical Constitution of 1863, the Conference occupies the fifth place in the list of Conferences, owing to the merging of the fourth and fifth into one Conference. In 1871, at a special meeting of the Ministerium, it was constituted as the Fifth District Conference, embracing Northumberland, Montour, Columbia, Lycoming counties, north to the New York State line, the Ringtown parish in Schuylkill county, Dauphin county north of the Blue Ridge, and all west of the Susquehanna river and north of the Juniata river.

The condition of the Church, on the territory of the old Fifth Conference, is presented in the following statement, by one who has had much to do in the development of the Church on this territory. Writing of the period prior to 1868, he says: "On that territory (the territory of the Fifth Conference) many of our churches had left us, because nearly all the English-speaking pastors had gone with or into the East Pennsylvania Synod. All of Snyder, as well as Union county had gone into the Central Synod. We had not a single church within the limits of the present Danville Conference, in a single one of the larger towns, except Danville, where we still had two—Trinity and St. John's. I accepted call to —, under express contract that it should return to the old Synod. After remaining about a year, I found that all those churches, which are now again with us, had never been made aware that they were supposed to have changed their synodical relations." This graphically describes the lamentable condition of things after the division in 1866 and at the time of the formation of the General Council. Many of the congregations were duped into the belief that they still retained their old synodical relations, whilst at the same time they were connected with other Synods and served by pastors selected by them; and quite a number of these congregations never returned to their old relations and are now numbered among some of the strongest congregations in the General Synod. Long and bitter were some of the contests, contemptible and unChristian were some of the means used to keep these churches from returning to their original synodical relations, but in many cases right prevailed and a new beginning could be made in the development of the interests of the Church.

As another evidence of the condition of affairs, attention is directed to the meeting of the Conference in the year 1867, the year of the organization of the General Council. There were, at that time, four pastors of our Ministerium in active work, on the territory of the Fifth Conference: The Rev. S. S. Kline, Conyngham; the Rev. W. J. Eyer, Catawissa; the Rev. J. F. Wampole, Turbotville, and the Rev. J. W Early, Selinsgrove. Father Erlenmeyer, though universally regarded as an "old Lutheran," had not yet united with the Ministerium, though that was effected a few years afterwards. This was the time when it was commonly reported on our territory that there was only one "old Lutheran minister" living and that he was getting to be an old man and could not live much longer. This was Father Erlenmeyer. When, therefore, the report spread that a young "old Lutheran minister" had settled at Selinsgrove, people at a distance of twenty miles sent for him, in order that he might visit them and that they might be able to see this curiosity. But to our Conference meeting. The meeting was held at Mifflinville, Columbia county. The Rev. J. W. Early was providentially prevented from attending. The other three were present, just enough to fill the necessary offices, though the office of treasurer was not burdened with funds. The Rev. Mr. Kline was elected president, the Rev. Mr. Wampole secretary, and the Rev. Mr. Eyer treasurer. This is the celebrated occasion of which our honored and highly-esteemed Father of Conference likes to speak when he wishes to impress upon the minds of the younger men, the importance of not despising the day of small things. He relates how the two men voted the third into office, and how each one took his turn in being a candidate for office, and that finally the Conference was officered to the universal satisfaction of all the pastors present. One made the motion, the other seconded it, and the president put it before the house, and the mover and second voted "aye." In this way every motion was carried with great unanimity; and everything was harmonious and satisfactory. They were all of one mind and heart.

At the meeting in 1869, held at Danville, eight ministers were present. One of those present at that meeting says: "As the number had increased a hundred per cent., we felt very much elated. Such a thing as eight ministers getting together in that Conference, had not been known for a long time, probably never before. We all felt that now there would be a regular Fifth Conference.' The good work of our self-sacrificing pastors was beginning to show its results, not only in the increased number of pastors and congregations, but also in the increasing activity and the ever-widening demands for the services of our men. Much of the lost ground had been recovered, and the prospects were daily growing brighter for the recovery of much more.

The fact has come to light that prior to this time, negotiations had been in progress and overtures made to unite our pastors and congregations and the pastors and congregations of the East Pennsylvania Synod, occupying this territory, into one synodical body. As a matter of fact, the writer of these lines can testify that he knows of a congregation, for whose development he has given the best part of his life, to which this proposition was actually made, with a view of bringing about the disbanding of the congregation, and in this way securing a most desirable and valuable property. This is only one of the instances referred to in the statement just made. But this threatened calamity was averted by the infusion of new blood into the working forces of our congregations. With the new life infused into the Conference, the tide of affairs began to turn in our favor and, instead of congregations continually leaving us and going over to the Synods of the General Synod, some came to us and others returned to their old synodical home. We give only two illustrations. In 1868, the Rev. Mr. Early brought the Selinsgrove parish back into the Ministerium, and in 1870 Father Erlenmeyer entered with his immense parish, embracing nearly all the rest of the congregations in Snyder county, that had formerly belonged to the Ministerium.

When Conference met at Jersey Shore, in 1871, eleven or twelve pastors were in attendance; and from that time, the growth of our Church, on the territory of the Conference, has been regular and healthy, so that at the time of the last readjustment of the districts, it numbered 25 ministers, 24 parishes, 64 congregations and 10,800 communicant members, and the meetings of Conference were generally attended by 18 or 20 ministers, besides a respectable number of lay delegates.

The history of the Danville Conference, as it is now constituted, is very brief. In 1893 it was constituted by authority of the Ministerium, in connection with the re-districting of its territory into nine Conference districts. The following districts were formed: 1. Philadelphia-German, embracing German congregations in Philadelphia, New Jersey (south of Trenton, including Newark), Baltimore, Delaware and Norristown. 2. Philadelphia-English, embracing English congregations in Philadelphia, New York City, New Jersey (south of Trenton, including Asbury Park), Baltimore, Delaware and Chester county, Pa., south of Chester. 3. Norristown, embracing Bucks, Montgomery and Chester counties. 4. Allentown, embracing Lehigh, Northampton and part of Monroe counties, and Phillipsburg, N. J. 5. Wilkes-Barre, embracing Western Monroe, Carbon, Luzerne, Wyoming, Lackawanna, Susquehanna, Bradford, Wayne and Pike counties. 6. Reading, embracing Berks county. 7. Pottsville, embracing Schuylkill county. 8. Lancaster, embracing Lancaster, Lebanon, lower Dauphin, Cumberland and York counties, and all west of the Susquehanna and south of the Juniata rivers. 9. Danville. embracing Northumberland, Montour, Columbia, Lycoming and all counties north to New York State line, Dauphin county north of the Blue Ridge, and all west of the Susquehanna and north of the Juniata rivers. To these the Ministerium added a tenth district, to wit: The Rajahmundry district, consisting of the missionaries and missions in India.

According to resolution of the Ministerium, the new arrangement of Conferences went into effect January 1, 1894. In the fall of 1893, the old Fifth Conference elected its officers as usual, with the understanding that on January 1, 1894, the old arrangement should cease and the new go into effect. Accordingly, on that date, its operations began under the new name, and at the spring meeting the election, previously held, was ratified. This was almost the only change that resulted from the new order of things. Some years prior to this, the Ringtown and Tower City parishes had been transferred to the old Third Conference. Under the re-districting of Conferences, Lykens fell into the Pottsville Conference; but in 1894 it was again restored to its old place in our Conference. This was the only change made, and after the congregation at Lykens had been restored to its former connection, the Conference was left with the same territory as before. A few years later the Line Mountain parish, owing to the residence of the pastor in Schuylkill county, was transferred to the Pottsville Conference. As now constituted, the Danville Conference embraces Dauphin county north of the Blue Ridge, Northumberland, Montour, Columbia, part of Luzerne, Lycoming, Sullivan, Tioga, Potter, Clinton, Snyder and Juniata counties, with 25 parishes, 26 ministers, 69 congregations and 12,000 communicant members.

The Conference occupies a large part of the missionary territory of the Ministerium. The vast extent of unoccupied territory is simply appalling. All over this vast extent of territory are cities and towns where our people are living without the means of grace and without that pastoral care which they need, many of them desire and all of them have a right to ask of the Chruch. Whole counties there are, where our people are found in large numbers without the ministrations of the Gospel. I think of Tioga county, with its growing towns and with Lutherans everywhere; of Mifflin county, where people have been known to travel thirty miles to attend service and have their children instructed in the catechetical class; of Union county, where we have not a single church, and where people attend divine service ten and fifteen miles away from their homes. This territory is lying waste, ready to be cultivated by the Church, whose children are as sheep without shepherds. We need more men. The men now laboring on this territory have already more than they can do; they cannot do more. I think of my own parish of about twenty miles in diameter, reaching into three counties, and often necessitating long and wearisome journeys in order to attend to pastoral duties, and permitting only the most necessary and urgent duties to be attended to. There are places right at our very doors, where work ought to be begun at once. It ought no longer to be delayed. Delay is fatal, not only to the interests of the Church, but especially to the souls of men.

Then, again, we need to re-adjust some of our large parishes in order to accomplish more efficient work. This can be done, as soon as we will be able to secure the right kind of men. But we need men who will be willing to make sacrifices for the Church. Ours is not a territory where large salaries are paid; but where pastors must be willing to labor hard and be satisfied with small salaries.

This may not be history; but it presents material from which history can and ought to be made in the future, and that without unnecessary delay. May God speed the day when the number of faithful pastors on this vast territory shall be quadrupled, and every town shall have become a centre of far-reaching activity.

CONFERENCE MEETINGS.

Sixth Conference, 1838-63.

Time	Place	President	Secretary	Treasurer
1838, Sept. 9-10	Turbotville, Pa.	Rev. J. P. Schindel.	Rev. G. Schultze.	
1839, August 30	Selinsgrove, Pa.	Rev. J. P. Schindel.	Rev. G. Schultze.	
1840, October 6-8	Milton, Pa.	Rev. W. J. Eyer.	Rev. G. Schultze.	
1840, Dec. 11-14	Selinsgrove, Pa.	Rev. J. P. Schindel	Rev. G. Schultze.	
1841, September 4-6	Williamsport, Pa.	Rev. G. Schultze.	Rev. J. F. Abele.	
1842, February 19-21	Lewisburg, Pa.	Rev. G. Schultze.	Rev. J. F. Abele.	
1842, August 1	Bloomsburg, Pa.	Rev. J. P. Schindel	Rev. W. J. Eyer.	
1843-1845	No Record of Meetings.			
1846, Sept. 16-17	Catawissa, Pa.	Rev. W. J. Eyer.	Rev. C. F. F. Sallman.	
1847, January 6-9	Conyngham, Pa.	Rev. W. J. Eyer.	Rev. C. F. F. Sallman.	
1847, April 28	Mifflinville, Pa.	Rev. W. J. Eyer.	Rev. C. F. F. Sallman.	
1847, September 5	Coal twp., Northumb'l'd Co., Pa.	Rev. W. J. Eyer.	Rev. C. F. F. Sallman.	
1848, January 12	Perry twp., Lycoming Co., Pa.	Rev. G. Schultze.	Rev. C. F. F. Sallman.	
1849-1854	No Record of Meetings.			
1855, October 31	Conyngham, Pa.	Rev. W. J. Eyer.	Rev. S. R. Boyer.	
1856, January 2	Catawissa, Pa.	Rev. W. J. Eyer.	Rev. S. R. Boyer.	
1856, December 10	Wash't'nville, Pa.	Rev. W. J. Eyer.	Rev. S. R. Boyer.	
1857, May 12	Briar Creek, Pa.	Rev. W. J. Eyer.	Rev. S. R. Boyer.	
1857, August 26	Danville, Pa.	Rev. W. J. Eyer.	Rev. S. R. Boyer.	
1857, October 29	Conyngham, Pa.	Rev. S. R. Boyer.	Rev. W. Hasskarl, Ph.D.	
1858, January 27	Williamsport, Pa.	Rev. S. R. Boyer.	Rev. W. Hasskarl, Ph.D.	
1858, April 28	Catawissa, Pa.	Rev. S. R. Boyer.	Rev. W. Hasskarl, Ph.D.	
1858, September 1	Cherry twp., Sull. Co., Pa.	Rev. S. R. Boyer.	Rev. G. Schultze.	
1858, November 9	Hazleton, Pa.	Rev. S. R. Boyer.	Rev. G. Schultze.	
1859, October 25	Catawissa, Pa.	Rev. G. Schultze.	Rev. D. M. Henkel.	
1860, April 24	Turbotville, Pa.	Rev. G. Schultze.	Rev. D. M. Henkel.	
1860, October 31	Danville, Pa.	Rev. G. Schultze.	Rev. D. M. Henkel.	

Sixth Conference, 1838-63. (Continued.)

Time	Place	President	Secretary	Treasurer
1861, January 12	Trevorton, Pa.	Rev. G. Schultze.	Rev. D. M. Henkel.	Rev. I. Bahl.
1861, October 2	Williamsport, Pa.	Rev. J. Albert.	Rev. D. M. Henkel.	Rev. D. M. Henkel.
1862, June 25	Catawissa, Pa.	Rev. J. Albert.	Rev. D. M. Henkel.	Rev. D. M. Henkel.
1862, November 5	Danville, Pa.	Rev. J. Albert.	Rev. R. S. Wagner.	Rev. D. M. Henkel.
1863, May 5	Danville, Pa.	Rev. J. Albert.	Rev. P. F. Zizelmann.	Rev. D. M. Henkel.
1863, September 30	Wash't'nville, Pa.	Rev. J. Albert.	Rev. P. F. Zizelmann.	

Fifth Conference, 1864-93.

Time	Place	President	Secretary	Treasurer
1864, May 10-11	Cogan Station, Pa.	Rev. J. Albert.	Rev. P. F. Zizelmann.	Rev. D. M. Henkel.
1864, Sept. 26-27	Wilkesbarre, Pa.	Rev. J. Albert.	Rev. P. F. Zizelmann.	Rev. D. M. Henkel.
1865, August 18-19	Scranton, Pa.	Rev. J. Albert.	Rev. P. F. Zizelmann.	Rev. D. M. Henkel.
1865, October 3-4	Danville, Pa.	Rev. J. Albert.	Rev. C. Oeffinger.	Rev. D. M. Henkel.
1866, May 1-2	Dewart, Pa.	Rev. J. Albert.	Rev. C. Oeffinger.	Rev. D. M. Henkel.
1866, Sept. 24-25	Catawissa, Pa.	Rev. J. Albert.	Rev. C. Oeffinger.	Rev. D. M. Henkel.
1867, May 20-21	Danville, Pa.	Rev. J. Albert.	Rev. W. O. Cornman, pro tem.	Rev. D. M. Henkel.
1867, October 8-9	Williamsport, Pa.	Rev. J. Albert.		
1868, April 13-14	Cross Roads, Pa.	Rev. J. Albert.	Rev. W. B. Fox.	Rev. D. M. Henkel.
1868, Sept. 29-30	Mifflinville, Pa.	Rev. S. S. Kline.	Rev. J. F. Wampole.	Rev. W. J. Eyer.
1869, May 22 (spec)	Reading, Pa.	Rev. J. M. Anspach, pro tem.	Rev. J. F. Wampole.	Rev. W. J. Eyer.
1869, October 5-6	Danville, Pa.	Rev. J. F. Wampole.	Rev. J. W. Early.	Rev. W. J. Eyer.
1870, January 11-12	Williamsport, Pa.	Rev. J. F. Wampole.	Rev. J. W. Early.	Rev. W. J. Eyer.
1870, May 10-11	Turbotville, Pa.	Rev. J. F. Wampole.	Rev. J. W. Early.	Rev. W. J. Eyer.
1870, Sept. 6-7	Jersey Shore, Pa.	Rev. J. F. Wampole.	Rev. J. W. Early.	Rev. W. J. Eyer.
1870, Nov. 29-30	Uniontown, Pa.	Rev. J. F. Wampole.	Rev. J. W. Early.	Rev. W. J. Eyer.
1871, February 14-15	Danville, Pa.	Rev. J. F. Wampole.	Rev. J. W. Early.	Rev. W. J. Eyer.
1871, May 2-3	Freeburg, Pa.	Rev. J. F. Wampole.	Rev. J. W. Early.	Rev. W. J. Eyer.
1871, October 3-4	Cogan Station, Pa.	Rev. J. F. Wampole.	Rev. J. W. Early.	Rev. W. J. Eyer.
1872, February 6-7	Williamsport, Pa.	Rev. T. Steck.	Rev. J. W. Early.	Rev. W. J. Eyer.
1872, May 27-28 (special)	Philadelphia, Pa.	Rev. T. Steck.	Rev. J. W. Early.	Rev. W. J. Eyer.

CONFERENCE HISTORY.

Date	Location		
1872, Sept. 17-18	Gratz, Pa.	Rev. T. Steck.	Rev. W. J. Eyer.
1872, Dec. 10-11	Turbotville, Pa.	Rev. T. Steck.	Rev. W. J. Eyer.
1873, April 15-16	Selinsgrove, Pa.	Rev. T. Steck.	Rev. J. F. Wampole.
1873, October 6-7	StoneVal.Ch.,Pa.	Rev. T. Steck.	Rev. J. F. Wampole.
1874, January 27-28	Wash't'nville, Pa.	Rev. J. W. Early.	Rev. J. F. Wampole.
1874, April 14-15	Jersey Shore, Pa.	Rev. H. H. Bruning.	Rev. J. F. Wampole.
1875, Sept. 22-23	Kratzerville, Pa.	Rev. H. H. Bruning.	Rev. J. F. Wampole.
1875, February 2-3	Danville, Pa.	Rev. J. W. Early.	Rev. J. F. Wampole.
1875, April 20-21	Catawissa, Pa.	Rev. W. H. Rickert.	Rev. J. F. Wampole.
1875, November 2-4	Selinsgrove, Pa.	Rev. W. H. Rickert.	Rev. J. F. Wampole.
1876, April 18-19	Williamsport, Pa.	Rev. W. H. R'ckert.	Rev. J. F. Wampole.
1876, October 3-5	Up. Mahanoy, Pa.	Rev. W. H. Rickert.	Rev. J. F. Wampole.
1877, April 17-18	Mifflinville, Pa.	Rev. J. M. Uhrich.	Rev. J. F. Wampole.
1877, October 16-17	Georgetown, Pa.	Rev. J. M. Uhrich.	Rev. J. F. Wampole.
1878, May 14-15	Turbotville, Pa.	Rev. M. C. Horine.	Rev. J. M. Uhrich.
1879, October 8-9	Beavertown, Pa.	Rev. M. C. Horine.	Rev. J. M. Uhrich.
1879, April 29-30	Freeburg, Pa.	Rev. M. C. Horine.	Rev. J. M. Uhrich.
1879, October 21-22	Cogan Station, Pa.	Rev. R. S. Wagner pro tem.	Rev. J. M. Uhrich.
1880, April 20-22	Lykens, Pa.	Rev. J. W. Early.	Rev. J. M. Uhrich.
1880, October 12-14	Mahoning, Pa.	Rev. J. W. Early.	Rev. J. M. Uhrich.
1881, May 10-12	Jersey Shore, Pa.	Rev. J. W. Early.	Rev. J. M. Uhrich.
1881, October 11-12	Lykens Valley, Pa.	Rev. J. W. Early.	Rev. J. F. Wampole.
1882, April 25-27	Vera Cruz, Pa.	Rev. J. W. Early.	Rev. J. F. Wampole.
1882, October 24-25	Wash't'nville, Pa.	Rev. J. R. Groff.	Rev. J. F. Wampole.
1883, April 17-19	Catawissa, Pa.	Rev. J. R. Groff.	Rev. J. F. Wampole.
1883, October 9-10	West Beaver, Pa.	Rev. J. R. Groff.	Rev. S. E. Ochsenford.
1884, May 6-8	Trevorton, Pa.	Rev. J. R. Groff.	Rev. S. E. Ochsenford.
1884, Sept. 30-Oct. 1	Williamsport, Pa.	Rev. J. R. Groff.	Rev. S. E. Ochsenford.
1885, April 28-30	Mifflinville, Pa.	Rev. A. P. Pflueger.	Rev. S. S. Henry.
1885, Sept. 22-24	Globe Mills, Pa.	Rev. A. P. Pflueger.	Rev. S. S. Henry.
1886, May 11-13	Selinsgrove, Pa.	Rev. A. P. Pflueger.	Rev. J. H. Neiman.
1886, October 12-14	Wash't'nville, Pa.	Rev. A. P. Pflueger.	Rev. C.K.Drumheller, pro tem.
1887, May 3-5	Lock Haven, Pa.	Rev. A. P. Pflueger.	Rev. J. H. Neiman.
1887, Sept. 26-29	Pillow, Pa.	Rev. A. P. Pflueger.	Rev. J. H. Neiman.
1888, April 10-12	Danville, Pa.	Rev. A. P. Pflueger.	Rev. J. H. Neiman.
1888, May 25-29 (special)	Lancaster, Pa.	Rev. A. P. Pflueger.	Rev. J. H. Neiman.
1888, Sept. 25-27	Tower City, Pa.	Rev. A. P. Pflueger.	Rev. J. H. Neiman.

Fifth Conference, 1864-93 (Continued).

Time	Place	President	Secretary	Treasurer
1889, April 29-30	Williamsport, Pa.	Rev. A. P. Pflueger.	Rev. J. H. Neiman.	Rev. J. F. Wampole.
1889, June 14 (spec)	Lebanon, Pa.	Rev. A. P. Pflueger.	Rev. J. H. Neiman.	Rev. J. F. Wampole.
1889, September 3-4	Dushore, Pa.	Rev. A. P. Pflueger.	Rev. J. H. Neiman.	Rev. J. F. Wampole.
1890, April 29-30	Oak Grove, Pa.	Rev. A. P. Pflueger.	Rev. J. H. Neiman.	Rev. J. F. Warmpole.
1890, October 21-23	Jersey Shore, Pa.	Rev. S. E. Ochsenford.	Rev. A. L. Yount.	Rev. A. P. Pflueger.
1891, April 21-22	Lykens, Pa.	Rev. S. E. Ochsenford.	Rev. O. E. Pflueger.	Rev. A. P. Pflueger.
1891, October 6-7	Augustaville, Pa.	Rev. S. E. Ochsenford.	Rev. O. E. Pflueger.	Rev. D. M. Stetler.
1892, May 3-4	Sellnsgrove, Pa.	Rev. S. E. Ochsenford.	Rev. O. E. Pflueger.	Rev. D. M. Stetler.
1892, Sept. 27-28	Elizabethville, Pa.	Rev. S. E. Ochsenford.	Rev. O. E. Pflueger.	Rev. D. M. Stetler.
1893, April 25-26	Grovania, Pa.	Rev. S. E. Ochsenford.	Rev. O. E. Pflueger.	Rev. D. M. Stetler.
1893, Sept. 26-27	Turbotville, Pa.	Rev. S. E. Ochsenford.	Rev. O. F. Pflueger.	Rev. D. M. Stetler.

Danville Conference, 1894.

Time	Place	President	Secretary	Treasurer
1894, April 17-18	Catawissa, Pa.	Rev. S. E. Ochsenford.	Rev. O. E. Pflueger.	Rev. D. M. Stetler.
1894, Sept. 11-12	Dushore, Pa.	Rev. S. E. Ochsenford.	Rev. O. E. Pflueger.	Rev. D. M. Stetler.
1895, Apr. 30-May 1	Shamokin, Pa.	Rev. S. E. Ochsenford.	Rev. O. E. Pflueger.	Rev. D. M. Stetler.
1895, Sept. 17-18	Beavertown, Pa.	Rev. S. E. Ochsenford.	Rev. O. E. Pflueger.	Rev. D. M. Stetler.
1896, April 21-22	Mifflinville, Pa.	Rev. S. E. Ochsenford.	Rev. O. E. Pflueger.	Rev. D. M. Stetler.
1896, Sept. 15-16	Elizabethville, Pa.	Rev. S. E. Ochsenford.	Rev. J. N. Wetzler, Ph. D.	Rev. D. M. Stetler.
1897, May 4-5	Jersey Shore, Pa.	Rev. O. E. Pflueger.	Rev. J. N. Wetzler, Ph. D.	Rev. D. M. Stetler.
1897, Sept. 21-22	Treverton, Pa.	Rev. O. E. Pflueger.	Rev. J. N. Wetzler, Ph. D.	Rev. D. M. Stetler.
1898, May 3-4	Elizabethville, Pa.	Rev. O. E. Pflueger.	Rev. J. N. Wetzler, Ph. D.	Rev. D. M. Stetler.

PLATE I.

J. P. SCHINDEL, SR.

J. N. HEMPING.

I. I. ALBERT.

ISAIAH BAHL.

W. J. EYER.

C. L. ERLE.

II. Congregational Histories

BEAVERTOWN PARISH.

BY REV. S. E. OCHSENFORD, D.D.

THIS parish consists, at present, of six congregations, five of which are located in Snyder county and one in Mifflin county. The combined membership of these six congregations is 552 communicants. The parish was organized January 11, 1885, and owns a neat frame parsonage, at Beavertown, which was secured during the pastorate of the Rev. O. E. Pflueger.

BEAVERTOWN.—St. Paul's congregation, at this place, was organized by the Rev. J. P. Schindel, Jr., in the year 1851. The members constituting the new congregation formerly belonged to the congregation at Adamsburg (Beaver dam, now Beaver Springs), dating back to about the year 1800, and served by the Revs. John Herbst, John Conrad Walter, J. P. Schindel, Sr., J. W. Smith and J. P. Schindel, Jr. At Beavertown a log church-building was erected for the use of the Lutheran and Reformed congregations, the corner-stone of which was laid April 27, 1851, in the presence of a large concourse of people, who were interested in the new enterprise. The ministers present were Revs. J. G. Anspach and J. P. Schindel, Lutheran, and Revs. J. H. Derr and Hackman, Reformed. On October 11th, of the same year, the church was consecrated, the same Lutheran ministers officiating, and Revs. R. Duenger and A. B. Casper of the Reformed Church. On the 4th of January, 1852, the Rev. J. P. Schindel, Jr., took charge of the Lutheran congregation as its pastor and continued to serve the congregation until January 24, 1869, a period of seventeen years, when he resigned on account of ill health. During his pastorate he confirmed 110 persons. He was succeeded by the Rev. D. O. Kempfer, who acted as supply during the summer of 1871, and the Rev. S. P. Orwig, from April, 1872, until October 1, 1873. Until this time the congregation was in connection with the General Synod, and served by pastors connected with that body; but after Rev. Orwig's resignation, a portion of the original congregation separated from it and organized a separate congregation on the confessional basis of the General Council, and called the Rev. D. M. Stetler, a member of the Ministerium of Pennsylvania, as its pastor, who served the congregation from 1873 until 1887. When Rev. Stetler became the pastor, the congregation numbered 90 members. A neat new frame church-building was erected by the congregation and consecrated in the year 1878. Rev. Stetler was succeeded by the Rev. O. E. Pflueger, who served the parish from 1887 to 1889, and the Rev. J. N. Wetzler, 1889-1894. February 14, 1892, the church, after having been remodeled, was reconsecrated. The Rev. O. S. Scheirer was the pastor, 1894-1896. The Rev. C. D. Zweier is the present pastor, having assumed the duties of his pastorate June 27, 1897. The church-building is owned jointly by the Lutheran and Reformed congregations and they have a Sunday School numbering 110 pupils. The Lutheran congregation has a membership of 104 communicants.

DORMANTOWN.—St. Mark's congregation, near Dormantown, Mifflin county, was organized by the Rev. D. M. Stetler, October 1, 1885, with twenty-five members, some of whom had been connected with Samuel's congregation, about five miles distant. The congregation worshiped in a school house until the year 1893, when they succeeded in erecting a small frame church-building, the corner-stone of which was laid July 23, 1893, the Revs. J. N. Wetzler, pastor, and S. E. Ochsenford, President of Conference, officiating. Rev. Stetler had served the congregation until 1887, and was succeeded by the Rev. O. E. Pflueger, 1887-1889, and the Rev. J. N. Wetzler, 1889-1894, during whose pastorate the church-building was erected, but not quite completed, though the congregation used it for worship. The Rev. O. S. Scheirer was the pastor, 1894-1896, during whose pastorate the church-building was completed, and consecrated, December 8, 1895, the pastor being assisted in the consecration services by the Rev. J. N. Wetzler, Ph.D. Since June 27, 1897, the Rev. C. D. Zweier has been pastor of the congregation. This is a Lutheran church, having a membership of 30, and a Sunday School with 100 pupils.

LOWELL (near).—St. John's congregation at "Black Oak Ridge," was organized about the year 1790. In the same year a tract of land was deeded to the Lutheran and Reformed congregations, and a small log church-building erected, either during this year or a few years later. The Lutheran congregation was probably served from the beginning by the pastors who also served Christ or Hassinger's congregation. Subsequently, at a time not known to the writer, a second church-building, a log-frame structure, was erected by the two congregations worshiping at this place. Somewhere about the seventies, some of the Lutherans seceded and organized St. Paul's congregation in connection with the General Synod and built a brick church not far from the original church. In the year 1873, old St. John's Lutheran congregation called the Rev. D. M. Stetler as its pastor, who re-organized the congregation in June, 1874, on the confessional basis of the General Council, the congregation adopting the Constitution for congregations recommended by the Ministerium of Pennsylvania. On June 14, 1874, the corner-stone of the present St. John's church was laid with appropriate services, Lutheran and Reformed ministers officiating, and the church, a neat frame structure, was consecrated, August 29, 1875. In the year 1876, the congregation was received into connection with the Ministerium of Pennsylvania. Rev. Stetler continued to serve the congregation until 1887, when he was succeeded by the Rev. O. E. Pflueger, 1887-1889, the Rev. J. N. Wetzler, 1889-1894, and the Rev. O. S. Scheirer, 1894-1896, during whose pastorate the church was remodeled at an expense of $700, and reconsecrated, November 10, 1897, the Lutheran pastor being assisted by the Rev. G. F. Spieker, D.D., professor in the Theological Seminary at Mt. Airy, Philadelphia, and the Rev. S. E. Ochsenford, President of the Danville Conference. The Rev. C. D. Zweier, ordained at the last meeting of the Ministerium of Pennsylvania, is the present pastor. The congregation has a membership of 132 communicants, and a "union" Sunday School, numbering 175 pupils.

McCLURE.—St. Matthew's congregation was organized by the Rev. D. M. Stetler, January 28, 1877, with twenty-four families, a number of whom had formerly been connected with St. John's congregation, at "Black Oak Ridge." The need of a church in town was felt by the pastor and people, the organization was effected and the congregation united with the Ministerium of Pennsylvania. The congregation worshiped for some years without having its own church-building. Rev. Stetler severed his pastoral relation in 1887, and was succeeded by the Rev. O. E. Pflueger, 1887-1889, and the Rev. J. N. Wetzler, 1889-1894. On March 23, 1890, a neat frame church-building was consecrated, free of debt. The Rev. O. S. Scheirer was the pastor, 1894-1896. Since June 27, 1897, the Rev. C. D. Zweier is the pastor. This congregation has lately organized a Luther League with encouraging prospects. The congregation also has a

Sunday School, numbering 80 pupils, and uses the General Council Sunday School literature. The membership of the congregation numbers 110 communicants.

PAXTONVILLE (near).—Christ (Hassinger's) congregation was organized in 1785. Prior to this, services were held in the homes of the Lutherans who had settled in that part of the country. In November of the year already stated, Joseph Simon, a converted Jew, and his wife Rose, conveyed to Jacob Walter, in trust for the Lutheran and Reformed congregations, sixteen and one-half acres of land for church and school purposes, and for a burial ground. On this tract of land, two miles west of Middleburg, a log church was erected for the use of both congregations. There is no record at hand of the time of the erection of this church, nor of the consecration. In 1790, the Rev. J. M. Enterline became the pastor and served the Lutheran congregation, probably until his death, March 6, 1800. During his ministry in what is now Snyder county, he had charge of numerous congregations and served them faithfully until his death, doing a vast amount of missionary work among the scattered Lutherans. In 1791 preparations were made for the erection of a new church-building and in 1798 the new church was consecrated as Christ church, Revs. Schultz, Lutheran, and Geistweit, Reformed, officiating. The building was a large square structure, built of logs, and had a seating capacity for 500 persons. For a short time after the death of Rev. Enterline, a certain Rev. Guensel seems to have served the congregation. He was an erratic character, and was drowned in the attempt to ford Middle creek, where Royer's bridge is now located. The Rev. John Herbst was the pastor, 1801-1804; the Rev. John Conrad Walter, 1805-1819. Both these pastors had charge of all the congregations on the territory now embraced in Snyder county, including Salem, Grubb's, Freeburg, Selinsgrove and others. During the pastorate of Rev. Walter, in 1807, the church-building was weatherboarded and painted white. Rev. Walter died as the pastor of this congregation and was buried near the church. His grave is marked: "John Conrad Walter (Preacher), born November 30, 1775, in Germany, died August 10, 1819." He was, therefore, a young man of thirty years, when he became the pastor of this vast parish in the wilds of Pennsylvania. The Rev. J. P. Schindel, Sr., of Sunbury, officiated at his funeral, and afterward served the congregation, as supply, during the year 1820. The following were the pastors after him during a period of fifty-two years: The Revs. J. W. Smith, 1821-1831; William German, 1831-1838; J. P. Schindel, Jr., 1838-1860; Geo. Greymiller, D. O. Kempfer, H. Breininger, R. Lazarus, 1867-1868; and C. G. Erlenmeyer, 1868-1873. About the year 1870 a division took place among the Lutherans on account of "New Measures," and those claiming to be General Synod Lutherans withdrew and in 1871-'72, erected a church-building of their own, not far away from the old church, whilst the General Council Lutherans retained the old property, jointly with the Reformed. The Lutherans and Reformed built a new frame church, the corner-stone of which was laid on Trinity Sunday, May 26, 1872, the Revs. C. G. Erlenmeyer, Lutheran, and A. B. Casper, T. J. Seiple and L. C. Edmonds, Reformed, officiating. On February 2, 1873, the new church was consecrated with appropriate services, the Rev. H. H. Bruning, of Selinsgrove, preaching the consecration sermon. The Lutheran congregation numbered then about forty members. The following pastors have since served the congregation, as pastors of the Beavertown parish, the Rev. D. M. Stetler, 1873-1887, during whose pastorate, in 1876, the congregation was received into connection with the Ministerium of Pennsylvania, having adopted the Constitution recommended by Synod; the Rev. O. E. Pflueger, 1887-1889; the Rev. J. N. Wetzler, 1889-1894; the Rev. O. S. Scheirer, 1894-1896; and the Rev. C. D. Zweier, since June 27, 1897.

TROXELVILLE.—St. James' congregation was probably organized about the year 1800. A church-building was erected on land donated to the Lutherans by Henry Swartz and was originally known as "Henry's Church," and later as "Musser's Valley Church." At first it was an exclusively Lutheran church, and was probably the first organization in this region. In 1805, the congregation, though small, called as its pastor the Rev. John Conrad Walter, who served it in connection with numerous other congregations until his death, in 1819. In the year 1811, the Lutheran congregation and the Reformed members of the community jointly erected a church-building, the corner-stone of which was laid April 28, 1811, the Revs. J. C. Walter and Geo. Heim, Lutheran ministers, officiating. During the War of 1812 the church remained in an unfinished condition, though it was used for worship, and in October, 1814, the building was consecrated by the Revs. J. C. Walter and Geo. Heim, Lutheran, and Y. Henry Fries and Isaac Walter, Reformed. The church was now a union church and remained so for many years. After the death of Rev. Walter, the Rev. J. P. Schindel, Sr., supplied the congregation with occasional services during the summer of 1820, and was succeeded by the Rev. J. W. Smith, as regular pastor, who remained about seven years, when the Rev. William German became the pastor, and served the congregation until 1840. The next pastor was the Rev. C. G. Erlenmeyer, who served the congregation in connection with numerous others in the lower end of the county, until 1851, and was succeeded by the Rev. J. P. Schindel, Jr., who preached his introductory sermon, October 25, 1851, and served the congregation until January 24, 1859. During his pastorate he confirmed 244 persons, and when he resigned the congregation had a membership of more than two hundred communicants. For several years the congregation was without a regular pastor; but in 1872 the Rev. D. O. Kempfer accepted a call and served one year. In 1873, the Rev. W. R. Wieand became the pastor; but during his pastorate a separation took place on account of the introduction of "new measures," the result of which was three churches, two Lutheran and one Reformed. Those Lutherans who remained faithful to the Lutheran doctrines and usages reorganized and in 1873 called the Rev. D. M. Stetler as their pastor, who labored here until the year 1887. During his pastorate, on June 13, 1880, the corner-stone of a new church was laid, and on July 3, 1881, a neat frame church, the present building, was consecrated. The church is located at the eastern end of the village, on the road leading to Centreville. The following have been the pastors of the congregation, in connection with the Beavertown parish, since Rev. Stetler's resignation: The Rev. O. E. Pflueger, 1887-1889; the Rev. J. N. Wetzler, 1889-1894; the Rev. O. S. Scheirer, 1894-1896; and the Rev. C. D. Zweier, since June 27, 1897. The congregation has a membership of 118 communicants and a Sunday School numbering 80 pupils.

PLATE II

L. G. EGGERS.

A. BERGNER.

J. SCHINDEL.

C. G. ERLENMEYER.

J. P. SCHINDEL, JR.

W. G. LAITZLE.

BERWICK PARISH.

BY THE REV. N. SCHEFFER.

FIVE congregations compose the Berwick parish. Three of them are located in Luzerne county and two in Columbia. Two are on the south side of the Susquehanna river and three on the north side. The history of two of them extends beyond the ken of the living and one is of recent date. In earlier days the whole valley along the north branch of the Susquehanna was one mission territory. Revs. Stock, Plitt and Fridrici were the earliest Lutheran pastors in the field. In the time of Rev. Engle this parish extended from Danville north. Rev. Peter Kessler's territory was between Danville and Hobbie. When Rev. Bahl entered upon his ministerial duties the extent of the field was somewhat contracted, though at first he had a dozen preaching places.

Rev. W. B. Fox came to this parish in January, 1863, and found the field anything but encouraging. The parish had been overrun by all kinds of revivalists who had scattered the flocks. The people were unsettled in their religious belief, but by his energetic activities, the congregations were strengthened in the faith. In one of the churches three persons composed his first audience. At this time the language question was an important factor in the congregations. Heretofore the services were all German, but the middle-aged and young desired English. The question was, however, settled by the introduction of some English services. During his pastorate two lots in the town of Berwick were purchased on Main street, and a commodious brick house was built in 1866 for a parsonage.

The parish was divided again in the year 1890, and six congregations were left to compose the parish. In the year 1892 the seventh congregation was added. Soon after Rev. Stupp entered the field he began services in Berwick, and in November, 1892, the eighth congrega-

BRIAR CREEK CHURCH.

tion was added to the parish. The parish was then too extensive to be cared for by one pastor, so in the summer of 1894 it was again divided, leaving Mt. Zion, St. James, St. Paul in Luzerne county, and Briar Creek and St. John in Columbia county to form the Berwick parish.

BRIAR CREEK CONGREGATION is the oldest in the parish. It was begun in the days when church records were considered of little value. There is no record extant of its organization, but well-authenticated tradition says that services were held in the homes of our Lutheran people for years before an organization, or a church was built. On the fly-leaf of an old record book this is written: "Upon the first day of August, Geo. M. Bauer and Jeremiah Kolb were installed elders, and Fred Hill and John Gower deacons." The year in which this first day of August occurred is not given. The first seven baptisms recorded were in the year 1800 and 1801. Then follow eight which are dated in the years 1798 and 1799. After that they follow in a chronological order.

On the ninth Sunday after Trinity, 1804, Henry Koelchner and Anthony Adam were elected elders, and Joseph Seibert and Geo. Schelhauser deacons. On Sunday after Easter, 1805, the holy communion was administered.

The history of Columbia county states that the first house of worship was built in 1805, which was owned conjointly by the Lutherans and Reformed, the Revs. Plitt and Adams being the respective pastors. In 1807 articles of agreement between the Lutherans and Reformed were drafted by Rev. M. Carl Solomon Fridrici, the Evangelical Lutheran pastor.

This paper states that the two congregations, Evangelical Lutheran and Reformed, in Briar Creek township, Northumberland county, Pa., resolved to build a union church on a half acre of land, bought from Jessie Bowman. This house was built for church and school purposes. The house was to be built at the expense of both congregations and neither should have the advantage. The pastor was to be elected and paid by both congregations, but must be a regularly ordained minister of either denomination. This church was to remain forever a German church. The alms were to be held in common. The pastor was to be elected every three years, once a Lutheran and the next time a Reformed, unless both congregations should be satisfied with the one serving them. There was but one treasury. All violators of the constitution were to have no right in the church.

This church ordinance was adopted June 5, 1807, at which time the corner-stone was laid. The articles are signed by the pastor, M. Carl Solomon Fridrici, and by the elders, deacons and trustees of both denominations. The first church was built of logs and had a gallery on three sides.

How long Rev. Fridrici remained their pastor is not known. From the year 1814 to 1816, Rev. J. F. Engel confirmed their children and administered the holy communion. In the year 1818 Rev. Peter Hall, a Lutheran pastor, confirmed fifteen children. In 1816 he baptized Henry Shaffer, who is still living and an active member of our church. In May, 1819, a Rev. J. K. Haal, a Lutheran pastor, administered the holy communion to 86 persons. On April 9, 1820, Rev. Peter Kessler's name appears on the church record for the first time, and on April 26, 1829, he administered the sacrament for the last time. Rev. Isaiah Bahl began his work here in 1830 and continued as pastor until his death, March 6, 1862. He was the first Lutheran pastor who made his home in Berwick.

In 1850 the old log church was displaced by a brick structure which stands near the old one. The foundation was laid and the brick hauled on the ground by the members. Mr. John Ent received $995 for building and furnishing it. It is a good substantial building, standing about one mile north of the river bank, and four miles north of west from Berwick.

Rev. W. B. Fox entered upon his pastoral duties the first week in January, 1863, and continued his labors until September 13, 1868. Rev. S. S. Henry succeeded him in 1869 and continued his labors until 1873. In the beginning of 1874, Rev. Thomas Steck took charge and labored here until February, 1880. Rev. J. P. German succeeded him in August, 1880. The church was remodeled and repaired on the inside in 1883. In 1885 a cabinet organ was purchased by the congregations. He removed from the field in October, 1892, to take charge of a congregation in Minersville. Rev. S. B. Stupp began his work here on November 20, 1892, and ended November 20, 1894. On April 21, 1895, Rev. G. G. Kunkle took charge and relinquished his labors October 11, 1896. On February 4, 1897, Rev. N. Scheffer took the pastoral oversight. A new supply of Church Books was purchased in June and the Morning Service of our Church Book is used in full. In August of the same year a communion set was purchased by the Lutheran congregation.

MT. ZION'S CONGREGATION.—This church is in Nescopeck township, Luzerne county, about four miles southeast from the town of Nescopeck along the old turnpike. The first part of the history of this congregation is buried in the past. On a few leaves of an old torn up and destroyed church record book we find that on the 17th of November, 1811, twenty persons were received into the Lutheran congregation by the rite of confirmation and eleven others received the Holy Communion. From 1812 to 1814 Herman Jacob Shellhardt, an applicant to the Pennsylvania Ministerium for license, seems to have been the pastor. From this time to 1821 the records are lost. The first baptisms recorded are the three children of Abraham and Sarah Shartz, who were baptized November 23, 1809. The parents were members of the

Lutheran Church. Who the pastor was is not known. Rev. Thos. Pomp, a German Reformed minister of Easton, preached here as early as 1809. The first Evangelical Lutheran pastor of whom we can gather any knowledge from the living was Rev. Peter Kessler. He lived in or near Bloomsburg and served this congregation from

MT. ZION CHURCH.

1820 to 1827, when he left very suddenly. He had a catechetical class here of twenty-three young persons, but left them before confirmation. They were then gathered into a class by the German Reformed minister and confirmed. Rev. John G. Binninger began preaching here in 1828 and continued until 1833 or 1834 when Rev. Bahl began preaching here.

In 1816 a piece of land was deeded by Geo. Keen to John Buss, Abraham Shartz, John Henry and Geo. Rouch, trustees of the German Church and Presbyterian Societies. Messrs. Keen, Buss and Shartz were Lutherans. To what church the other two belonged cannot be learned.

The history of the county states that a church was built on this ground in 1811. This was a log church with galleries on three sides. Later on it was weather-boarded and painted. Rev. I. Bahl served this congregation during his pastorate of the parish. Rev. R. S. Wagner, of Hazleton, had the congregation under his care from Rev. Bahl's death until the summer of 1863, when Rev. W. B. Fox began work here, and continued until September, 1868.

In the spring of 1868 they began to build a brick church. It is a large structure with a basement. It stands as an honor to the congregations which built it. The history states that the Lutherans united with the Reformed in building this church, intimating that the Lutherans had nothing in the old church, whilst the Lutherans formerly were by far the stronger of the two congregations. In 1882 the church underwent some repairs. A cabinet organ was purchased in 1885 by the two congregations. On July 11, 1897, the Morning Service of our Church Book was introduced, and used to the satisfaction of all.

In August, 1897, at a congregational meeting it was decided to petition the Court to become incorporated as Mt. Zion's Evangelical Lutheran Congregation. This petition was delayed until January, 1898, and was granted by the Court on the 29th of the month. The Reformed became incorporated at the same time. The congregations have enlarged their cemetery by purchase at two different times.

The pastors from Rev. Fox's time were the same as those of Briar Creek congregation.

ST. PAUL'S CHURCH.

ST PAUL'S CONGREGATION.—The first church was known as the Salem church. It is in Luzerne county about two miles northwest from Beach Haven and four miles northeast of Berwick. It was built on a piece of ground purchased from Christian Bilheimer. The church was built of stone, and had a gallery at the two sides and end. The church was a union church of the German Lutheran and Reformed; however, it was provided that either could have English services, though all others were debarred. The building was begun in the spring of 1824, the cornerstone being laid on the 27th day of May by Rev. Peter Kessler on the Lutheran side, and Rev. J. N. Zeiser and Jacob Diefenbach on the Reformed, the first two being the pastors. Bastian Seybert and Adam Breder were the trustees. The church was dedicated on October 30, 1825, by Revs. Kessler, Schindel and Bahl on the Lutheran side, and Rev. Zeiser, German, and Rev. W. Wott, English Reformed ministers.

Stephen Hill, son of Jacob and Catharine, was the first child baptized in the church, which took place on November 5, 1825. On the same day Rev. Kessler confirmed a class of 33 and 26 others received the holy communion. The last communion Rev. Kessler administered was on May 31, 1829. Rev. Bahl began his work some time before May 2, 1830, as on that day he confirmed a class of nine and administered the holy communion to 38 persons. He continued to serve this congregation until his last sickness.

In 1883 the old stone church was sold to the Grange organization. The congregations then built a frame church on land given by Philip Seely about one mile north of Beach Haven. The name at this time seems to have been changed to St. Paul. This is also a union church. In 1885 a cabinet organ was presented to the congregations by Mrs. Leah Seely. In August, 1897, the full Morning Service of our Church Book was introduced. The pastors which served this congregation after Rev. Bahl were Revs. Fox, Henry, Steck, German, Stupp, Kunkle and the present pastor.

ST. JAMES' CONGREGATION is located in Luzerne county, about three miles south of the town of Nescopeck. The first services were held in a log building popularly known as the Shaffer school-house. This house was built by the

ST. JAMES' CHURCH.

citizens and subscription school was held in it until 1849 when the public schools were introduced into these parts. The school-house was enlarged for church purposes. Rev. John Jacob Benninger, of Mountain Grove began to labor here about 1830, and continued until about 1840.

In 1835 Jacob Shaffer deeded a little over an acre of land on which the school-house stood to the German and English Lutheran and Presbyterian churches, for church and school purposes and for burying grounds. Rev. Sallman of Conyngham labored here for several years. Rev. Isaiah Bahl then began his labors here. On account of the extent of his field he could at first preach for them only every fourth Saturday. In 1861 the corner-stone for a church was laid. In November of the same year the church was dedicated but Rev. Bahl was unable to attend. Rev. R. S. Wagner, of Hazleton, attended the dedication. The German Reformed assisted in building the church. Rev. Wagner administered the first communion in the church on June 28, 1862, when 111 communed. Rev. Wagner confirmed a class of nine on April 4th, and on April 5th, 1863, administered the communion for the last time. The Lord's Supper was never administered in the school-house. Previous to this time the members attended the communions at Mifflin and Mt. Zion. The record of baptisms has been kept since 1837, but not by whom administered.

Rev. Fox succeeded him, and the congregation has continued in the Berwick parish ever since. In 1885 a reed organ was purchased by the congregation. In May, 1897, the Morning Service of our Church Book was introduced and used in full to the entire satisfaction of all.

On August 7th, 1897, at a congregational meeting after preparatory service, the constitution recommended by the General Council of the Evangelical Lutheran Church was unanimously adopted. On August 28 certain by-laws were adopted. The congregation voted unanimously also to petition the Court to become incorporated as St. James' Evangelical Lutheran Congregation. On December 18 this petition was granted by the Court of Luzerne county.

The pastors succeeding Rev. Fox are the same as those in the other churches of the parish.

ST. JOHN'S CONGREGATION, BERWICK.—This is the latest of the congregations organized in the parish. It

ST. JOHN'S CHURCH.

is located in Berwick. In the year 1794 Evan Owen, the founder of the town of Berwick, donated and deeded a lot about the center of the town to Jacob Kisner, William Martz and Sebastian Seibert in trust for a German Lutheran church of Berwick. This lot was exchanged for another one on Market street, in 1873.

Several of the pastors had preached in the town hall but there was no permanent result therefrom until 1892. In that year Rev. Stupp became the pastor of the parish and moved into the parsonage. He soon took in the situation and began to canvass the town for our people. His energetic labors proved successful. On Wednesday evening, November 30, 1892, an Evangelical Lutheran congregation was organized with twenty members. The first services were held in the parlor of the parsonage; but later on the Y. M. C. A. Hall was secured in which to hold the services. The Court granted the petition of incorporation on Feb. 13th, 1893. On April 9, 1893, arrangements were made to build a chapel on the ground belonging to the parish, agreeing to purchase the shares of any of the congregations which might withdraw at any time from this parish to form another. The ground was broken for the chapel on the 18th of April. The corner-stone was laid by the pastor on May 10, at 2 o'clock, p. m. The services of dedication took place on Sunday, December 10, 1893. Rev. D. M. Henkel, D.D., and Rev. J. W. Early assisted the pastor in the dedicatory service, the former preaching in the morning and the latter in the evening. Services were held every evening during the week, the neighboring Lutheran pastors preaching for the pastor.

The first year's service of the pastor was given free. In November, 1894, Rev. Stupp accepted a call to the Lime Mountain parish. Rev. G. G. Kunkle was his successor. He resigned in October, 1896. The present pastor entered upon his duties in the parish February 4, 1897, with anything but flattering prospects ahead. In April, 1897, a full supply of Church Books was purchased and the liturgical service of our Church Book was introduced.

St. John's, Catawissa.

BY REV. E. L. REED.

ACCORDING to the meager accounts which are at hand, it appears that St. John's Evangelical Lutheran congregation, Catawissa, Pa., was organized, May 1, 1796, with thirteen members. The stone building which served as their first house of worship, dating from 1804, was replaced by a brick building in 1852. The Reformed occupied, and held ownership in the same.

In 1881, the Lutheran congregation purchased the Reformed interest, and July 13, 1890, they laid the corner-stone for the present new and attractive house of worship.

The first pastor of whom there is any record, was Rev. G. V. Stochs, who began his ministry in 1796. Rev. Frederick Plitt was his successor, but there is a blank as to dates. The Rev. Peter Hall began his ministry in 1817; Rev. Peter Kessler in 1820, and the Rev. Jeremiah Shindle, in 1831. Rev. Wm. J. Eyer's pastorate covers a period of thirty-seven years, viz., from October, 1837, to February, 1874; Rev. W. G. Laitzle from Oct. 15, 1874, to Jan. 20, 1878; Rev. L. Lindenstruth, Feb. 1, 1878, to June 1, 1881; Rev. J. H. Neiman, Aug. 1, 1881, to April 1, 1892; Rev. E. L. Reed, Nov. 1, 1892, to Nov. 15, 1897.*

Owing to the scarcity of ministers in the early history of our Church in this country, it was not an unusual matter for one pastor to have charge of six, eight or even more congregations, scattered over a territory of many

---

* The Rev. P. Altpeter assumed pastoral charge of St. John's, Palm Sunday 1898.—Ed.

miles. There are at present no less than nine Lutheran pastors in the territory formerly occupied by one man.

Inasmuch as the people were scattered so greatly and the interval between preaching days was so great, it was thought a stroke of policy to permit several denominations to occupy the same building, and share the burden of expense. The unwisdom of this policy has been shown, time and again. In many cases it occasioned strife and litigation in the courts, creating scandal, estrangements among relatives and neighbors, besides giving a set-back to the common cause for which each was pledged to strive.

The district of which St. John's was a part, was no exception to this rule. The so-called union churches were, however, gradually brought to realize the necessity of a separation of interests, and either by the aid of the court, or otherwise, one by one the congregations comprising the Catawissa charge, acquired their own properties.

The pastor to whom much of this result is due, was the Rev. J. H. Neiman. The charge during his ministry consisted of St. John's, Catawissa, St. Paul's, Numidia, and Emanuel, Mainville; in each congregation, a separation from the Reformed was effected, and new churches built.

Besides the difficulty occasioned by the union churches, the subject of language was often a perplexing question. At first, the German language was exclusively used in the ministrations in St. John's, but as surrounding conditions and circumstances were altogether favorable to the development of the English language, it became necessary occasionally to preach in that language.

This sentiment among the younger people in the congregation grew faster than the privilege, and finally, in 1845, under the pastorate of the Rev. W. J. Eyer, a colony went out from the mother church and organized St.

Matthew's English Evangelical Lutheran Church. And though the same pastor continued for a time to minister to both congregations, the new organization finally switched off the solid, well-founded and safely historic track of the unaltered Augsburg Confessional Lutheran faith and practice, and ended in the fanatical, so-called new Lutheranism, saturated with the ideas of the anxious-bench system and its new-fangled measures.

ST. JOHN'S CHURCH.

It is, however, gratifying that the present generation is again learning something of its true heritage, and is approaching nearer the old historic faith.

St. John's, the mother church, continued in the use of both the German and the English language, until the close of Rev. Neiman's pastorate. The German then ceased altogether.

It is a matter of great satisfaction that St. John's, in confession and practice, never betrayed her birth-right. From the very beginning, the congregation was in connection with the Ministerium of Pennsylvania, and her pastors have never had occasion to adopt the sensational methods of those who are of a different spirit, to gain a hearing. Catechetical instruction has always been faithfully pursued, with satisfactory results.

The congregation delights in the use of the full liturgical service found in the Church Book, and the pastor wears the clerical robe.

The Sunday-school uses the excellent lesson system furnished by the General Council.

The festival seasons of the Church year are faithfully observed; and the congregation, in all its appointments, is not a whit behind those of our larger cities.

St. John's has enrolled more than three hundred and fifty members with a Sunday-school of nearly the same number, having over ninety in its infant department.

Since November, 1892, when the present pastor began his ministry, the congregation stands alone, and rejoices in the exclusive services of its pastor. The present new and up-to-date house of worship was completed in November, 1893. In the same year, St. John's purchased from the congregations formerly connected with the charge, their individual rights in the parsonage.

The Aid Society, which is a most efficient organization, assumed the debt and will complete their payments within the present year.

The Luther League movement has been an interesting feature in St. John's. The League conducts a devotional service each Sunday evening an hour before the regular service, faithfully using the League topics.

May 10, 1896, the congregation began the celebration of the centennial of its organization, with appropriate services, and continued the same with much interest and profit for a week. The President of Synod and the President of Conference, besides a number of neighboring brethren, assisted on the occasion. Rev. D. M. Henkel, D.D., prepared and read a short history of the congregation at that time. We are indebted to that pamphlet for a few facts in this sketch.

PLATE III

H. WEICKSEL.

R. S. WAGNER.

D. M. HENKEL.

THOS. STECK.

F. WALZ.

J. F. BAYER.

COGAN STATION PARISH.

BY REV. O. REBER.

THE Cogan Station parish is located in Lycoming county, Pa., ten miles north of Williamsport, and embraces the territory around the station.

The church itself is located in the village of Lycoming, two miles northwest from the railroad station.

The parsonage is at Perryville. The first Lutheran minister who came into this section of the State, was the Rev. Gustavus Schulze, who preached around in the houses of the settlers about the year 1835.

The first confirmation administered by this pioneer servant of the Lord took place in the spring of 1848, in the log school-house at Perryville, sixteen persons, mostly married, being confirmed at that time.

In 1849, a school-house was built in Quigelville, which was used by the Lutherans and Evangelicals for divine services until the present church was erected, in 1862.

From 1845 to 1865, many Lutherans from Germany moved into the parish, and right in the midst of the Civil War, it was decided to build a church.

Messrs. J. M. Sander, Adam Schaefer and Frederick Drumm were the Building Committee; through their influence as well as of others who had come from Germany, some money was contributed by the Gustavus Adolphus Society towards building this church.

It was dedicated on Christmas Day, 1862, by the highly-esteemed pastor, Father Schulze, who continued to serve the parish until he was prevented by the feebleness of old age.

In 1867, Father Schulze not being able to serve any

longer, the Rev. Joseph Hillpot became pastor; during his time the parsonage was built and English was introduced, which things gave prestige and stability to the parish.

Rev. Hillpot was succeeded by Rev. W. H. Kuntz, who came in 1873, and was pastor but a little more than one year, when he was followed by the Rev. Harrman Eggers, who became pastor in 1875, and remained until

ST. MICHAEL'S CHURCH.

1878, during his time the debt on the parsonage was liquidated.

In 1879, the Rev. Lewis Smith became pastor. Up to this date a union Sunday School was in existence, but through his influence, the Sunday School became exclusively Lutheran.

Rev. D. E. Reed succeeded Rev. Smith in 1885, and remained pastor until the time of his death, in 1889. His remains are interred in the cemetery belonging to the church.

Up to this time the congregation at Jersey Shore was served most of the time by the pastors of this parish, but when Rev. A. M. Strauss was called as pastor, in 1890, that congregation also called a pastor and thus two services every Lord's Day have been conducted from that time on till to the present.

Rev. J. W. Klingler followed Rev. Strauss, in January, 1892. Through the influence of Rev. Klingler and his wife, the Ladies' Home and Foreign Missionary Society was organized. This society has been very active from the beginning, having raised about $500.00 already towards building a new church.

Rev. Klingler was succeeded by the Rev. L. Rosenberg, and he in turn by the present writer, in October, 1896. A Luther League has been organized and is doing good work.

The membership of the congregation is 200; that of the Sunday School about 90.

TRINITY, DANVILLE.

BY THE REV. W. E. RONEY.

THE history of Trinity Lutheran Church, Danville, is similar in many respects to the early history of the Lutheran Church in America. Stern opposition confronted her; trials of various kinds obstructed her pathway, and for a brief period seemingly clogged the wheels of progress; but as the crucible tests and purifies the gold, as the storm and tempest give strength and beauty to the cedar, thus opposition and bitter trials gave firmness of purpose and unity of labor to the little band of the Master's servants who prayed and labored for the establishment of the church now known as Trinity of Danville.

Trinity church is a daughter of St. John's church (German), Danville, and, as is the case with so many of our English Lutheran churches, owes her origin to the language question. Believing it to be more in accord with the spirit of the gospel to separate in peace than to live in continual strife and discord, the English element separated from the mother church during the year 1851. No sooner had they left the threshold of the mother church than they were confronted with another perplexing question, to wit: to secure a location for the erection of a church that would be satisfactory to all. The solution of this question resulted in a second division, the division of the English element; one faction going to the north side of the city, now known as Pine street Evangelical Lutheran church, and the other party remaining on the south side, known as Trinity Evangelical Lutheran church. The members on the south side being the minority, were compelled to struggle for an existence. A Sunday-school was started in the store room now owned by Mr. Wm. Roat, and there the little band labored and toiled, buoyed up with the hope and prayer that some day they might

TRINITY CHURCH.

procure the services of a pastor. At length their hopes were realized, their prayers were answered, when in 1859 Rev. D. M. Henkel, providentially passed through Danville, and being apprised of the little band on the south side and their need of a pastor, stopped off and inquired into the status of things. This was found to be anything but encouraging, yet upon the urgent request of the little band, Rev. Henkel kindly consented to revisit them, which he did, and March 24th, 1859, organized the congregation under the name of Trinity Evangelical Lutheran church.

The congregation at that time numbered 45 members and immediately extended a call to Rev. Henkel. The call was conditionally accepted and on May 30th, 1859, the newly-elected pastor took charge of the newly-organized congregation. Under the skilful leadership and faithful labor of Rev. Henkel the congregation began slowly but steadily to increase and prosper.

In 1862 the lot on the corner of Church and Market streets was purchased for the erection of a church building. In the spring of 1863 the ground was broken for the foundation of the new church; the corner-stone was laid on the 23d of July, 1863, and on February 26th, 1865, the building was consecrated to the service of God. Brethren present on that occasion were: Rev. C. F. Schaeffer, D.D., filling the pulpit at the morning service, Rev. E. Greenwald, D.D., administered communion in the afternoon, and Rev. S. Sprecher filled the pulpit at the evening service. Rev. W. J. Eyer was present at the afternoon service.

In 1866, one Lord's Day, a cyclone passed through Danville, striking the beautiful steeple of Trinity church, completely demolishing the steeple and damaging the church. The damage was quickly repaired through the activity of the members, but the steeple was never rebuilt.

Rev. Henkel's pastorate at Danville was a long and successful one. But as best of friends must part, so the most dearly beloved and successful pastor is called in the providence of God to other fields of labor. Having resigned as pastor of Trinity church, he preached his farewell sermon March 31st, 1867, and amid the tears and with the prayers of the congregation, took his departure to minister elsewhere in the Master's vineyard. The membership at the close of Rev. Henkel's pastorate numbered about 100.

Rev. Henkel's successor was Rev. W. O. Cornman, who on account of impaired health, served the congregation but one year, April 1st, 1867, to April 1st, 1868.

Rev. Cornman was followed by Rev. J. M. Anspach, April, 1868. During the pastorate of Rev. Anspach, the parsonage was built at a cost of $5,000. By the efficient services of Rev. Anspach, as pastor and pulpit orator, the membership assumed a rapid growth, so that at the time of Rev. Anspach's resignation, April 28th, 1872, Trinity church numbered 180 members.

Rev. M. C. Horine began his pastorate at Danville September 1st, 1872. During Rev. Horine's pastorate the panic of 1876 came on, which impeded the progress of all church work. It is due to the self-sacrificing labors of Rev. Horine that the doors of Trinity church remained open, and the gospel message of peace and cheer continued to be proclaimed to the people at the time of special need. At the time of Rev. Horine's resignation, September 1st, 1881, the membership numbered 220.

Rev. Horine's successor was Rev. J. R. Groff, who became pastor of Trinity church October 12th, 1881. During Rev. Groff's pastorate the church building was remodeled and repaired to the extent of about $1600, and reconsecrated January 17th, 1886, by Revs. Henkel, Anspach, and Groff. Rev. Groff resigned February 9th, 1886. Membership 206.

Rev. C. K. Drumheller succeeded Rev. Groff, June 3d,

1886, and resigned December 1st, 1889. For many years the church was hampered in its work by a heavy debt; Rev. Drumheller put into execution a most admirable plan for the liquidation of the debt, but unfortunately it failed. At the close of Rev. Drumheller's pastorate the church numbered 190 members.

Rev. Drumheller was succeeded by the present pastor, Rev. W. E. Roney, who entered this, his first charge, March 1st, 1890. During Rev. Roney's pastorate the church was beautified with beautiful stain-glass windows, a two-manual pipe-organ was purchased and the church cleared from all debt. It enjoys two active Luther Leagues, Senior and Junior, and a Ladies' Aid Society, which has been and is an indispensable help to the congregation.

The history of Trinity Lutheran church, of Danville, has been one from shadow to sunshine; from the cross to the crown, a fulfillment of the promise: "Weeping may endure for a night, but joy cometh in the morning." Ps. 30:5. Trinity church has at the present a membership of 350, and a flourishing Sunday-school of over 300 members. All her pastors, seven in number, are still among the living, whilst the mother church and the twin sister churches are harmoniously laboring together in the Lord's vineyard, "in the unity of the Spirit, in the bond of peace."

THE DANVILLE GERMAN PARISH.

BY THE REV. D. L. FOGELMAN.

THIS parish consists of four congregations, all in Montour county.

ST. JOHN'S, GERMAN, DANVILLE.—This is the mother of the Lutheran churches in the city. In the year 1820, the Rev. Peter Kessler came into this part of the State as the only Lutheran pastor. He took charge of the congregations in this and adjoining counties. By his efforts the Lutherans were brought together and served until 1829. The Lutherans now joined the Episcopalians in the erection of a church, hoping that after its completion they would have the privilege to worship in it. About this time, 1830, Rev. Jer. Shindel came from Bloomsburg and held services in the union church about a year or two, when a disappointment was sprung upon the Lutheran members, finding themselves shut out on account of some disagreement relative to the occupancy of the church. The Lutherans, however, together with Rev. Shindel, proceeded to the old court house where services were held and an organization effected. His labors were abundantly blessed until 1835 or 1836, when he resigned. During these years of struggles for the establishment of a Lutheran church many Lutheran families renounced the faith of their fathers and were lost to the Church.

The hopeful Lutherans were served, once a month, by Rev. Wm. J. Eyer, from 1838 to 1840, when they were united with the Catawissa parish. After a vacancy of about three years, Rev. Elias Swartz, sustained by the Home Missionary Society, ministered to the remaining members of about 20. Yet by his services, which were favored by God's blessing, he was able to receive into the Church between 40 and 50 members. Through his instrumentality a design of a church edifice was drawn and for its execution a committee was appointed. The corner-stone was laid in 1844, and the building was consecrated to the service of Almighty God in June, 1845. Revs. E. Swartz, W. J. Eyer and Jacob Smith officiated. The congregation was rapidly increasing, but was hampered by a church debt, which caused the pastor's resignation in 1845.

Subsequently the congregation was served in connection with the Milton parish by Rev. F. Ruthrauff, for about nine months in 1846. Rev. M. J. Alleman then began his labors in 1847, but resigned in 1848. The congregation was again without a regular pastor for about two years, when Rev. P. Willard was called in 1850. Through his efforts the disheartened members were infused with new zeal and once more emerged from their spirit of despondency to emulate the spirit of their fathers and came rejoicing to the help of the Lord against the mighty. Many members were added to the church, a cemetery lot and a parsonage were purchased.

So rapidly did the congregation increase as to consider the advisability of building a larger church. During these extended proceedings discord and contention reigned supreme, quickened by the language question, as is the case in so many similar instances. The ultimate end of dissatisfaction and the beginning of pacification was the withdrawal of the English portion to the north ward, approved by a majority of votes previously taken, in about 1851. Thus came to be incorporated the Evangelical Lutheran church, April 29, 1852. Subsequently the English members living in the southward desired an English Lutheran church in that locality and were incorporated as Trinity Evangelical Lutheran church, May 18, 1863. Rev. Willard was still pastor during this turbulent period of the German congregation, but resigned and held his farewell discourse May 11, 1856.

The congregation was without a pastor until the Rev. Wm. J. Eyer was again called in January, 1858. He, together with some of the German members, at once proceeded to the purchase of the old church and succeeded. In 1859 they applied for a charter, which was granted, and incorporated as St. John's German Evangelical Lutheran church. Rev. Eyer served faithfully until his death in the spring of 1874.

Vacant until May, 1875, when Rev. J. W. Early was called, ministering to this people in connection with the aforesaid congregations and supplying Trinity Lutheran church in Liberty township, thus practically forming the present parish. He resigned April 1, 1883.

Rev. J. R. Groff succeeded him as pastor in 1883, serving it in connection with Trinity Lutheran church for the first three years, when he accepted a call from the German parish proper. He resigned in the spring of 1888. The Rev. D. L. Fogelman entered upon his pastoral duties at the same time, April of 1888. The church was generally renovated. A Luther League was organized and is doing good work.

ST. JAMES', RIDGEVILLE.—Prior to 1800 an unordained person by the name of Mr. Schellhardt occasionally came from Northampton or Lehigh counties to preach in what was then popularly called "Mahoning church," erected by Lutherans and Reformed people. It is a union church to this day. However, the first record of a church organization seems dated 1803, at which time Johann Paul Ferdinand Kramer was pastor, and remained until 1805. An unknown minister with the initials, M. C. S. F., served the congregation from 1805 to 1808.

The congregation was without a pastor from 1808 to 1810, when Rev. J. F. Engel became the pastor until his resignation in 1816. He lived at Bloomsburg, Pa., and served four other congregations. Then follows another vacancy of about four years, after which Rev. J. P. Kessler entered upon the duties as pastor about 1820, remaining until 1828. His successor, Rev. J. J. Ungerer, doubtful as to him being a Lutheran, ministered to this people until 1830. The Rev. Jer. Shindel was then called and labored here until 1833. He was succeeded by Rev. I. Bahl, 1833 until 1840 or 1841. The Rev. W. J. Eyer assumed the pastoral duties in 1841 until 1843, when Rev. E. Schwartz began his labors, until 1844. For a short time Rev. F. Ruthrauff held services during the year 1845, as also Rev. J. W. Smith. After a vacancy of several years Rev. Eyer was recalled as pastor in 1848, continued until 1858, when Rev. M. J. Stover became pastor a year later, preaching in the English language, and Rev. J. F. Hornberger in German. The Rev. D. M. Henkel was then called, assuming the pastoral duties in 1860 to 1863 or 1864, after which Rev. Eyer was again urged to take charge of their spiritual welfare, which was in 1864.

On February 22, 1870, the congregations were granted a charter of incorporation to be known as Lutheran and Reformed church. During the fall and winter of 1870, the church edifice, which had been constructed of logs, with galleries on three sides and a wine-cup-like pulpit, and "back-breakers" for pews, was entirely remodeled, after which it was reconsecrated to Almighty God. Revs. W. J. Ever and his Reformed colleague, J. W. Steinmetz, officiated. In May, 1875, the Rev. J. W. Early assumed the pastorate and ended with his resignation in April, 1883. The Rev. J. R. Groff succeeded him in 1883, until 1888. In the spring of the same year, April, 1888, the Rev. D. L. Fogelman entered upon the pastoral duties and is the present pastor.

ST. PETER'S, GROVANIA.—At first services were held by Rev. Isaiah Bahl in the school-house near the present church, which was erected as a union church—Lutheran and Reformed—12 or 13 years after the organization of the congregation. Rev. Bahl labored here from 1842 or 1843 to 1856.

The land on which a church was ultimately built was donated by Mr. Leonard Lazarus. The corner-stone of the church was laid with appropriate services June 1, 1856, and the church consecrated in May, 1857, as St. Peter's Evangelical Lutheran and Reformed church. It is popularly called "Lazarus" church.

The first Lutheran pastor was Rev. W. R. Hasskarl, who served the congregation between 1856 and 1859. He was followed by Rev. J. F. Hornberger, in 1859. From 1860 to 1862 the Rev. W. J. Eyer ministered to the congregation. Rev. J. R. Dimm served them from 1862 to 1864 or 1865. Subsequently Rev. Eyer again assumed the pastoral duties in 1865, continuing until his death in 1874. Rev. J. W. Early was then called and began his pastorship in May, 1875. In view of dissatisfaction which arose from the want of support by the Reformed, the Lutherans applied for a charter of incorporation to be known as the St. Peter's Evangelical Lutheran church, Grovania, Pa., which, in the face of a counter petition, was granted December 21, 1877. During these fiery trials and for several years afterward, Rev. Early earnestly labored until his resignation in April, 1883. Rev. D. M. Henkel, D.D., succeeded him in 1883 to 1885. The Rev. J. R. Groff followed in 1886 until 1888. The writer of this sketch assumed the pastoral duties in April, 1888. Up to this time no Sunday-school was permitted in the church, though several efforts at different times had been made to introduce it, but proved unsuccessful, nor was a light allowed in the church after sun-set, to prevent holding evening services. In 1889, however, another effort was made to organize a Sunday-school in the church, and to introduce evening services, which, after several pleadings and by the majority of votes, was granted. The result is a flourishing Sunday-school, together with evening services.

TRINITY, OAK GROVE.—The initial steps toward the establishment of a Lutheran church were taken by Rev. Jacob Albert, who held frequent services in the school-house at the cross-roads, popularly called "Rowdy Corners," in the fall of 1868 and spring of 1869. In the meantime the Lutheran families living in this vicinity concluded to erect a church edifice, the cornerstone of which was laid June 5, 1869. Revs. Jacob Albert and J. F. Wampole officiated. On November 7, 1869, said church was consecrated to Almighty God by Revs. J. F. Wampole and J. M. Anspach, at the same time effecting an organization. The congregation was supplied with services every two weeks by Revs. J. M. Anspach and J. F. Wampole, preaching alternately, the former in the English and the latter in the German language. At the communion November 12, 1871, Rev. J. F. Wampole resigned, on account of his other pastoral duties.

Rev. J. M. Anspach continued his services until April 21, 1872, when he resigned. After a vacancy of several months, Rev. M. C. Horine, then pastor of Trinity Lutheran church, Danville, assumed the pastorate, in September, 1872, until September, 1875. On the acceptance of a call to the German charge Rev. J. W. Early, also supplied the pulpit of this church, beginning September, 1875. About this time a "church quarrel" occurred. The seceders wished to exercise unprincipled authority, whilst the conservatives adhered to congregational as well as synodical preferences and rights. The conservatives, showing themselves equal to the emergency, liquidated their obligations to the seceders, and secured a deed to their church property as well as a grant of a charter of incorporation as Trinity Evangelical Lutheran Church, Oak Grove, dated September 25, 1878. The seceders, finding their "names stricken from the list of members," erected a church on the opposite corner, and are recognized by the Susquehanna Synod to this day.

Rev. M. C. Horine again rendered his services as a supply from October, 1880, to 1881. Rev. J. R. Groff supplied the pulpit in 1881 to 1888. In the spring of the same year the writer assumed the pastorate, April, 1888, and is the present pastor. About the year 1890, by vote, Trinity was connected with the other three congregations.

DUSHORE PARISH.

BY THE REV. J. W. KLINGLER.

THE EVENTS leading to the establishment of a large parish of the Lutheran Church connected with our General Council, located north of the Alleghenies, 50 or 60 miles distant from neighboring Lutheran parishes are a source of wonder; and when we realize that it is probably the largest Protestant parish in Sullivan county, our surprise is in no way diminished. Gratitude to God for the wonderful establishment and preservation of our Luthern Zion here prompts us to voice our thanksgiving and should certainly direct us to give tangible evidence of our love to the Church and her institutions in this year of Jubilee.

FRIEDEN'S, OR PEACE.—A number of families from Berks, Luzerne and Columbia counties, about 1825, came to this county, at that time a part of Lycoming, and settled here in the wilderness. It is difficult to conceive the hardships and privations they endured in providing new homes for themselves. It was not long after their arrival that the Gospel was preached to them. A log church was built and called Frieden's. This must have been as early as 1826. The earliest record of baptism is that of Caroline, daughter of Jacob and Catherine Hoffa in June, 1827, and to this is added, "in Frieden's church, Cherry township." The person baptized is still living, the wife of John Dieffenbach, and a communicant of our Zion's church, Dushore. In April, 1830, the Holy Communion was administered to 39 persons, including eight catechumens. Ministers of the Reformed and Lutheran churches served rather irregularly. It is possible that the old log church was built a few years later but certainly not many. Services were conducted in the school house situated on the turnpike, not far from the present borough limits and the people who assembled there might have constituted the Frieden's church. We are told, however, that the log church "stood many years and in such a ruinous condition that the congregation resolved to erect a frame church but owing to the poverty of the members, several years passed by before its completion."

In 1839 the Rev. C. L. Erle arrived and assumed the duties of pastorate, which included the entire parish as now composed of the three congregations. He preached his introductory sermon on June 2, 1839. He instructed a class of 18 catchumens and on April 13, 1840, they were confirmed and the Lord's Supper administered to them and to 69 members of the congregation. Rev. Erle was not a member of our Synod at this time and because of this, he requested Rev. Benninger, of Black Creek, near Conyngham, to confirm the young people and administer the Holy Communion. Rev. Benninger was approached by a few Reformed members who expressed the wish that he should hand them bread, to which request he acceded. Rev. Erle, having been received into connection with our Synod, followed the example of Father Benninger, believing, as he expressed himself, that the "worthy communicant can receive the body of our Lord Jesus Christ for the remission of sins with the bread as well as with the hostiens." For many years he labored in Frieden's as also in old Zion's, until the Reformed organized a congregation of their own in the borough. The work and expense of the church properties devolved upon the Lutheran people and a few Reformed who believed that the labors of Rev. Erle had been prosecuted with singular fidelity and with satisfaction to themselves.

The site of the old log church was abandoned and the new frame church was erected on the burial ground. It was consecrated to the service of the Triune God on August 28, 1859, the Rev. Isaiah Bahl assisting the pastor. The first communion in the new church was administered to 43 communicants on June 11, 1864, the congregation celebrated the 25th anniversary of the pastorate of Rev. Erle, who preached the sermon on the occasion. He relinquished the duties as pastor at the close of 1872, having served a period of nearly 34 years. His successors were the following: Rev. H. B. Strodach, June, 1874-1876; Rev. Lewis Smith, 1877-1880; Rev. R. S. Wagner, February, 1881-May, 1884; Rev. S. Wenrich, August 17, 1884-July, 1893; Rev. J. W. Klingler, since March 4, 1894. The membership now numbers 72.

St. John's.—Rev. C. L. Erle directed his labors in other directions. Towards the North Branch of the Susquehanna six to seven miles from Dushore, he found a number of German families, some living in Bradford and others in Sullivan county. They had no sanctuary, no conveyances, a road hewn through the forest, traveling on foot an arduous task, and yet with all these inconveniences, these people, desirous of worshiping God and hearing the precious truths of the Gospel, wended their way, with their children on their arms to the house of a neighbor, where services were most frequently held, in the home of J. George Eberlin, in Wilmot township, Bradford county. In the Eberlin home, already on March 23, 1845, five persons were confirmed and communion administered to twenty persons. Services were also held in the home of George Schock, owing to the illness of Mrs. Eberlin. Steps were taken to build a log church not far from the Eberlin homestead and with the following in charge: J. George Eberlin, architect and elder; Jacob Hollacher and George Eberlin, Jr., trustees;

Jacob Eberlin, Adam Messersmith and Thomas Messersmith, deacons, to which David Frey, sr., and Joseph Eberlin were later added as deacons. Of the above named only Joseph Eberlin survives—a father in Israel and who, though growing old, has not grown cold in the service of the Master. The work was finished in 1851 and on June 14 was dedicated to God. The first Lord's Supper in the new church was administered on July 13, 1851, to 40 communicants. On October 31, 1867, the congregation assembled at the house of Joseph Eberlin and marched in a body to the church to celebrate the 350th Jubilee of the Reformation. Several were present who attended a similar service in the Fatherland in 1817, among whom was the pastor of the church. An offering of $14.50 was gathered as a "token of gratitude to God for his mercy and grace." In the spring of 1872 the congregation determined to build a neat frame church and on July 7, 1872, the corner-stone was laid and the edifice dedicated in the fall of the same year. Pastor Erle discontinued his services at St. John's the same time he relinquished the duties of the pastorate of Frieden's. There was a strong sentiment for English services and Rev. Erle, then about 70 years of age, unable to preach in that language with any satisfaction to the young people, retired from the active duties of the ministerial office. He was succeeded by the same pastors as in Frieden's church. Rev. Strodach entering upon the work introduced English and at present English is used in connection with the German service. During the pastorate of Rev. S. Wenrich, a steeple was added to the church and a 750-pound bell was purchased by the Women's Working Association and presented to the congregation. The church was rededicated and the bell consecrated on October 26, 1892, Revs. C. J. Cooper and J. W. Early assisting him.

ZION'S.—Prior to the erection of Zion's church, two

miles northeast of Dushore, on the Wyalusing road, Rev. Erle held services in his humble home near the present location of the church. In 1851 the corner-stone was laid on a part of the ground which had been donated for church and burial purposes by George Thrasher. The work progressed slowly, due to the few members and their limited means. It was completed in 1853 and set apart for public worship on September 1, by the pastor,

ZION CHURCH.

assisted by Revs. Bahl and Boyer. Services were held here regularly by the succeeding pastors of the parish. A movement was inaugurated in 1890, Rev. S. Wenrich, pastor, to erect a church in the borough of Dushore. Meetings were regularly called and held in the old church and by resolution the congregation determined to build its church in the borough, convinced that it would be conducive to the best interests of our Zion. Two lots were purchased for $500 on Carpenter street at the eastern end of Dushore. A building committee composed of Rev. S. Wenrich, S. Cole, C. W. Hoffa, J. H. Yonkin and L. M. Barth began the work. On October 26, 1890, the corner-stone was laid, Revs. A. L. Yount, D.D., and J. W. Mayne assisted the pastor. Rev. Wenrich continued to hold services in the old Zion's while the new church was in course of erection, and on September 4, 1892, the people assembled in the edifice, that was henceforth to be the home of the congregation, to join in the dedicatory services. The pastor was assisted by the Rev. H. B. Strodach, a former pastor, and the Rev. S. E. Ochsenford, D.D., president of the Conference. The building is frame, octagonal in its proportions, with a graceful steeple tapering high above the structure. The main audience-room is exceptionally beautiful, bright and attractive, pulpit and pew furniture as durable as beautiful. The room in which the Sunday-school assembles every Lord's day, is located in the northern end of the building and is connected with the main room by a movable door. The sacristy is in the southwest corner of the building. It is one of the finest churches in the county. Since the completion of new Zion's but few services have been held in the old church. From August, 1893, to March 4, 1894, Rev. J. W. Early supplied the parish with the Word and Sacrament. Rev. J. W. Klingler was installed pastor on March 4, by Revs. J. W Early and J. H. Umbenhen.

FREEBURG PARISH.

BY THE REV. G. D. DRUCKENMILLER.

THE history of the Freeburg Parish would be incomplete, if no mention were made of the first house of worship in the immediate neighborhood of what is now called Freeburg.

Shortly before the Revolutionary War this neighborhood was settled with people who believed in the Christian religion, the Lutherans, through Andrew Morr, Peter Straub and Casper Roush, the latter a soldier in the Revolutionary War, applied in the year 1770, and had patented for the use of the Lutheran church, 42 acres of land in the year 1774, one mile north of Freeburg, Washington township, Snyder county. On this ground they erected a school-house in which they held services, school and lectures. Rev. Enterline, Lutheran, occasionally preached as a visiting minister.

After the congregation had increased in numbers, they resolved, in the year 1787, to erect a church on this land. At the laying of the corner-stone they named it Zion's. This church was never finished, but used in its unfinished condition until the completion of St. Peter's church, in Freeburg, in the year 1815. Rev. Enterline, Lutheran, preached nine years in this congregation. Rev. Herbst, Lutheran, from 1802 to 1804; Rev. J. Conrad Walter, Lutheran, 1804 till the completion of St. Peter's church, in Freeburg, 1815. About six acres of the original tract still remains as the property of the Lutheran congregation. The old cemetery is kept in order and occasional interments are made there.

ST. PETER'S CHURCH AT FREEBURG.—The motives

and reasons that actuated our forefathers to build this church are as follows:

1st. Because in the year 1796 the town of Freeburg was laid out by Andrew Straub, and he donated four lots —one acre—of ground for school and church purposes.

2d. Because after the town of Freeburg had been located and buildings erected, and increasing in population, and Zion's church situated one mile distant, it became too inconvenient for the majority to attend public worship.

3d. Because Zion's church was becoming dilapidated, and according to the changed order of population it was not considered expedient or proper to make any repairs on it.

4th. Because the Reformed congregation had no share or interest in Zion's church or the grounds on which it was erected, and the cemetery.

After a number of meetings at which numerous difficulties were discussed which presented themselves in the building of a union church, and which had retarded the building of a new church, it was finally agreed that a Lutheran and Reformed church be erected in Freeburg, and on the grounds donated by Andrew Straub.

The corner-stone was laid May 7, 1812. Rev. J. Conrad Walter, Lutheran pastor in charge, laid the corner-stone. A large audience had assembled.

The consecration occurred Sunday, Oct. 27, 1815. Rev. J. P. Shindel, of Sunbury, preached in the forenoon, Ps. 9:12; Rev. Gearhart, of Bedford, in the afternoon, from Gen. 28:11, 17; Rev. H. Fries, of Youngmanstown (now Mifflinburg), in the evening, Ps. 87:3. Rev. Walter preached on Monday, text, Hag. 2:10. Rev. J. C. Walter and Rev. Gearhart, regular pastor in charge, conducted the consecration ceremonies.

The stone church, after standing fifty-five years, became dilapidated, the walls were cracked, and dissatisfaction with its arrangements was expressed by nearly all of the members of the church. Dec. 22, 1867, after ser-

ST. PETER'S CHURCH.

vice by Rev. Erlenmyer, a meeting was called. Edward Bassler presided, and Daniel S. Boyer, secretary. It was then unanimously resolved to erect a new church on the union basis, Lutheran and Reformed. A number of meetings were held, progress reported at every meeting. Feb. 16, 1868, the Building Committee was elected: Lutherans, Francis Boyer and John Hummel; Reformed, Geo. C. Moyer and George Hilbish.

It now became necessary to take down the old church. Sunday, March 15, 1868, Rev. Erlenmyer preached his last sermon in the old stone church, text, "Remember the Sabbath Day to keep it holy."

The corner-stone ceremonies of the brick church at Freeburg took place on Sunday, Aug. 2, 1868. About eight hundred persons were in attendance. A stand and temporary seats were arranged on the foundation of the church and on the adjoining grounds. Rev. C. F. Hoffmeier, Reformed, of New Berlin, preached the opening sermon from Isaiah 28:16, and was followed on the same text, by Rev. J. W. Early, Lutheran minister from Selinsgrove. A shower of rain interfered. Repairing to the town hall, where Rev. Millet, of Walker, addressed the audience in the English language, from 1 Cor. 3:11. After the services had concluded, the audience assembled around the corner-stone. Rev. Erlenmyer then laid the corner-stone.

The brick church was consecrated June 19, 1870. Rev. J. G. Anspach, Rev. J. M. Anspach, Rev. J. W. Early and Dr. Gearhard preached appropriate discourses. Rev. Erlenmyer, Lutheran, and Rev. J. S. Shade, Reformed, ministers in charge, were also present. The Lutheran congregation, in order to meet the requirements of the Synod of Pennsylvania, to which body they belong, and of the General Council of the Lutheran Church in the United States, had a constitution prepared by Rev. J. F. Wampole, which was regularly adopted and transcribed into a book into which the annual meetings of the church council are regularly recorded. The conditions for church membership require of every member to contribute annually according to their means, a reasonable amount to the support of the minister or ministers, or forfeit all claims to the burial ground and church membership.

Lutheran ministers, in St. Peter's church: Rev. J. Conrad Walter, from 1804 to 1819; Rev. J. P. Shindel, Sr., from 1819 to 1820; Rev. J. W. Smith, from 1821 to 1831; Rev. W. German, from 1832 to 1842; Rev. C. G. Erlenmyer, from 1842 to 1876; Rev. J. F. Wampole, from 1876 to 1892; Rev. H. G. Snable, from 1892 to 1896; Rev. G. D. Druckenmiller, from June, 1897, to the present time The names of the Lutheran ministers, Enterline, Jasensky and Herbst have already been given in the sketch of Zion's church, also Adams, Reformed.

BOTSCHAFT'S OR GRUBB'S CHURCH, Chapman township.—The territory embraced by those who founded this church and congregation was included in Penn's township, Cumberland county, and then Northumberland county, and in 1795 this portion was formed into Mahantongo township, and about 1820, the same portion was embraced in parts of Chapman, Perry and Union townships.

John Shamory was one of the earliest settlers, who emigrated from Germany to this country, and was sold for a term of three years, to pay his passage, serving out his time in Baltimore, and then coming up the Susquehanna, took up a tract of land and built a hut, where the old house, on the premises of George Heintzleman, deceased, was afterwards built. He was a carpenter by trade, and is said to have built the old Grubb's church, and was the second person to be buried in the graveyard, behind the church. Here a piece of ground, of about 42 acres, was selected, about 1770, on which to put a church and school-house and graveyard, but they neglected to secure the right to the possession of it, by applying for a warrant to have it surveyed, and take out the patent deed, until 1790.

The early settlers, being mostly Lutherans, at once provided for the religious and educational wants of themselves and their children. Rev. Michael Enterline, who resided in Lykens Valley, came over the river occasionally and preached for them, baptized their children and buried their dead, and urged them to build a church and school-house on the tract of land which they had selected for that purpose.

The first church was built of logs, without being plastered outside or inside, about 30 by 35 feet, with pulpit to the north, and one door on the east side and one on the west side, with a gallery on three sides, and stood at the southwest corner of the present graveyard, with the upper wall just inside of the present fence. In the year 1836, the old log church was repaired and partly rebuilt. It was plastered inside and outside. It was reconsecrated Nov. 20, 1836, by Revs. W. German and Isaac Gearhart, pastors at that time, and given the name of Botschaft's church. The Building Committee was Philip Arnold, Reformed, and Jacob Richenbach, Lutheran.

The old log school-house and dwelling house having become unfit for use, and the public schools having been introduced, it was determined, in the year 1865, to build a new house on the church property, and William Heiges and Daniel Eisenhart were elected as building committee. The lumber and frame were taken from the church woods, and thus the present house was erected, right across from the old church. In the year 1871, having determined to build a new church, a preliminary meeting was held, Aug. 12th, to consider plans, etc., for the new church. At this meeting it was decided to build a brick church, with basement 45 by 60 feet, with an audience room of suitable height, with a gallery at one end for the choir, and a steeple of suitable height on top of said church, and that said church should be an Evangelical Lutheran and Reformed, as heretofore. Oct. 23, a meeting was called

BOTSCHAFT'S (GRUBE'S) CHURCH.

to select a site for the new church, when three sites were proposed, and on a vote being taken, the present site was chosen by the majority over all the rest. The cornerstone was laid Aug. 18, 1872; the basement, having been first finished, was consecrated Aug. 24, 1873. The church proper was consecrated Sunday, Nov. 5, 1876.

Rev. M. B. Lenker, of Lykens, preached in German, and Rev. E. L. Reed, of Selinsgrove, in English.

Following are the names of the pastors who served this congregation from the beginning to the present time: Rev. Michael Enterline, as before stated, was the first minister who served this congregation, and he organized the congregation and was the pastor during the building of the first church and school-house. After him came Rev. Mathias Gentzel, Frederick Hinze and John Herbst, until the year 1804, when the congregation called Rev. John Conrad Walter, who served them until his death, Aug. 11, 1819. Rev. J. P. Shindel, Sr, served one year, when Rev. J. W. Smith became pastor, in 1820, and, after serving nearly ten years, resigned in 1830, and Rev. Wm. German took charge, Oct. 10, 1830, and continued until Nov., 1839, when he resigned, and the congregation was without a pastor until Feb. 20, 1842, when Rev. C. G. Erlenmyer became the pastor, continued to preach for this congregation until his death, when Rev. J. F. Wampole took charge, Nov. 5th, 1876, the very Sunday that the present church was consecrated, and was the pastor in this congregation until 1892. Rev. H. G. Snable became the pastor of this church in 1892, and continued until 1896. On the 4th of July, 1897, Rev. G. D. Druckenmiller took charge of this congregation and is the present pastor.

ST. JOHN'S OR SCHNEE'S CHURCH, AT FREMONT.—The first Lutheran and Reformed of this neighborhood, who had settled here before 1800, worshiped at the "Bauerman's or Kruppe Kirche," and Mohr's or Zion's church, near Freeburg, where congregations had been organized and churches built, as early as 1776 and 1781. Among the first Lutherans here, was Frederick Stees, who owned the farm including all of Mt. Pleasant Mills and Fremont. He built a school-house on the spot where the present one now stands, and had it arranged with a partition, so that one part could be used for school,

ST. JOHN'S CHURCH.

and by removing the partition, the whole could be used for church purposes.

About the year 1810 the Lutherans and Reformed began to form a congregation, and called Rev. J. Conrad Walter to become their regular pastor, who preached for them on New Year's Day, 1811, and preached his introductory sermon on Feb. 2d, on Hezek. 3:17, 18. He supplied them with regular preaching for three years, when he was compelled to stop, on account of his abundant labors elsewhere. Before this time and after, Revs. Adams and Gearhart preached for the Reformed, one year each, and also left. For several years after, Revs. Walter and Gearhart occasionally visited them and preached for them, but in the year 1818, Rev. Walter was again recalled to become their regular pastor, and having accepted the call, he preached his first sermon, Oct. 4th, on Matt. 22:1, 5. About this time the first church council was elected.

Up to this time the congregation had no building of their own in which to worship, and no graveyard in which to bury their dead, though the school-house was always open to them free of charge. Soon after Rev. Walter had again taken charge of the congregation, they bought the school-house and two acres of land; in 1818 they prepared and adopted a "Kirchen Ordnung." Rev. Walter continued to serve the congregation until his death, Aug. 11, 1819.

After Rev. Walter's death, Rev. J. P. Shindel, of Sunbury, who had preached his funeral sermon, was most earnestly implored to become his successor, and he agreed to supply them until they could be regularly supplied with a pastor. Accordingly he preached for this congregation, as often as his other engagements would permit, until Rev. J. W. Smith, who was then a student under him, and assisted in preaching, was licensed, and in May, 1823, took regular charge of this congregation, and he continued to preach here until 1830, when Rev. Wm. German became his successor, and he preached here until the year 1836, when Rev. C. G. Erlenmyer became the pastor and served this congregation for forty successive years, until his death, March 6th, 1876. Rev. J. F. Wampole became his successor, the 5th of November, 1876; he continued his pastorate here until 1892, when Rev. H. G. Snable became his successor and served until 1896. The present pastor, Rev. G. D. Druckenmiller, took charge of this congregation July, 1897. In the year 1853, the present brick church was built. Building Committee was Philip Arbogast, Frederick Rathfon, John Haas, Jacob Stiever.

ST. PAUL'S CONGREGATION.—This congregation was organized by Rev. S. E. Ochsenford, D.D., in June, 1886, it being the successor of "Keiser's Church," which probably was organized early in this century. In 1840 a church was erected by the Lutherans and Reformed. Many years before this date, Jacob Keiser had donated two acres of ground for a cemetery. Jacob Keiser, according to the date on his tombstone, died May, 1829, aged 42 years. Other stones show that earlier burials took place here. One stone bears the date of the year 1801. Funeral sermons were preached in the house of Jacob Keiser, which was located near the place where the church now stands. No names of pastors are known prior to the year 1869. From 1869 to 1870, the Rev. J. W. Early served the congregation. He found there "a small tumble-down frame building." After 1870 the few Lutherans had no services and finally the congregation disbanded. It was again re-organized as stated above, and the church renovated and reconsecrated by Revs. S. E. Ochsenford, Lutheran, and J. W. Haas, Reformed. Rev. S. E. Ochsenford served the congregation from 1886 until July 1st, 1897, when the congregation was united with the Freeburg parish and is now served by the Rev. G. D. Druckenmiller.

ZION CHURCH, JERSEY SHORE.

BY THE REV. LUDWIG ROSENBERG.

THE congregation was organized through the agency of Rev. C. F. Welden in 1867. Mr. Borkstahler was the first minister who served it until March, 1869. In the same year a Sunday-school was organized and an organ purchased.

Rev. G. F. W. Guensch then took charge of the congregation and served it until 1871. In his time the congregation secured a church building of their own, having previous to that worshiped in the engine-house and town-hall.

After a short vacancy Rev. Carl Weber took charge of the field. During this time there was some difficulty about the payment of a balance still owing on account of the building of the church. Rev. W. H. Kuntz took charge of the congregation in May, 1873. He resided at Cogan Station and served the congregation for one year and six months.

He was succeeded by Rev. H. Eggers, also residing at Cogan Station, who remained in charge until September, 1878, thus serving the congregation about three years and nine months.

Rev. A. Linsz, residing at Lock Haven, then served the congregation until August, 1880. During his pastorate the church was renovated and a new pulpit bought.

He was followed by Rev. F. J. Hennicke who also served the congregation at Lock Haven. He preached for about one year.

He was succeeded by Rev. Lewis Smith, also residing

at Cogan Station. His successor was Rev. S. S. Henry, who preached besides in some neighboring churches, White Deer and Dewalds church, in Lycoming county. He also supplied Cogan Station a part of the time.

Rev. D. E. Reed, pastor of Cogan Station, then took charge of the field and served it faithfully until his death. Though often prevented by sickness to preach, he is nevertheless gratefully remembered by the congregation for whose spiritual welfare he consumed his health. He died in February, 1889.

Rev. J. W. Early was then called to the field and served for a little more than four years. Under his pastorate a parsonage was built and, as far as can be seen from the church records, English services introduced. He also did some missionary work in Tioga County. He preached his last sermon on the evening of Whitsunday, 1893.

He was succeeded by Rev. E. F. Steinhagen who served the congregation until September 30, 1895.

He was succeeded by Rev. L. Rosenberg who is serving the congregation at present.

St. JOHN'S PARISH, LYKENS, PA.

BY THE REV. H. E. C. WAHRMANN.

THE EARLY history of this congregation is shrouded in obscurity because of lack of any early records. The Rev. N. Jaeger preached here in the year 1852, but left at the close of the year. The Rev. D. Sell came in 1853 and organized a Lutheran congregation. In 1859 they built the first church. Soon after it had been consecrated, the Rev. D. Sell introduced protracted meetings, with all their concomitants, and distracted the congregation. The German element protested against the introduction of un-Lutheran practices and quietly withdrew. In 1862 they sent a committee to the Rev. F. Walz, at that time pastor of the Lykens Valley parish, asking him to supply them with the preaching of the Word. At first he declined, but perseverance finally induced him to come and keep the little flock together, "because," as he himself says, "I was aware that the material would scatter and be lost to our Church if I did not take hold of the matter." Early in 1863 the congregation was organized as "St. John's Evangelical Lutheran Church of Lykens and Wiconisco," with the following church council: Carl Seifert, Andrew Weis, Geo. Weber, Fred. Schindler, John Schand and Mr. Schroeder. The Rev. F. Walz supplied these people with the means of grace until 1869, when he accepted a call to Sellersville. Deprived of the services of a pastor, the little flock soon scattered. Some returned to the old congregation, others went to some of the denominations, and the rest lost all interest in church matters.

In 1871 revival meetings were again held in Zion's

church, as a result of which the conservative Germans again protested; but they were in the minority and had to submit or withdraw. They decided upon the latter course, and during the year 1872 applied to neighboring pastors for services, which were "cheerfully and promptly given." On March 15, 1872, the Revs. Thos. Steck, then president of Conference, and J. W. Early, secretary of Conference, organized or re-organized St. John's congregation. In February, of the same year, the president of Conference had invited the Rev. M. B. Lenker, of Circleville, O., to visit the field, with a view of becoming the pastor. He visited the congregation and was elected. In June, of the same year, both pastor and congregation were received as members of the Ministerium of Pennsylvania. After he had labored here about a year, writes the Rev. M. B. Lenker, in 1874, "the congregation felt itself sufficiently strengthened to erect a church edifice, to its own edification and comfort, and to the honor and glory of God." The corner-stone was laid August 16, 1874, the pastor being assisted by Revs. F. Walz and J. W. Early. The building was consecrated on November 22, of the same year, the pastor being assisted by Revs. J. W. Early and R. S Wagner.

The congregation now began to prosper; but, alas! all was not to go on smoothly, for in 1876 the church building was entirely destroyed by fire. Pastor Lenker writes, "supposed cause of this misfortune was a defective flue." Much better and to the point is the statement of the Rev. J. W. Early, in his Conference Chart: "The first church was destroyed by fire—most probably of incendiary origin, almost certainly so." Much more could be said about this "misfortune," and facts adduced to prove the origin of it. But enough. 'Tis past. In the year 1877, the great fire in the mines occurred, and as a consequence all the members were out of employment and no money could be raised to erect a new church. It was not until January 1, 1879, that steps were taken in this direction. July 27, 1879, the corner-stone of the second church was laid, the pastor being assisted by Revs. F. Walz, R. S. Wagner, and J. M. Uhrich. The consecration of the present church building took place, Oc-

ST. JOHN'S CHURCH.

tober 19, 1879. Ministers present on this joyous occasion, besides the pastor: Revs. D. Sanner, Prof. D. Worley, M. C. Horine and J. M. Uhrich. In 1881 a new organ was purchased and was consecrated on the 17th of July.

In connection with this congregation, Pastor Lenker also served Trinity, at Williamstown, and St. Paul's, at Tower City. In 1891 the latter called its own pastor; whilst the former was abandoned, most of the members uniting with the General Synod congregation. Since then St. John's has supported its own pastor. Had Pastor Lenker lived two months longer, he would have served this congregation twenty-four years—May, 1873, to March, 1897.

The present pastor, the second of St. John's, preached his first sermon May 16, 1897, and on the 22d he was unanimously elected pastor. He took charge July 6th and was installed August 8th by the Rev. Drs. Ochsenford and Prof. G. F. Spieker.

PLATE IV.

J. R. GROFF.

J. F. WAMPOLE.

A. R. HORNE.

A. M. STRAUSS.

H. H. BRUNING.

J. W. EARLY.

LYKENS VALLEY PARISH.

BY THE REV. O. E. PFLUEGER.

IN this parish there is preserved the name of what was one of the oldest and most extensive Lutheran parishes in this part of the State. On the territory which was originally covered by the pastors of this Lykens Valley parish, there are now no less than 12 separate parishes of our Church, with about 40 congregations. As late as the year 1864, it included the following eight congregations: St. John's in Mifflin township, Salem at Elizabethville, Zion at Rife, Fetterhoff's and St. Jacob's in Armstrong Valley, and the congregation at Vera Cruz. Beginning with 1870, the parish was constituted, for a period of 25 years, of the following five congregations, all in Dauphin county: St. John's in Mifflin township, Simeon's at Gratz, Salem at Elizabethville, Zion at Rife, and St. Jacob's in Armstrong Valley. At a joint meeting of the church councils, held November 10, 1894, it was agreed that the four congregations last named should constitute a parish by themselves, said action to go into effect January 1, 1895, since which time Simeon's, Salem, Zion and St. Jacob's congregations have composed the Lykens Valley parish.

PARSONAGE.—Provision has always been made in this parish for the property, which, next to the church edifice itself, is the most interesting and honorable,—the parsonage. The first parsonage property was a farm of 24 acres, located in Washington township, about one mile west of St. John's Church. The substantial house on this tract of land was erected and first occupied in 1809 by the Rev. Daniel Ulrich. Realizing that the pastor should spend no part of his time in the cultivation of land, but that his undivided energy is required in the care of the congregations, this parsonage farm was sold in 1870, and the house purchased in Berrysburg, which is now the property of A. J. Kantz, M.D. This was used as a parsonage only during one pastorate of three years, that of the Rev. Thomas Steck. The location was not

PARSONAGE.

thought favorable, and the property was sold. In the summer of 1874, the house was erected in Elizabethville, which has served ever since as the home of the pastors At the late dissolution of the former Lykens Valley parish, the property was sold at public sale, and purchased by the four congregations of the present Lykens Valley parish, by whom it is now owned in equal shares.

PASTORS.—The following is a list of the pastors who have successively served this parish, as far back as the organization of the oldest of the congregations now belonging to it, and is therefore the correct list of pastors of all the present congregations of the parish, with the single exception that Simeon's congregation at Gratz was not in this parish from 1827 till 1865, and that instead of its being served by the Pastors Welden, Yeager and Walz, it was served during that time by the pastors whose names appear in the appended history of that congregation:

1. The Rev. John Nicholas Hemping, who first came to Lykens Valley in 1811, and continued as pastor of this parish till 1850, organized each one of the present congregations of the parish. He was a man of thorough education and great powers of endurance, and as a result of his labors, many new congregations were organized.

2. The Rev. C. F. Welden was pastor from September, 1850, to September, 1851, and as a comment on this brief pastorate, we quote his own words: "At the end of the first year, finding my strength insufficient for the extensive field of labor, I reluctantly left the kind-hearted and very friendly people of Dauphin county, and moved to Bethlehem."

3. The Rev. Nathan Yeager, from 1852 to 1853.

4. The Rev. Frederick Walz became pastor January 1, 1854, and his pastorate marked a period of aggressive work, during which organizations were effected at Vera Cruz, Lykens, Tower City, and other places, until, as Rev. Walz puts it, "the work outgrew his strength." and he requested a division of the parish. The congregations not being willing to take this step, the pastoral relation was severed December 31, 1864.

5. The Rev. Jeremiah Schindel was pastor from 1865 till the time of his death, in March, 1870.

6. The Rev. Thomas Steck succeeded Rev. Schindel in November of the same year, and remained three years.

7. The Rev. Reuben S. Wagner served from October, 1874, to June 1, 1881.

8. The Rev. Joseph Hillpot was pastor from July 31, 1881, to April 24, 1889. During his pastorate, the Zion Church was erected and the Salem Church begun.

9. The writer assumed pastoral charge July 1, 1889, and continues to the present. This pastorate has so far been marked by the completion of Salem Church, the organization of the congregations of the parish with an annual meeting for the transaction of business, and, as we think, a development of interest in the life of the Church, largely by means of the holding of an annual mission festival and the circulation of the literature of the Church more extensively than is usual in rural congregations. The parish has been divided by the mother congregation becoming self-sustaining, and the four congregations having learned to support their pastor more comfortably than the five had previously done. There are at this time two young men at the Theological Seminary at Mt. Airy, the first fruits of these congregations. The ministrations are now about equally divided between the English and German languages.

SIMEON'S AT GRATZ.—The Rev. J. N. Hemping organized this congregation, chiefly from members of St. John's, in the year 1822. For a period of about 10 years, the congregation worshiped in a building which was the property of Mr. Simon Gratz, which was later converted into a dwelling and is now owned and occupied by Mr. William S. Boyer. The first baptism on record, was entered June 30, 1822. Eight baptisms are recorded that year on the Lutheran side, and the following year ten. At the first communion, May, 1822, there were 59 participants, of whom 23 were confirmed that day.

The Rev. John Peter Schindel, of Sunbury, succeeded the Rev. Hemping, in 1827, and continued till 1843.

In the years 1831-2, the Lutherans and Reformed

united in the erection of the present church edifice, the land for the building and the cemetery having been donated by the above-mentioned Simon Gratz. The corner-stone was laid August 14, 1831.

With the close of the pastorate of the Rev. Schindel, sensational religion, under the popular name of "new measures," had been introduced, so that both the Luth-

SIMEON'S CHURCH.

eran and Reformed congregations became very much distracted. The choice of a successor of the Rev. Schindel fell on the Rev. August Bergner, who was also pastor of the territory now comprised in the Line Mountain and Mahanoy parishes, and served this congregation till his death, in the fall of 1860. The "new measure" party separated from the old congregation, and, under the guidance of the Rev. C. F. Stoever, erected the other church in town. The new congregation did not prosper, and after a number of years, the property was sold to the Evangelical Association, by whom it is still held May 9, 1852, the Rev. Bergner recorded a communion of 92 guests, and during his pastorate the church building was improved by the addition of a steeple, with a bell, and the alteration of the gables.

The Rev. W. R. C. Hasskarl, who succeeded the Rev. Bergner in his large field, was pastor of this congregation from the spring of 1861 to 1865, when he was succeeded by one August Unkerer, who remained less than a year, and left an odious record behind him.

With the succession of the Rev. Jeremiah Schindel to the pastorate of the Lykens Valley parish, in 1865, this congregation, after having been supplied for almost 40 years from the other side of the mountain, was received back again into its mother parish, to which it has belonged from that time to this.

In the year 1883, the church building was materially improved by the walls being cemented and the woodwork being painted without and within, the old steeple being replaced by a new one, and a furnishing with new pews. These improvements were made at a cost of $2,618.06.

December 4-5, 1897, the congregation engaged in interesting services commemorative of its own 75th anniversary, as well as the 150th anniversary of the organization of the Ministerium of Pennsylvania. At these services, the pastor was assisted by the Revs. C. J. Cooper, W. H. Geiger and C. A. Kerschner. The congregation supports a flourishing union Sunday-school, as well as a Luther League. The record shows the communion of 215 guests in the year 1897, and the congregation is in a prosperous condition.

SALEM AT ELIZABETHVILLE.—A translation of the earliest bit of history of this congregation, on a fly-leaf of an old record, is as follows: "In the year 1835 the citizens in and around Elizabethville organized themselves into a Christian congregation and built a church named Salem." This first union church is built of stone, and while it has not been used for ten years, is standing still. The Building Committee at its erection was John Heller, Ludwig Lenker and Simon Salada. At the lay-

OLD SALEM CHURCH.

ing of its corner-stone the offerings amounted to $19.37, and at its consecration, September 6, 1835, they were $43.75. Public school was taught for some time in the basement. About 1866 a steeple and bell were added to the building. The Sunday-school had fallen into the influence of the United Brethren, but through the remonstrances of the Rev. J. Schindel, during his pastorate, was re-organized as a Lutheran and Reformed Sunday-school. The Reformed congregation, having built for itself a substantial brick church edifice, abandoned the old church in 1884, and thus left the Lutheran congregation in sole possession.

April 18, 1887, the Lutheran members held a meeting to consider the question of erecting a new Lutheran church building, and in two days, more than $2,700 were subscribed, and Jonas Swab, L. R. Bender and Hiram Smith were elected a building committee to erect a "brick

SALEM CHURCH.

church with a slate roof," on three town lots which were purchased from Miss Persida Bender, for $325. The corner-stone was laid September 18, 1887, when the pastor was assisted by the Revs. M. B. Lenker and W. H. Geiger, the offerings of the day amounting to $467.23. Credit is due the Rev. J. Hillpot, under whose pastorate the erection of this church was begun, and who himself was a liberal contributor, for the part which he took in launching this important project under very adverse circumstances. The last communion in the old church showed the presence of 42 guests. The Rev. Hillpot having been called to another field of labor, the completion of the church was left to his successor, the present writer. The Sunday-school room of the new building was first occupied December 23, 1888, but the auditorium was not finished and the church consecrated till November 16, 1890, at which time the pastor was assisted by the Revs. O. Leopold, A. P. Pflueger, W. H. Geiger and M. B. Lenker. The total cost of the edifice was about $6,500.

The congregation supports a Sunday-school which is in excellent condition, using the literature of the General Council, and a Luther League, through which the church is open every Sunday evening. The number of communicants in 1897 was 123.

ZION AT RIFE.—The organization of Zion congregation of Upper Paxton township, was occasioned by the sensational wave of "new measureism" which spread over our territory more than 50 years ago. Dissension in Salem Evangelical Lutheran congregation at Killinger (known as Wert's) was so sharp as to end the pastoral work there of the Rev. J. N. Hemping, who thereupon started to preach to such as sympathized with him in a schoolhouse at what is now Rife. At the first communion there were 21 guests. Early in the spring of 1843, steps were taken towards building a union church for the Lutheran and Reformed congregations which were organized under the name of Zion, a constitution having been drawn up by the Rev. Hemping and adopted by the two congregations. The first church was a modest log building, 26x32 feet, and stood in the cemetery, across the road from the present building, on about one-fourth acre of land, donated the previous year by Andrew Kieffer, Sr., who was likewise largely the donor of the lumber. It was completed and dedicated to the service of Almighty God towards the fall of the same year, 1843.

After almost 40 years of service in the first church, the congregations felt the need of a larger and more commodious place of worship, and one more in keeping with the times. This resulted in the erection of the present

ZION CHURCH.

brick building. The ground on which the present building stands was purchased, and the building begun in 1882, the corner-stone being laid June 25, with appropriate services, the pastor, the Rev. J. Hillpot, being assisted by the Rev. M. B. Lenker, and, in the absence of the Reformed pastor, by the Reformed Elder, Henry Paul. The church was completed and dedicatory services held, June 6, 1883, participated in by the Lutheran ministers, the Revs. M. B. Lenker, J. N. Wetzler and C. K.

Drumheller, and by the Reformed pastor, the Rev. S. Kuhn. The Revs. J. Hillpot and J. B. Kerschner, Lutheran and Reformed pastors loci respectively, performed the act of consecration. The building committee which superintended the erection of this church consisted of George Webner, Henry Bonawitz, George Holtzman and Silas Cooper, and the treasurer was George I. Bordner. The total expenditure was $3,000, which was all provided for before the consecration.

The semi-centennial of the congregation was celebrated with appropriate services, December 31, 1893, in which the pastor, the present writer, was assisted by the Rev. I. B. Ritter. The congregation supports a flourishing union Sunday-school. In 1897 there were 85 communicants.

ST. JACOB'S, IN JACKSON TOWNSHIP.—The early record of this congregation, popularly known as Miller's, in Armstrong Valley, bears a date of baptism as early as April 23, 1828, and deeds show that the nine acres of land now the joint property of the Lutheran and Reformed congregations, were donated in small tracts by several of the members, a number of years after the date of the first baptism.

The first house in which worship was held was a combination school-house and church with a shifting partition. January 1, 1849, a congregational meeting was held, at which it was resolved to erect a new church building, the result of which was the present frame edifice, built in the summer of 1849 and consecrated in the fall of the same year. In the year 1873 this building was improved by the erection of an addition to the church with a steeple and bell.

This Lutheran congregation was organized by the Rev. Hemping and has constantly been a part of the Lykens Valley Parish, excepting that during the "new measure" excitement of the forties, the Revs. W. G. Laitzle and E. J. Neiman preached for the congregation during brief pastorates. At this time a split took place in the congregation and the "new measure" faction built what is known as Strow's church, about one mile distant.

ST. JACOB'S CHURCH.

The record gives the names of 31 communicants in 1834. In the year 1897 there were 50. The location is not favorable to great growth of the congregation, but it supports a flourishing Sunday-school which is exclusively under Lutheran influences because of the fact that there are very few Reformed members of the congregation and they have had no pastor for several years.

PLATE V

M. B. LENKER.

JOS. HILLPOT.

D. E. REED.

S. S. HENRY.

J. S. RENNINGER.

W. O. CORNMAN.

MAHANOY PARISH.

BY REV. D. M. STETLER.

THE Mahanoy Parish in its present arrangement comprises six congregations, spreading over a territory of twenty-five miles, with the parsonage at Mahanoy, Northumberland county, Pa. This territory originally belonged to the old and extensive Lykens Valley Charge, whose pastors ministered to the congregations for almost three-fourths of a century (1773 to 1847), with the exception of two pastors from other sources, who served for brief periods. Since 1847 the congregations have constituted a separate parish.

The following is as accurate a list of the succession of pastors as can be secured: The Rev. J. Michael Enterline, the Lutheran pioneer in this part of the State, was pastor on this territory from the time of the first Lutheran organization, in 1773, to the year 1787. In 1790, the name of Rev. Carl Christopher Getz appears as pastor, but very little is known of him by historians. In 1795 Rev. Christian Espich was pastor. He left an odious record because of immorality of life, and afterwards went to Fayette county, and later to the State of Ohio. From 1803 to 1805 Rev. J. P. F. Kramer was pastor, having come from Bucks county, and from 1805 to 1809 Rev. J. Conrad Walter. The latter's labors extended over into Snyder county, where he died August 10, 1819, and his remains were laid to rest on the cemetery of Christ church near Middleburgh. Rev. Daniel Ulrich, who was licensed by the Ministerium in 1809, served on this territory as a part of his first charge till 1811, when he accepted the call from the Tulpehocken district, the reception of which call was prevented at the beginning by a want of harmony. Next followed the long pastorate of Rev. John Nicholas Hemping, who served on this territory from 1812 to 1847, and whose faithful service and promptness in meeting all appointments notwithstanding heat and cold and storm, are still fondly remembered by his spiritual children. The Rev. Augustus Bergner was the first of the pastors, except Getz and Espich, who did not reside in Lykens Val-

PARSONAGE, MAHANOY.

ley. His successful pastorate extended from 1848 to the time of his death, October 26, 1860, his remains being interred on the cemetery of Himmel's church. His faithful wife survived him till September 3, 1893, when her remains were tenderly laid to rest beside those of her husband, the present pastor officiating. We glean from the records of Rev. J. W. Early, that prior to the pastorate of Rev. J. N. Hemping, a division had already been made, as Rev. J. P. Schindel is represented as having charge of part of the territory again occupied by Father Hemping.

Rev. A. Bergner is shown to have served parts of it only. Rev. J. W. R. Hasskarl served in 1861, but his pastorate was short because he refused to affiliate with the Reformed. In the years 1862 to 1863, the charge was supplied for a time by Rev. P. Anstadt, D.D., from Selinsgrove. About this time a division of this extensive field was made, so that when Rev. J. C. Schmidt, who served so long and faithfully, and still resides on the territory as the pastor of St. Peter's congregation, came to the Mahanoy Parish in 1864, his services were limited to the Line Mountain and Mahanoy congregations, till about the year 1874, when Himmel's church became the eastern limit of the Mahanoy Parish. This active and faithful pastor served the congregations from 1864 to 1869, and again from 1870 to 1881. A monument to his painstaking labors are the beautifully kept church records. The Rev. J. F. Bayer twice succeeded Father Schmidt, his pastorates extending from 1869 to 1870 and from 1881 to 1887, when he died. His labors were marked by strong opposition to the prevailing unionistic spirit and advocacy of the worship and cultus of the Lutheran Church, to such an extent as to arouse strenuous opposition, culminating in the withdrawal of St. Peter's congregation, of Mahanoy, from the charge and its organization as a separate Parish. The writer assumed the pastoral duties of the Parish April 1, 1887.

HIMMEL'S.—This church is located in Washington township, four miles east of Mahanoy, and one-half mile east of the village of Rebuck. This is one of the oldest congregations of the county, its congregational record dating back to the year 1776. In 1773 the Lutherans received from the State a title to sixty acres of land, on which there was erected the following year a school house in which Charles Henry Kauffman imparted instruction.

This building still stands, having been converted into a residence for the organist.

In the same year, 1774, a log church was erected conjointly with the Reformed, near the sight of the present stone edifice, and inasmuch as the Reformed were not mentioned in the title but had taken part in the erection

HIMMEL'S CHURCH.

of the buildings, the following action was taken and recorded September 22, 1781: "The Evangelical Lutheran and Reformed congregations shall have equal rights and privileges to land, church and school house."

In June, 1817, it was decided at a meeting of the Lutheran and Reformed members to build a new union church, which church was built of stone, on an eminence about twenty rods away from the place where the first church stood. The Building Committee consisted of Michael Reitz, Michael Rebuck and Leonard Reitz. The corner-stone was laid in the spring of 1818, and at the dedication Revs. John Nicholas Hemping, John Felix, Philip Moyer and George Mening officiated. This church is of the old Pennsylvania style of architecture, one-story high, one room with gallery, and a "pigeon box" pulpit with a seating capacity for 400 persons. From the large pipe organ which it contains the church is popularly known as the "Organ Church," and also as the "Stone Church," because of its stone walls.

The first Lutheran Church Council consisted of J. Nicholas Brosius and Peter Ferster, deacons; and Daniel Kobel and George Heim, elders. The first baptisms are recorded June 7, 1774, and are those of John and Maria, children of Henry and Catharine Kobel. The first communion was administered June 30, 1776, to 64 guests.

When the present church edifice was erected in 1818, the Church Council consisted of Christian Thomas, George Miller, David Haas, Abram Hoch, Frederick Kahler, Godfried Thomas, Peter Reitz and Jacob Falk. The communicant record of the same year, April 12, gives the names of 79 communicants.

While the younger portion of the congregation would favor the erection of a new church building, and while such erection has been considered, as well as the matter of remodeling the present one, the majority of the members are still inclined to preserve the church as it stands, a sacred heirloom of the fathers and a reminder of a period when the foundations of our nation were laid. The present membership of the congregation is 235, and during the decade of the present pastor's minstrations he has administered baptism to 99 children and received 100 by confirmation.

The pastors of this congregation were those named as the pastors of the Parish, at the beginning of this article.

IMMANUEL'S.—The location of this church is four miles north of the parsonage, in Little Mahanoy township, on the road leading from Herndon to Shamokin. Although nominally a union church, the deed being given to the

IMMANUEL'S CHURCH.

Lutherans and Presbyterians, and although the Reformed had assumed the right of the property, practically it is an exclusively Lutheran church, the Reformed having been without pastor and service since 1866.

The congregation was organized during the pastorate of Rev. J. P. Schindel, the corner-stone of the church building having been laid April 12, 1828. This building is of logs, 30 feet square, weather-boarded, with gallery and small old style pulpit, and is in use to this day. The Susquehanna Classis of the Reformed Church has given a release permitting the Lutherans to build a new church upon the ground without interfering in any way in the use of said church.

The Rev. J. P. Schindel, with the assistance of his son, J. P. Schindel, Jr., was pastor of the congregation from its organization, in 1828, to 1840. Rev. E. J. Neiman served about 1842, Rev. Augustus Bergner from 1847 to 1860, Rev. J. G. Hornberger from 1861 to 1862, Rev. J.

DAVID'S CHURCH.

C. Schmidt from 1864 to 1869, from which time the pastors of this charge followed regularly as named at the beginning of this article.

During the present pastorate of 10 years, there were 53 children baptized and 60 young persons confirmed. The present membership is 90.

DAVID'S.—Eight miles southeast of the parsonage, is located David's union church, at Hebe. The first church-building was erected, in 1829, and was constructed of logs, weather-boarded. In 1864 it was destroyed by fire, on the occasion of a funeral, the fire being caused by a defective flue. The records of the congregation were also destroyed, so that the information for the historian is limited.

The present building is constructed of stone, 30 by 45 feet, and was erected in 1864, the Building Committee having been Abraham and Elias Troutman, and Daniel W. Shaffer. After having undergone extensive repairs, the church was re-dedicated, November 26, 1893.

The early pastors were Rev. John Nicholas Hemping, Rev. E. J. Neiman, Mr. Sapper and Mr. Porr. Beginning with Rev. J. C. Schmidt, the congregation was a regular part of the Mahanoy Parish, and was served by its pastors as they are enumerated at the beginning of this article.

The congregation now numbers 50 members and helps to support a Union Sunday School.

ST. PAUL'S.—St. Paul's union church, of Urban, is located four miles southeast of the parsonage. This congregation was organized by Rev. A. Bergner, with a communicant membership of 40. The first church was erected in 1855, and was a wooden structure, 30 by 40 feet. The corner-stone of the present frame building was laid May 18, 1890, and the church consecrated in the fall of the same year. The building is 35 by 65 feet, and was erected under the supervision of Elias Phillips and Gabriel Adams. The half-acre of land on which the church stands was donated by Aaron Schaffer.

The following have been the pastors of the congregation: Rev. A. Bergner, 1855 to 1860; Rev. J. W. R. Hasskarl, 1861; Rev. F. Waltz, 1863, and from Rev. J. C. Schmidt on down to the present time, the regular pastors of the Mahanoy Parish, as given at the beginning of this article.

The present membership of the congregation is 125. The congregation supports a Sunday School with an auxiliary in a school house. During the present pastorate of ten years, 92 young persons were confirmed and 85 were baptized.

Zion.—This union church is located at Herndon, four miles west of the parsonage. Services were first held by

ST. PAUL'S CHURCH.

Rev. M. C. Horine, President of the Fifth, now the Danville Conference, as early as 1877. Later on Rev. J. W. Early preached in the school house about one-fourth mile north of the church. The organization was effected in 1882, at the house of Elias Lahr, during the pastorate of Rev. J. F. Bayer, and the first communion was attended by 19 guests, formerly members of St. Peter's, at Mahanoy. Services were held in the Methodist Episcopal church. Rev. J. F. Bayer was pastor from 1882 to 1886, when he died, and the present pastor succeeded him April 1, 1887, since which the congregation has prospered well and promises still greater things.

The church-building had been erected as a union church, but had come into the exclusive possession of the Methodist Church. In the spring of 1887 it was purchased by the Lutheran and Reformed congregations. May 5, 1888, steps were taken to remodel the building, and a bell was placed in the tower, an organ procured and other improvements made, and on August 12, 1888, the corner-stone was relaid and the building dedicated to the service of the triune God. The congregation numbers 80 members and supports a flourishing Sunday School.

ZION CHURCH.

St. John's.—This church stands about one mile north of the parsonage and five miles east of Herndon. The congregation was formed of members who formerly belonged to St. Peter's congregation, of Mahanoy, and was the result of an unfortunate misunderstanding between the pastor and many of the members of St. Peter's, which resulted in the pastor and his adherents being locked out. As a result St. John's congregation was organized at the house of John S. Klock, where services were held. The first council consisted of John Carl and Abraham Deppen, elders; Jorias S. Lahr and George L. Snyder, deacons, and Elias F. Zartman, John S. Klock and George Malich, trustees.

The church was erected in 1885, the corner-stone having been laid in March, and the dedication having taken place September 20. It is a frame building, 35 by 45 feet, with a tower, bell and basement. The first pastor was Rev. J. F. Bayer, from 1884 to 1886, and the present pastor since April 1, 1887. The church is exclusively Lutheran. The congregation has adopted the constitu-

ST. JOHN'S CHURCH.

tion for congregations recommended by the General Council. The Church Book and the Sunday School literature of the General Council are in use, and while the congregation has suffered by the removal of many members, it holds its own, numbering 35 members.

Mahanoy, Penn'a, July, 1897.

THE MAINVILLE PARISH.

BY REV. C. F. DRY.

THE Mainville parish consists of three congregations —Emmanuel's at Mainville, St. John's at Mifflinville, and St. Peter's in Beaver township, all in Columbia county.

This parish was formed in the year 1890. Prior to that time, Emmanuel's congregation belonged to the Catawissa parish; St. John's at Mifflinville to the Berwick parish, and St. Peter's to the Ringtown parish. After the formation of this new parish, the Rev. W. E. Roney served it for a short time, until he accepted a call from Danville.

These congregations were all union at first, but the only one that worships in a union building at present, is St. Peter's in Beaver township.

EMMANUEL'S.—This congregation formed a part of what, prior to the year 1888, was known as Emmanuel's Evangelical Lutheran and Reformed Church, popularly called Fisher's. This union church was organized in the year of our Lord 1822. The corner-stone of the first union church was laid with appropriate services, September 23, 1832. In the following year, January 16, 1833, this church edifice (frame) was dedicated. The corner-stone of the second union church, a brick structure, was laid July 15, 1877. On the 11th day of November, this new edifice was solemnly set apart for divine services. Rev. M. C. Horine, D.D., at this time pastor of Trinity Lutheran Church, Danville, preached the dedicatory sermon, and Rev. W. G. Laitzle, then pastor of the Lutheran congregation, assisted by Rev. Long, pastor of a Reformed congregation at Williamsport, consecrated the church. The building, as well as the furniture, was greatly damaged by a storm which visited this section of country, November 18, 1886.

EMANUEL'S CHURCH.

The Lutherans then decided to sell their interest in this church to the Reformed, and build a church edifice for their exclusive use. After this step had been taken, Mr Frank Shuman donated the piece of ground upon which the church now stands. The corner-stone of this neat frame building was laid June 23, 1888. Rev. U. Myers, pastor of St. Matthews' Evangelical Lutheran Church, Catawissa, preached an appropriate sermon on this occasion, from Ezekiel xxxiv:26. On the 24th day of March, 1889, the pastor, Rev. J. H. Neiman, assisted by Revs. Drumheller of Danville, A. P. Pflueger of Turbotville, and O. D. Bartholomew of Ringtown, consecrated the newly-erected house of worship. The cost of the church as it now stands is about $4,300.

The present membership of Emmanuel's is about 150, and that of the Sunday-school about 80.

October 18, 1893, a Luther League was organized, which has rendered material assistance to the congregation in several instances. We hope for good from this source in the future.

RECORD OF PASTORS.

Since its organization, this Lutheran congregation has been served by the following pastors: Rev. John Benninger, Rev. Jeremiah Schindel, Rev. Wm. Eyer, who ministered to the spiritual wants of the people in this section for a period of 37 years; Rev. W. G. Laitzle from 1874 to 1877; Rev. L. Lindenstruth from 1878 to 1881; Rev. J. H.. Neiman from 1881 to 1889; Rev. W. E. Roney.

The Rev. C. F. Dry assumed the pastorate on October 31, 1890.

St. John's.—The members of this congregation worshiped in a union building up to the year 1882. The corner-stone of this union church bears the date 1809. In 1882, steps were taken toward the erection of a new church, which was also to have been union, but, on account of the language question, the Lutherans, under the leadership of Rev. J. P. German, resolved to withdraw and build a church-home for themselves. At this time, the congregation consisted of about sixty members. The following spring, 1883, ground was broken, and at the laying of the corner-stone the pastor was assisted by Rev. J. H. Neiman, of Catawissa. By November of the same

ST. JOHN'S CHURCH.

year, the new house of worship, a brick structure, was completed. It was consecrated in November, the pastor being assisted on this occasion by Rev. J. W. Early and Rev. D. M. Henkel, D.D. The cost of the church and furniture was about $3,000.

During the summer of 1892, the church was remodeled.

November 6th it was re-opened with appropriate services conducted by Rev. W. E. Roney and the pastor.

Prior to 1890, the congregation had services only every four weeks, English and German services alternating. Since the new parish was formed, services have been held every two weeks, and are now conducted in the English language altogether.

The membership is about 150; that of the Sunday-school about 100. A Luther League has also been organized, and has rendered valuable service to the congregation in various ways.

The following is a list of pastors who served the congregation: Rev. Barnitz, but it is not known which one; Rev. J. Schindel, Rev. Isaiah Bahl; Rev. W. B. Fox from 1862 to 1868; Rev. S. S. Henry from 1869 to 1873; Rev. Thomas Steck from 1874 to 1880; Rev. J. P. German from 1880 to 1890; Rev. W. E. Roney; and since October 31, 1890, by the writer.

ST. PETER'S.—As nearly as can be ascertained from the incomplete records, this congregation, popularly called Harger's Church, was organized in the year 1848. Within the memory of some of the oldest members now living, occasional services were held in barns in the neighborhood. Before the organization was effected, people crossed the Nescopeck Mountain to attend services at the union church, Mifflinville. For a number of years, prior to the regular organization of this congregation, the people were supplied with the means of grace, as may be learned from the record of baptisms, the first one entered bearing the date December 28, 1817. The first regular worshiping place was a log building, probably also used for school purposes. The first church edifice, after the organization had been effected in 1848, was a frame structure, erected during the summer of 1849. In the spring of the same year, the corner-stone of the new church, which was union, was laid with appropriate services. Some time in the fall of this same year, it was solemnly set apart for divine services. In the course of time, this building proved to be too small for the growing congregation. In

ST. PETER'S CHURCH.

the summer of 1892, another neat frame house of worship was erected on the site of the old one. At the dedicatory services, held November 13, 1892, the following brethren assisted the pastors: Revs. D. L. Fogleman of Danville, J. Gruhler of Shenandoah, and J. W. Bell. The Lutherans have services every two weeks. At the beginning of the present pastorate (1890), English and German services alternated. At present, every fourth service is conducted in the German language.

There are two Sunday-schools under the auspices of this congregation, but they hold their sessions in school-houses. It would be a great benefit to the congregation and the Sunday-schools if the sessions could be held in the church. We hope that the difficulties which have thus far prevented this, may soon be removed.

The following is a list of pastors who have served this congregation, but the length of their pastorates is not on record: Rev. J. Benninger from 1822 or 1823, about 27 years; Rev. Isaiah Bahl about 19 years; Rev. R. S. Wagner, Rev. J. S. Renninger, Rev. S. S. Kline, Rev. H. Weicksel, Rev. J. P. German, Rev. W. H. Geiger about five years, Rev. O. D. Bartholomew, and Rev. C. F. Dry since 1890.

PLATE VI

J. M. ANSPACH.

E. L. REED.

D. M. STETLER.

S. WENRICH.

J. H. NEIMAN.

W. H. RICKERT.

NUMIDIA PARISH.

BY REV. F. A. WEICKSEL.

ST. PAUL'S EVANGELICAL LUTHERAN CHURCH.—The early history of this congregation is very meagre, owing to the lack of records which were either not kept at all, or have been lost.

It had its origin most likely amongst the pioneer settlers of this valley, but was not formally organized until about 1800 A. D.

In the earlier days it was known as the Roaring Creek Church, and belonged to the large mission charge including the Catawissa, Fisher's, Danville, Lazarus and Mahoning congregations.

This St. Paul's Ev. Lutheran congregation, prior to 1816, held divine services in a barn near the present town of Numidia. About that time, in union with the German Reformed congregation, a place for a church building was selected in the southeast corner of the old burying ground, and on July 5th, 1816, the corner-stone was laid. This building was so far completed that same year as to enable them to hold services in it, but was not dedicated until about 1830 or '31.

Prior to this time the pastors' names who served this charge cannot be ascertained, excepting that of the Rev. J. Benninger, who most likely was the immediate predecessor of the Rev. J. Schindel, who was pastor of this charge as early as 1831. Rev. Schindel was succeeded by the Rev. W. J. Eyer, who took charge in the year 1839, and for 35 years continued the faithful laborer in this part of the Lord's vineyard. During his pastorate the congregation increased, slowly but surely, and in 1870, still in union with the German Reformed congregation, the work of building a new church was commenced. The site of this building was near the old church, on an adjoining lot bought for this purpose. The corner-stone

ST. PAUL'S CHURCH.

was laid on Oct. 13th, 1870, and in the autumn of 1871 it was dedicated. This is the brick church which still stands, and which was remodeled by the Reformed congregation and rededicated in 1893 as a Lutheran and Reformed church, although the Lutherans do not worship there any more; but have never relinquished their rights on the property.

On the 9th day of February, 1874, the Rev. W. J. Eyer was called from his labors on earth to his reward in heaven. He came to his death by injuries received from being kicked and trampled upon by his horse. His labors were many and arduous, and he made full proof of his ministry. He died at an age of 71 years, 1 month and 4 days, and was buried at Bloomsburg, Pa., the Rev. A. L. Geisenhainer conducting the funeral services.

After the death of Father Eyer, the charge was divided, Catawissa, Fisher's and Numidia forming one charge, and Danville, Lazarus and Mahoning, another.

The Rev. William G. Laitzle, then of Pottstown, Pa., was next called as pastor, and having accepted, entered upon his labors on Oct. 15th, 1874, and served until 1878.

During his pastorate of this congregation, the names of 285 members were enrolled on the church record. He officiated at 65 baptisms, 19 marriages and 22 funerals.

Pastor Laitzle was succeeded by the Rev. L. Lindenstruth, then of Philadelphia, Pa. He was unanimously elected by the congregation, and accepting the call, he entered upon his labors on Jan. 28th, 1878, the installation taking place on March 3d, 1878, the former pastor, Rev. Laitzle, officiating. Pastor Lindenstruth faithfully served this charge for nearly three and one-half years, when, on June 1st, 1881, he resigned this charge to accept a call from St. John's Ev. Lutheran Church of Mauch Chunk, Pa.

During his pastorate, 335 names were enrolled. The actual membership averaged about 295. He officiated at 96 baptisms, 14 marriages and 50 funerals.

After the resignation of Rev. L. Lindenstruth, the Rev. J. H. Neiman, of Conyngham, Luzerne county, Pa., was elected on June 19th, 1881. He accepted the call and entered upon his pastoral duties on August 1st, 1881. He was installed by the Rev. J. W. Early, on Sept. 4th, 1881.

Up to this time, this congregation had no Sunday-School. Pastor Neiman lost no time in placing this important matter before the people, and as the Reformed members had apparently no interest in this branch of the Christian work, he, with the approval of the church council, decided to begin Sunday School on the Sundays when there was Lutheran services. Lutheran officers were elected, Lutheran Sunday School literature secured, and the school was opened on May 27th, 1883. The next year an appeal was made to the German Reformed congregation, that they should begin Sunday School on *their* Sunday, but they would not. It was therefore concluded by the Lutherans to hold Sunday School on every Sunday. This was bitterly opposed by the Reformed members and caused the beginning of a long and bitter discord between the two congregations. Contention also arose concerning an organ which had been purchased by the congregations conjointly. The German Reformed people persistently opposed any and all efforts made by the Lutherans in whatever advancements and improvements they endeavored to bring about. On July 14, 1884, it was decided by vote that the Lutheran and Reformed congregations separate, and on August 16, 1884, it was decided to exclude the Sunday School from the church. According to the choice of the Reformed members, their congregation was to retain the church property, paying to the Lutherans $1200 for their interest. The transfer was to be made before legal authorities, June 20, 1885. But this was again foiled by the objections made by the Reformed members to a so-called protest which was presented by a number of persons who claimed to be members of the Lutheran congregation. Court proceedings were then entered upon, but after a long delay, and the expenditure of about $500, the judge decided that "the Church declaration gave him no power to decide in favor of a separation."

Some time after this unfavorable decision, the Lutherans held a meeting and agreed, "in the name of God, to erect for ourselves a church." Land was purchased, and on Nov. 1st, 1888, the first stake was set to mark off the church site.

On March 31st, 1889, the corner-stone was laid, and on Jan. 19th, 1890, the church was dedicated. This, it must be admitted, is one of the most beautiful country church-buildings in the State. The cost of erecting this church was $8,000.

Upon the church record, in conclusion to the account of this work, are these words: "We do not feel proud, but with joy and gladness we say, '*Hitherto hath the Lord helped us.*'"

At the corner-stone laying, Pastor Neiman was assisted by the Rev. Lewis Smith, of Weatherly, Pa., and at the dedication, by the former pastor, Rev. L. Lindenstruth, and Rev. S. E. Ochsenford, D.D., of Selinsgrove, Pa.

Rev. Neiman had in this charge eleven years of hard labor, but he accomplished a commendable work, and started the congregation on the way of prosperity and peace. At the close of his pastorate he had enrolled 332 members. He confirmed 198 members, and officiated at 286 baptisms, 53 marriages, and 113 funerals. He resigned this charge on Oct. 1st, 1892, to accept a call to Grace Lutheran church, at Royersford, Pa.

Soon after this, the congregation at Catawissa called a pastor independently, and so left this congregation alone. Fisher's (Emanuel's) at Mainville, having been connected with the Mifflinville charge. F. A. Weicksel, then a student of theology at Missionary Institute, Selinsgrove, Pa., was sent by the President of Conference, to supply this congregation. On Nov. 8th, 1892, a call was proffered him to become their regular pastor after his ordination, which should take place the next spring. The call

PARSONAGE.

was accepted and accordingly he continued to supply the congregation with services until July 1st, 1893, when he took regular charge, having been ordained by the Ministerium of Pennsylvania, on May 29th, 1893. The installation took place on August 13th, 1893. Rev. S. E. Ochsenford, D.D., officiating, assisted by Rev. H. Weicksel.

A new and convenient parsonage was built during the year of 1893 on a lot adjoining the church property. This makes a decidedly fine church property, now valued at ten thousand dollars.

It is now nearly five years since Pastor Weicksel has entered upon the work of this field, and during this time he has confirmed 122 members, officiated at 95 baptisms, 22 marriages, and 52 funerals. The membership now numbers 375.

Ever since the separation with the German Reformed congregation and the completion of the new church, a flourishing Sunday School has existed. The school rooms, one for the primary scholars, and one for the advanced scholars, are usually well filled every Sunday throughout the whole year. The school is organized with 7 officers, 15 teachers and 280 scholars.

A Luther League was organized March 1st, 1894, and has grown steadily until now its membership numbers seventy-five.

The Ladies' Aid Society has given very efficient assistance to the congregation in many ways. With these auxiliaries the church work is prospering, and while there is little prospect of any great numerical increase, yet they will hold their own in the firm Christian doctrine of the Lutheran Church.

ST. PETER'S EVANGELICAL LUTHERAN CHURCH, AT MONTANA, PA.—This little congregation was organized by Rev. F. A. Weicksel, Sept. 10th, 1893. It is in a little mining village, on top of the mountain, north of Centralia.

Some 20 faithful Lutherans, eager to hear God's Word and receive the Sacraments as administered in the Lutheran Church, petitioned Rev. Weicksel to visit them and see if a congregation could be organized. By the directions of Rev. S. E. Ochsenford, D.D., President of the Conference, Rev. Weicksel visited them and organized a congregation.

Immediately following this organization, the financial

depressions of the country fell heavily upon the mining districts, and this little congregation has simply struggled along as best they could. Having confirmed 24 members, there now remains a membership of 42. They hope and pray for better prosperity in the near future.

Numidia, Pa., Aug 17, 1897.

RICHFIELD PARISH.

BY THE REV. A. P. LENTZ.

THIS parish was organized about seventeen years ago, and comprises five congregations, located in Juniata and Snyder counties. The first regular pastor was the Rev. D. E. Reed, of Middleburg, Pa., 1880-85. He was succeeded by the Rev. Geo. J. Schaeffer, 1887-97.

RICHFIELD.—This church is located at the eastern end of the village. The building is a frame structure; but the date of its erection is not known. The congregation was organized May 17, 1842, by the Rev. C. G. Erlenmeyer. He served this congregation as pastor of the Freeburg parish, about twenty-five years, until 1867, when he relinquished the work on account of the labors in his own extensive parish. After a vacancy of two or three years, the Rev. D. E. Reed, a member of the East Pennsylvania Synod, became the pastor about the year 1870, and remained about two years. Then there was another vacancy of nine years, when Pastor Reed, having, during this time, become a member of our Synod, became the pastor a second time, and labored here 1880-85. When he came, in 1880, there were not more than a dozen families and about twenty members left. He was succeeded by the Rev. Geo. J. Schaeffer, 1887-97. This congregation has, according to the last report, fifty-six members.

ST. PAUL'S, ORIENTAL.—This church, known as Leininger's, is located about one mile west of Oriental and six miles southeast of Richfield, in Juniata county. The congregation was organized by the Rev. C. G. Erlenmeyer, September 21, 1834, evidently while he was residing near Liverpool. The first building was constructed of logs and was erected about the year 1834. The corner-stone of a new frame church was laid in 1884, and the building consecrated June 3, 1888. Father Erlenmeyer served the congregation until 1867. The regular pastors afterwards were Revs. Reed and Schaeffer. The congregation has eighteen members.

ZION'S.—This church, also called Arbogast's, is situated about five miles southeast of Richfield, in Perry township, Snyder county. The congregation was organized by Father Erlenmeyer in 1860, and served by him until 1867. The church is a frame building, and is in urgent need of repairs. The date of its erection is unknown. The later pastors were the same as those at Richfield. The congregation numbers 17 members.

ST. PETER'S is located about four miles south of Richfield, in Monroe township, Juniata county, and was organized by the Rev. Geo. J. Schaeffer, March 14, 1888. The corner-stone of a small frame church was laid July 29, 1888, and the building consecrated October, 1890. At present the congregation numbers 35 members, and maintains a flourishing Sunday-school during the summer months.

ST. JOHN'S, situated about six miles west of Richfield, in Fayette township, Juniata county, is the youngest of all the congregations of the parish, having been organized by Pastor Schaeffer September 11, 1888. The congregation has no house of worship. Formerly they held their services in another church; but the members of that church having recently built a new house of worship, no longer permit the Lutherans to hold services in their building. The membership has dwindled down to almost nothing, many of the members having sought a church-home among some of the denominations. The last report gave eight members.

This parish needs at once an active pastor, who will devote all his time to the work of the parish. One of the great hindrances to the prosperity of the parish is that all the churches are union churches. Besides, the members are widely scattered and are not in a condition to give the pastor a living support. It is one of the missions supported by our Ministerium.

St. John's, Lykens Valley.

BY THE REV. JER. H. RITTER.

ST. JOHN'S congregation of Lykens Valley, Dauphin County, occupies in various particulars a unique position among sister congregations. She was never fettered with union churches. She had almost continuously a pastor right in her midst. Latterly, altho a country congregation, she has had the exclusive services of a pastor—with church privileges equal to any town congregation. Highly favored in location and temporal possessions and more so in spiritual privileges,—what has thus far been her history?

LOCATION.—Lykens Valley, noted for its beauty, fertility of soil, and coal, is in the most northern part of Dauphin County, and extending eastward from the Susquehanna River. St. John's is seated in the very centre of this valley with the church on an elevation overlooking the country in every direction for many miles and therefore the popular name—"the hill church." A stranger on seeing this beautiful two-story brick church, with handsome steeple—cross surmounted—is led to exclaim in the words of the Psalmist in his description of Mt. Zion—Ps. 47.

EARLY HISTORY.—The congregation, according to date of organization, stands second to those in the valley and of Conference, altho preaching began here simultaneously with that of other points. The Rev. J. Mich. Enderline—pioneer missionary—began his labors in this vicinity in the year 1773 and extended them from Upper Dauphin into Schuylkill, Northumberland, and Snyder Counties.

In 1780 this congregation was organized by Rev. Enderline with Christian Schnug and John Matter as deacons.

CHURCHES.—For twenty years the infant congregation employed a log school house for its place of worship, which gave it the name in early years of "the school house

OLD ST. JOHN'S CHURCH.

congregation." January 19, 1797, at a congregational meeting a committee was elected and charged with the erection of a "new" church. This church—without corner stone—was built of logs on the present site with galleries on three sides—a stately church in its day.

Dedicated October 24, 1802, by Rev. John Herbst, pastor, and Dr. George Lochman, of Harrisburg. Later this edifice was weatherboarded and in 1856 the steeple with belfry added.

NEW ST. JOHN'S CHURCH.

In the year 1876 the log church gave way to the present handsome church. The corner-stone was laid May 21, 1876, by the pastor, the Rev. R. S. Wagner, assisted by

Dr. F. J. F. Schantz, and Revs. M. B. Lenker and J. M. Uhrich. The dedication took place November 11, 1877. Dimensions, 50 by 87 feet. Steeple and pulpit recess. Ample basement for Sunday school purposes, divided into three departments. Cost of church, $13,122. The last of the debt on this church was paid in 1890.

PARISHES.—In 1808 the parish consisted of the following congregations: St. John's, Wert's, Fetterhoff's, Stone Valley, Himmel's, Swabencreeck, Hohwaerter's, Klinger's and Herb's. From October, 1815 to 1843 St. John's was supplied from Sunbury by the Rev. John Peter Schindel, Sr., the congregation not yielding to the will of the majority—the other congregations having elected the Rev. John N. Hemping. The congregation, however, paid dearly for this irregularity, insubordination, and pride—said pastorate ending with a division—the "new measure" party withdrawing and organizing in Berrysburg, less than a mile from the mother church,—and other serious troubles. This evil was, however, somewhat counterbalanced by organizations being effected during this period at four surrounding points through the faithful labors of Father Hemping, namely at Rife—five miles west; at Elizabethville—three miles south; at Uniontown —four miles north; and at Gratz—five miles east. In August, 1828, representatives of eight congregations met at the parsonage to consider the question of dividing the parish but concluded to continue as before. In 1843 St. John's came back again to its former relations which together with Stone Valley, Uniontown, Elizabethville, Huber's Fetterhoff's and Miller's now comprised the parish. The upper or notheastern section, viz: Gratz, Coleman's, Herb's, Himmel's, Krebs' and Swartz's having through the "new measure" influences withdrawn. In 1864, November 5, the question of division was again voted on—St. John's having five wide-awake and aggressive members who voted for, with thirty-five against. In some congregations the majority were in favor of division, one unanimously so—but the total majority was against dividing, which result led to the resignation of the laborious and successful pastor—the Rev. F. Walz. In 1870 another division was effected—forming the Lykens Valley and Stone Valley parishes with five and four congregations respectively. The former again divided in the fall of 1894 by four congregations—the present Lykens Valley parish—withdrawing and thus leaving St. John's to its own abundant resources, and spirit and mode of conducting church affairs.

CHURCH PROPERTY.—Besides church and parsonage the congregation has a farm of over sixty-one acres surrounding the church and cemetery, which is operated by the person serving as janitor of the church. This land was donated to the congregation in the beginning of the century by John Matter.

PARSONAGES.—In the year 1809 nine congregations united in purchasing a property for parsonage purposes located a mile southwest of St. John's Church and consisting of thirty acres of land with timber and insufficient buildings. Cost, £220. After house and barn were erected the property cost $1,647.99. St. John's portion, $335. In 1870 this property was sold for $3,756. St. John's portion, $1,127. A well adapted property in Berrysburg was then bought and occupied three years by the pastor, the Rev. Thomas Steck, when it was sold. Elizabethville was now tried and found to be a more suitable residence for the pastor. After the dissolution of the old Lykens Valley parish, this parsonage was sold at auction to the new Lykens Valley parish. St. John's realized out of the one-half interest, $627.50. This was again invested in a home in Berrysburg, which after extensive repairs and building, cost the congregation nearly $3,500. The present parsonage—like the church—occupies a prominent position, is beautiful and very commodious.

PASTORATES.—The pioneer missionary in these parts—the Rev. J. M. Enderline—was pastor from 1780 to 1793. His body rests in St. John's cemetery. Rev. H. E. Hinze, pastor from 1795 to 1797. Rev. H. Moeller,

PARSONAGE.

1797-1802. Rev. J. Herbst, 1802-1805. Rev. J. P. F. Kramer, 1805-1806. Rev. J. C. Walter, 1807-1809. Rev. D. Ulrich, 1809-1811. Rev. J. C. Walter, 1813-1814. Rev. J. P. Schindel, Sr., October, 1815-1843. Rev. J. N. Hemping, August, 1843-1850. Rev. C. F. Welden, September, 1850-September, 1851. Rev. N. Yeager, 1852-1853. Rev. F. Walz, January 1, 1854-December 31, 1864. Rev. J. Schindel, 1865-March, 1870. Rev. T.

Steck, November, 1870-November, 1873. Rev. R. S. Wagner, October, 1874-June 1, 1881. Rev. J. Hillpot, July 31, 1881-April 24, 1889. Rev. O. E. Pflueger, July 1, 1889-December 31, 1894. Rev. J. H. Ritter, May 1, 1895-May 1, 1898. The congregation has furnished the church with one minister of the Gospel—the Rev. J. N. Wetzler, Ph.D.

St. Peter's Parish.

BY THE REV. J. C. SCHMIDT.

ST. PETER'S CHURCH is located at Mahanoy, Pa., a small town, about four miles east of Herndon, and within three-fourths of a mile of the Philadelphia and Reading railroad running from Shamokin to Herndon, Otto being the nearest station, about a mile distant.

When St. Peter's Lutheran congregation came into existence is not known. From historic fragments, however, it would seem that this congregation was organized about the year 1788. There is an old book at hand which served as a record of baptisms from 1788 to 1812, when it commenced to give also a list of communicants. As to who the first pastor of the congregation was, nothing further is given than that Rev. Mathias Guensel baptized children in the congregation as early as February 15, 1789. Several entries of baptisms were made in 1788, but there is a blank as to who officiated at those baptisms. From this record of baptisms, it is probable that the following pastors served the congregation from its beginning up to 1812: Revs. Mathias Guensel, J. M. Enterline, Henry Moeller, Jacob Schontz, John Herbst, J. C. Walter, and Daniel Ulrich.

According to an old saying, the congregation at first worshiped in a school-house, but for how long a time is not known. In the course of time, probably at about the close of the last century, the Lutherans and the Reformed jointly erected a log church and worshiped therein. Some time, perhaps several years, after its erection, this log church-building was weather-boarded and painted yellow.

On February 1, 1821, a deed for twenty-seven acres and ten perches of land was given by the State of Pennsylvania to John Haas, Martin Zartman and Jacob Tressler, in trust for the Lutheran and Presbyterian (Reformed) congregations at Mahanoy. How it came that these congregations erected a church-building and also a school-house on land to which they seem to have had no legal title until the year 1821, is a thing which we are unable to explain.

From 1812 to 1884, the following pastors have served the congregation: Rev. J. N. Hemping, 1812-1848; Rev. A. Bergner, 1848-1860; Rev. W. R. Hasskarl. 1860-1861; Rev. P. Anstadt, 1861-1863; Rev. F. Walz, Feb. to Sept., 1863, Rev. J. C. Schmidt, Nov., 1863, to April, 1869; Rev. J. F Bayer, 1869-1870; Rev. J. C. Schmidt, 1870 to July, 1880; Rev. J. F. Bayer, 1881 to June, 1884.

In 1859 the Lutheran and Reformed congregations united to build the present beautiful and substantial brick church, to replace the old yellow church, which had long enough served its noble purpose. The corner-stone was laid June 12, 1859, the ministers present were Rev. A. Bergner and Rev. J. F Bayer, Lutheran; Rev. J. Fritzinger and J. W Steinmetz, Reformed. On the 8th day of May, 1860, the church was consecrated. The building committee consisted of Isaac Reitz, William Deppen, and Abraham Klock.

In 1884 St. Peter's Lutheran congregation separated from the Mahanoy parish of which it was a part, and formed a parish by itself. This is a small parish, indeed! and without a parsonage. It is, however, large enough for a pastor who has been in the ministry for a period of nearly fifty-four years. The members are a peaceable, well-meaning people, and would by no means let their pastor starve.

During the summer of 1885 the inside of St. Peter's

church building was partly remodeled and repainted, and the walls and ceiling frescoed. And on August 16th, of the same year, it was reconsecrated. The ministers present were Revs. W. H. Geiger and Joseph Hillpot, Lutheran, and Revs. A. R. Hottenstein and W. Engel, Reformed.

This congregation has a membership of about 165 communicants, has divine services every other Sunday, and helps to support a flourishing union Sunday-school of at least 125 children. Since its separation, the following pastors have served this congregation: Rev. J. F Wampole, from Sept., 1884, to June, 1885; Rev. W. H. Geiger, from July, 1885, to July, 1887; and Rev. J. C. Schmidt, from August 5, 1887, to the present time.

In 1885 Mr. Samuel Melich donated to the Lutheran congregation, of which he was a member, one acre of land for a cemetery, as also a sum of money amply sufficient to pay the cost of inclosing said land with an iron fence on three sides, the fourth side opens into the old graveyard, in front of which the church stands. The proposed inclosure has since been made. The same member, at the same time, also donated half an acre of land for Sunday-school purposes, such as the holding of festivals, etc.

St. Peter's church, it is true, is a union church, but only so far as the church building and the land on which it stands are concerned. The Lutherans own one-half of this union property, and the Reformed the other half; the former occupy the church for divine services one Sunday, and the latter the following Sunday, so that there is divine service every Sunday throughout the year. In doctrine, as well as in the management of denominational church affairs, each of these two congregations is as independent of the other as if it had a church building of its own. Each has even a charter for its own sake.

THE SALEM PARISH.

BY THE REV. H. G. SNABLE.

THE Salem church, located at Salem, Snyder county, Pa., it is proper to state, prior to November, 1896, was included in the Freeburg parish. This was a very large parish, considered both territorially and numerically extending over an area of country about sixteen miles square, and embracing within its confines some 1,200 people. Dissatisfaction arose among themselves regarding certain internal pastoral administrations and the Salem congregation, numbering some 400 Lutherans, determined in the autumn of 1896 to detach themselves from the Freeburg parish, which they did by a unanimous vote, forming a parish by themselves consisting of Salem church, Sieber's and Erdley's, the Rev. H. G. Snable being unanimously voted for by all three congregations as pastor. The charge as now constituted contains about 600 communicants and is more compact with reference to territory, the pastor residing at Salem, one of the oldest villages of the county, on the public road leading from Sunbury to Lewistown.

SALEM CHURCH, SALEM.—The Salem church is the oldest Lutheran congregation in Central Pennsylvania west of the Susquehanna river. It was organized as early as the year 1775. The Rev. Isaac Gerhart, a Reformed minister, was chosen secretary at a joint church meeting held at Salem, Pa., March 26, A. D. 1817. The Rev. J. Conrad Walter, Lutheran, presiding, wrote in the minutes of the church, then newly erected, "that as before the Revolutionary War this community was inhabited by a people solicitous of spreading the Gospel and providing for the introduction of the Word of God, resolved to erect a church, and for this purpose secured from the Province of Pennsylvania a tract of land comprising 92 acres 137 perches, upon which a church subsequently was built, which was the first house of God this (west) side the Susquehanna." This community, well favored by nature, early became the home of the settlers who, pushing out into the remote frontier, established themselves on the western banks of the River Susquehanna, and as early as 1744 we find Thos. McKee, an Irish trader, located at McKees, a trading post between Harris Ferry and Shamokin.

On April 4, 1776, Melchior Stock and others made application to the Province for the tract of land above mentioned, and "on Dec. 19, 1811, upon the payment of $22.64, in full since paid by George Miller and Andrew Berger, in trust for the Lutheran and Calvinist congregations of Penn township, Northumberland (later Union, now Snyder) county, the State conveyed a plot of land containing 92 acres 137 perches, they to have and to hold the said tract or parcel of land, with the appurtenances, in trust for the said Lutheran and Calvinist congregations and their successors forever. Said land to be held free and clear of all restrictions and reservations, as to Mines, Royalties, Quit Rents, or otherwise excepting and reserving only the one-fifth part of all Gold and Silver ore, for the use of this Commonwealth to be delivered at the Pit's Mouth, clear of all charges." This conveyance is attested on behalf of the Commonwealth by Richd. M. Crain, Depty. Secy. Ld. Office. The congregation first organized in 1775, built a log church, which weathered the storms for 40 years, when it was torn down and replaced by a new brick church commenced in 1812 and finished in 1816, the work being interrupted by the second war with England, several of the Building Committee and officers being drafted for military service whilst engaged in working on the new church. The corner-stone was laid August 7, 1814, and the church was dedicated May 15, 1816. Thereafter the extension of this congregation was rapid and during the period of its growth there have been received into the church and carried on the rolls over 5,000 members of the Lutheran faith, nearly all the early settlers and first families of this county being at one time or the other resident and visiting members here.

The church of 1812-16 stood until 1897, when it was torn down and a modern church building, seating some 600 people, erected in its stead.

This makes the third church erected on this historic spot. The corner stone of 1814 was relaid after a lapse of 83 years, on May 30, 1897, amid impressive services, 2,000 people being present. Rev. Dr. Spieker, of Philadelphia, preached, and on April 24, 1898, the new church was formally consecrated, the Rev. Dr. Jacob Fry, Philadelphia, leading the services, Rev. H. G. Snable reading the consecration rites. Some $1,400 were raised on the day of dedication, and the impending indebtedness practically wiped out.

The records of this congregation have been remarkably well preserved by the officers and trustees from 1774 down to the present time, and it would be interesting to present in detail some salient features of the history of this time-honored and well-known congregation, such as lists of pastors with dates and terms of service, the financial exhibits in connection with the erection of the early churches, the papers, resolutions and deliverances drawn and made from time to time regarding the internal administration of its affairs, but limited space forbids such an attempt.   W. K. MILLER, ESQ.

ST. PETER'S CHURCH, GLOBE MILLS, PA.—The people of this community, about a century ago, worshiped in the church at Salem. Some time about the year 1799, initial steps were taken toward the erection of a house of worship more conveniently located. In 1799 something of an organization was effected; Samuel Moyer, Melchior Yoder, Peter Godshalk and John Yoder were elected trustees; and a plot of ground was donated to the congregation for church purposes, on which a school house was erected and used for religious services.

In 1840 the congregation decided to erect a church edifice. The lot owned by the congregation was exchanged for another more suitably located, and the church erected. Jacob Kessler and Daniel Zieber were elected trustees. The new building, called St. Peter's church, was consecrated May 28, 1840. It was soon found that the building was too small to accommodate the congregation and so it was decided, in 1850, to enlarge it. During a period of nineteen years, the congregation increased to such an extent that a larger building was found to be necessary, the Lutheran congregation having attained a numerical strength of over 200 members.

Additional ground was secured and the building was enlarged. The corner-stone laying and dedication took place on the same day.

Rev. J. Peter Shindel, Jr., served the Lutheran congregation from 1840, when the church was built, until 1853, when Revs. Peter Rizer and Frederick Ruthrauf served about two years each. J. Peter Shindel was again called June 21, 1856, and served until May, 1866. From this time on, the congregation was served by Revs Brenninger, Orwig and Lazarus, until 1874, when Rev. C. G. Erlenmeyer became pastor, and continued until his death, March 6, 1876. Revs. D. M. Stettler and D. E. Reed followed, until 1884, when Rev. J. F. Wampole became pastor, who served until fall of 1891. Rev. H. G. Snable took charge of this congregation July 2d, 1892, and is the present pastor of the congregation.

ST. PAUL'S CHURCH, Middlecreek township, was organized July 24, 1857. About this time, Mrs. Eve Erdley, widow of Henry Erdley, gave an acre of ground in one of the prettiest localities in Middlecreek township, Snyder county, upon which a church should be erected. The church is popularly called "Erdley's Church." The Lutherans, in connection with the Reformed, agreed to build a union church, a brick building, to be called St. Paul's Lutheran and Reformed church. The cornerstone was laid August 16, 1857, the Revs. C. G. Erlenmeyer, Lutheran, and A. B. Casper, Reformed, officiating. The work was carried on with great energy throughout the year and the church was consecrated August 29, 1858, the Revs. Reuben Weiser, Lutheran, and Dr. J. C. Bucher, Reformed, officiating. The second edifice, as it now stands, has stood for so many years, was erected at a cost of $2,000.

Rev. Erlenmeyer served the Lutheran congregation until his death. His successor, Rev. J. F. Wampole, took charge of the congregation Nov. 5, 1876, and served until the fall of 1891. The Rev. H. G. Snable, the present pastor, entered upon his duties in this field of work July 2, 1892, and with marked success has been ministering to the wants of the congregation until the present time.

PLATE VII

G. G. KUNKLE.

J. M. UHRICH.

J. P. GERMAN.

A. P. PFLUEGER.

SELINSGROVE PARISH.

BY THE REV. S. E. OCHSENFORD.

THE Selinsgrove parish consists of the following two congregations:

THE FIRST EVANGELICAL LUTHERAN CHURCH, Selinsgrove.—This congregation was organized about the year 1790, though the exact date is not known. It is known, however, that at this time there existed a Lutheran congregation here, which worshiped with the Reformed in the school-house, barns or private houses. About the year 1800, Conrad Weiser, a member of the Lutheran Church, donated several lots of ground to the Lutheran and Reformed congregations to be used for church and school purposes and another lot for a burial ground. These lots are located on the corner of Market and Bow streets, and extend to High street. The deed, in fee simple, bears the date, March 9, 1811.

The act of building the contemplated union church was delayed for some time after the lots had been donated. Meanwhile the following articles of agreement had been adopted:

"In the name of the Father, of the Son and of the Holy Ghost. Amen.

"1. The church is to be built and held as a union property by the Lutheran and Reformed congregations.

"2. The regular services are to be held alternately.

"3. No minister—a stranger, or one of a different denomination—shall be permitted to officiate therein, unless by permission of the joint consistories. II Chron. 2:4."

During the years 1801-02 two subscriptions were taken which resulted in the collection of $1,950.10. With this amount in hand, building operations were begun. On June 7, 1802, the corner-stone was laid, and during the following year the first church building was consecrated. The building, 40x38 feet, was constructed of pine logs, which were donated by the members. It was a one-story building, with two entrances, galleries on three sides, and the pulpit on the west side, and cost $2,284.22. The ad-

OLD FIRST CHURCH.

ditional amounts necessary to pay for the church were secured at the corner-stone laying and consecration of the church. The various subscription lists, bills of sale, receipts, etc., are preserved in the archives of the congregation. The two congregations, now, after long waiting and many privations, had their own church building, in which they could gather to worship God. Each congregation worshiped every alternate Sunday. But to build and support a church was much more difficult at that time than now. There were only a few families in each congregation which could give material aid in the work. That they did what they could appears from the fact that they donated timber, gave their time and labor and money. And in order to secure the new building for both congregations, it is said, that one man—John Ulrich —pledged all his property, until all the debts were paid. Here we find a spirit of devotion and self-sacrifice for the cause of the Lord that deserves to be held in grateful remembrance and to be imitated by the people of our time. The two congregations worshiped in this building until February 10, 1855, when the Reformed disposed of their interest in the "Union Church Property" to the Lutherans for $1,000, and built a separate church in the upper end of town.

In 1843 a split occurred in the Lutheran congregation on account of the introduction of the so-called "new measures." The pastor, with a number of Lutherans, withdrew and organized a second Lutheran congregation, which now belongs to the General Synod. The fight was long and bitter, and for many years retarded the work of the church.

Since the separation in 1855, the old congregation is known by its present title. Its charter bears the date of February 28, 1845, signed by the Lutheran Governor, Fr. R. Shunk, with a supplement bearing the date, March 22, 1862, signed by Gov. A. G. Curtin. For a number of years the congregation belonged, first, to the West Pennsylvania Synod, later to the Central Synod; but in 1868 it was received into the Ministerium of Pennsylvania (to which it had originally belonged) through the efforts of the Rev. J. W. Early, the pastor at that time. The congregation had to pass through many severe trials and difficulties; but many of its members were staunch Lutherans, were willing to endure persecution for the truth's sake, and finally saw their fidelity rewarded and their congregation firmly grounded on the principles and usages of the Church of the Reformation.

The old church remained in use for eighty years,

NEW FIRST CHURCH.

though during this time it had undergone material changes. In 1862 it was remodeled, an additional floor was put in the building, making it two stories, and the interior was improved. In 1883, the present pastor suggested the propriety of taking steps towards the erection of a new church-building during the Luther-Memorial year. The suggestion was favorably received and steps were at once taken to carry it into effect. On May 12, 1884, the beginning was made in tearing down the old building, on Sunday, August 3, 1884, the corner-stone of the new church was laid, the venerable Dr. C. W. Schaeffer preaching the sermon, and on October 25, 1885,

PARSONAGE.

the new building was consecrated to the service of God. The building is a brick structure, Gothic in style of architecture, and cruciform. The auditorium is 60x36 feet, with a tower on the southeast corner, furnished with a thousand-pound bell. The pulpit recess is on the west side, and is furnished with approved Lutheran chancel furniture. The Sunday-school Chapel, 47x32 feet, constitutes the arms of the cross, and the Infant Room, 20x20 feet, the head of the cross. The cost of the building, including labor, etc., donated, was about $9,000. In 1894 the congregation erected a frame parsonage, on the north side of the church, at an expense of $2,000. The congregation now has one of the most valuable church properties in the county.

The early pastorates of the congregation are somewhat in doubt, as far as the time of service is concerned; but the following list is approximately correct. Tradition has it that the Rev. Frederick William Jasensky came in 1790, and the Rev. Christian Espich, of Sunbury, in 1794, and served this congregation in connection with a number of others; and that at a later period, a Rev. Mr. Guensel and Rev. George Heim were pastors of the congregation. We give the following list of pastors: John Herbst, 1801-1804; John Conrad Walther, 1805-19; J. P. Schindel, Sr., 1820-43; C. G. Erlenmeyer, 1843-59; vacant, September, 1859-April, 1860; Peter Anstadt, 1860-63; C. G. Erlenmeyer (supply), 1863-68; J. W. Early, May, 1868-November, 1870; C. G. Erlenmeyer (supply), 1870-72; H. H. Bruning, November, 1872-October 1, 1874; E. L. Reed, 1875-December, 1878; J. F. Wampole, (supply), December, 1878-August 31, 1879; S. E. Ochsenford, since September 1, 1879.

The congregation now has a communicant membership of 300, a Sunday-school numbering 225 scholars, a Luther League with fifty members and a Woman's Home and Foreign Missionary Society. Since January 1, 1892, this congregation has been carrying on its operations under the Constitution recommended to congregations by the General Council. Its Council consists of ten deacons, with the pastor, ex-officio, president of the Council and congregation, a condition of things as should be found in every congregation connected with our Ministerium. The deacons, according to apostolic usage, are installed with the laying on of hands and with prayer. The congregation uses the full Liturgy in all its services, with clerical robe and altar vestments. In the midst of a community, permeated and influenced by un-Lutheran practices, it occupies a position which frequently calls down upon it abuse from those who are influenced by another spirit, and demands, on the part of its members, an unflinching fidelity and loyalty to the faith and usages of the Lutheran Church. The congregation, today, stands as a monument to the fidelity of the fathers, as well as of the present generation of workers.

The congregation was, at first, exclusively German; but about the middle of the present century it became German-English; and for the last twenty-five years it has been exclusively English in all its services. The congregation deserves great credit for what, under God, it has been able to accomplish within the last twenty-five years of its history. It has furnished two ministers to the Lutheran Church,—the Rev. S. J. Ulrich and the Rev. H. P. Miller, and has, at present, two young men in the Theological Seminary, at Mt. Airy, Philadelphia.

ZION CHURCH, Kratzerville.—This congregation was organized probably about the year 1790, or perhaps at an earlier date; but the first extant record bears the date already given. The early history of the congregation is shrouded in obscurity. Tradition has it, that the first church-building was a log building, which was used in an unfinished condition. The second building was erected about the year 1817, constructed of logs, and was erected on land donated by a man named Hessler; and hence for many years the church was known as "Hessler's Church." The Rev. John Conrad Walther was present at the consecration of this building. It was erected by the Lutherans and Reformed, and was jointly used by these two congregations. On September 28, 1817, the constitution of the "United Evangelical Lutheran and Evangelical Reformed Congregation of Zion's Church" was adopted and signed by Geo. Heim, Evangelical Lutheran minister; Jacob Hermann, trustee; Conrad Walter, elder; Heinrich Mattheis and Geo. Bieber, deacons. Daniel Kratzer, John Hermann, Adam Brans and John Erdle, members of the congregation, also signed the constitution. This is almost literally the Constitution prepared by Henry Melchoir Muhlenberg for the congregations in Philadel-

ZION CHURCH.

phia and elsewhere, embracing only a few verbal changes and adding the word "Reformed" wherever Lutherans are mentioned; and this constitution is still in force as it was originally adopted by the fathers. It bears the following date: "Given in the year of our Lord and Saviour Jesus Christ, one thousand eight hundred and seventeen, the twenty-eighth day of September, Monroe being President of the United States, Simon Schneider Governor of Pennsylvania." In 1847 the old log church was torn down and on June 20th the corner-stone of a new building was laid, the Revs. J. P. Schindel and J. B. Anspach, Lutheran ministers, assisting in the services on this occasion. The new church was consecrated on October 24, 1847, the Revs. J. P. Schindel and C. G. Erlenmeyer taking part in the consecration services, on the side of the Lutheran congregation. This is a brick structure, erected by the Lutheran and Reformed congregations, and cost about $2,500.

The Lutheran congregation was organized by a minister in connection with our Ministerium and for years maintained its connection with this body. Its Lutheran character is seen in the adoption of the Muhlenberg Constitution; and whatever changes may have occurred afterwards, this constitution has never undergone any changes. The congregation, also, refused to be drawn away by the revival excitement of later years, although it was brought into numerous conflicts on account of it. At what time it ceased its connection with the Ministerium is not known; but it is known, as a fact, that for many years it was connected with the Central Pennsylvania Synod, and was served by pastors of the same. But when the Rev. J. W. Early became the pastor, in 1868, the congregation asked to be dismissed to our Ministerium. The Central Synod hesitated to grant this request, questioned the validity of Rev. Early's election and sent a committee to the congregation to investigate matters and, if possible, avert the withdrawal. But the congregation was determined to carry out its intention, made application and was received into the Ministerium in 1868. At the same time the congregation at Selinsgrove and the congregations constituting the Freeburg parish, with their pastor, the Rev. C. G. Erlenmeyer, were received into the Ministerium of Pennsylvania. With this movement began the enlargement of the work of the Ministerium in this part of Pennsylvania, which has resulted in the establishment of four large parishes in this county, with fifteen congregations.

The early records of this congregation are very meager and give only a few hints with reference to the early history. Tradition has it that the Rev. Mr. Guensel was the first pastor and served the congregation until about the year 1800. He was succeeded by the Rev. George Heim, who began his labor about the year 1800; but how long he labored here is not known, though the present pastor has come across baptismal records bearing the date of 1827. The Rev. J. P. Schindel, Sr., it appears, served this congregation in connection with the one at Selinsgrove, until 1835, beginning his labors some time after 1820. He was succeeded by the Rev. J. P. Schindel, Jr., June 21, 1835-58 (a period of twenty-three years). The later records are more reliable, and present the following succession of pastors, who served this congregation in connection with Selinsgrove, the two congregations constituting one parish, as they do today: C. G. Erlenmeyer (supply), 1858-60; Peter Anstadt, 1860-63; C. G. Erlenmeyer (supply), 1863-68; J. W. Early, 1868-70; C. G. Erlenmeyer (supply), 1870-72; H. H. Bruning, 1872-74; E. L. Reed, 1875-78; J. F. Wampole (supply), 1878-79; S. E. Ochsenford, since September 1, 1879.

The congregation has, at present, a communicant membership of 522, and a "union" Sunday-school with about 100 scholars. The congregation is now large and strong enough to support its own pastor, and the sentiment is growing for this desirable change in carrying on the work of the congregation.

PLATE VIII

C. F. DRY.

W. H. GEIGER.

H. T. CLYMER.

L. LINDENSTRUTH.

J. N. WETZLER.

C. K. DRUMHELLER.

SHAMOKIN PARISH.

*BY REV. J. F. WAMPOLE.

GRACE LUTHERAN CHURCH.—From the time that Shamokin had a beginning, in 1840, there was occasional preaching, for the benefit of the few Lutheran families which had settled in the town, by Revs. Williard and Alleman, who were preaching in the Shamokin valley, until Rev. C. J. Ehrhard took charge of the three Lutheran congregations in Shamokin valley, and organized a congregation in Shamokin, and established the Shamokin Collegiate Institute in connection with Rev. Reuben Hill as assistant teacher, and organized a joint stock association to erect a suitable building, and after spending $8,000 on the building, one of the large property-holders conceived the idea of establishing a free university in Shamokin with a large endowment, and had the cornerstone laid, which discouraged the stockholders of the Collegiate Institute, who refused to contribute any more money on the building, and finally the building was given to the projector of the free university, on the simple condition that he would assume the debt of $2,000 still remaining unpaid on the building, and the creditors were mostly paid in building lots at exorbitant prices. That was the end of both educational enterprises.

Rev. Ehrhard was succeeded by Rev. J. F. Wampole, in 1857, and he was succeeded by Rev. I. B. Keller, in 1865, during whose pastorate the fine, large church was built on Sunbury street. But up to this time no provision was made for the Germans, and thus many families were lost to the Lutheran church and were drawn into the Reformed church, where regular services were held in the German. During 1866, and 1867, Rev. J. H. Schmidt, of Trevorton, came and preached regularly every four weeks in the Sunday-school room of the Reformed church and organized a congregation of 50 members or more, and had a church council, consisting of Martin Hofman, Lewis Marquart, Jacob Pfeifer and Henry Bach, until he left Trevorton in 1868, when the members continued to hold services every two weeks in Trinity Lutheran church, conducted by Rev. Kurtz, a retired Reformed minister, at 9 o'clock in the morning for about two years, when for various reasons the German services were discontinued and the congregation was dissolved and the members scattered, until the year 1884, when Rev. Henry Weicksel was prevailed upon to come and administer the communion to some German Lutherans who desired to have it administered as they were accustomed to receive it in Germany. He was also requested to give them regular Lutheran services in German every four weeks, which he consented to do if a suitable place could be secured. At first these services were held in Trinity Lutheran church, Aug. 16, 1885, but as the only hour at which these services could be held (3:30 o'clock p. m.) was very inconvenient to most of the members, Seiler's Hall, on Spruce street, was secured, and here a congregation was organized, Oct. 31, 1885, and a church council elected, consisting of Christian Lehner and Samuel Wagner, as deacons, and Ludwig Marquartt as treasurer; and it was resolved to hold public services every fourth Sunday, at 2 p. m. These services were regularly continued, with an encouraging increase of the membership and interest in the cause, and on the 8th of January, 1888, a constitution was adopted by the congregation, and a full church council elected: Christian Lehner and Martin Hofman, elders; Jacob Bummersbach and George Krach, deacons; Gotthilf C.

Crone, John G. Yeager and Herman Bartschat trustees; and Jacob Schankweiler, treasurer. Father Weicksel continued to serve the congregation, and with the assistance of his son, William, was able to preach every two

PARSONAGE.

weeks and give English services half the time, when on March 4, 1888, his son, Rev. William Weicksel, was elected pastor and on June 1, he entered upon the regular discharge of his duties as pastor. During his pastorate, two lots and a house were purchased, at the corner of

Seventh and Chestnut streets, for $3,600, on which in the future to erect a church.

On March 29, 1891, he resigned, and preached his farewell sermon on April 12th. On Trinity Sunday, May 24, 1891, Rev. J. F. Wampole preached for the congregation, and having received a call, entered upon his labors as pastor, on Sunday, July 5, 1891, preaching every other Sunday until November 1, when he moved to Shamokin, and after that preached every other Sunday morning in German, and every Sunday evening in English. In August of the same year, the congregation secured the use of the old Reformed church at a rental of $60 a year, which gave a fresh impulse to the work, and a large increase in the attendance of the congregation and Sunday-school. In the spring of 1893, the congregation had to vacate the building, as it was to be torn down to be replaced by a new church, and it was resolved to build a church on our own lot, 38 by 50 feet, with basement for Sunday-school. The corner-stone was laid June 4, 1893. The congregation and Sunday-school were able to occupy the Sunday-school room on Sunday, Aug. 13, and the church was dedicated Sunday, Nov. 19, 1893, by Rev. Father Weicksel, the founder of the congregation, having preached in German at 10 a. m., on Ps. 84:1-4, and Rev. T. Zuber, of Trevorton, preaching English in the evening. Collections, $354.57.

The church was regularly incorporated and received the name of Grace Lutheran Church of Shamokin. There was no Sunday-school until 1887, when a beginning was made with three scholars, and this number was not increased for three Sundays, but on the fourth Sunday 13 attended, and from that time the school grew until now there are 175 in the English Sunday-school and 100 in the German Sunday-school.

Now the congregation has nearly 250 members, and

has regular services every Sunday—German in the morning and English in the evening—with the German Sunday-school in the morning and English Sunday-school in the afternoon.

The church building with its furniture, cost $2,800, and

GRACE CHURCH.

is almost entirely paid for, with more than enough on the subscriptions to pay the balance.

ZION'S EVANGELICAL LUTHERAN CHURCH, Mt. Carmel.—This congregation was organized by Rev. William Weicksel, after frequent requests for German services, while he was pastor at Shamokin. After one German service in the summer of 1888, the first regular German service was held, February 17, 1889, in the English Lutheran church of the Susquehanna Synod, and was continued once every four weeks, at 3:30 p. m., after Sunday-school. On the 9th of June, 1889, a communion service was held at 8:30 a. m., when twelve persons communed. In the afternoon of the same day, a congregational meeting was held at the house of Henry Schweinhart, where Jacob Lupold and Henry Schweinhart were elected elders, and John Lupold and Andrew Wetzel, deacons. In the fall, in order to be able to have the services at a more convenient hour, the services were held at the house of Henry Schweinhart. At a communion held on Sunday, May 18, 1890, sixteen participated, and in the fall of this year, after a course of instruction in the catechism, an interesting class was confirmed, including Joseph Deppen and his four children, and at the communion held Nov. 2, 1890, 22 persons communed. In the spring of 1891, Rev. Weicksel resigned and preached his last sermon and administered the communion, on April 19, 1891, when 24 communed.

Rev. J. F. Wampole having been elected pastor of the Shamokin and Mt. Carmel Mission, commenced his labors as pastor of this congregation on Sunday, July 5th, 1891, and preached every two weeks, alternately in English and German, the German services being held at the house of Henry Schweinhart, and the English services at the house of Joseph Deppen. In the spring, he confirmed a class of six, and held communion, May 29, 1892, when 33 persons appeared at the Lord's table. During the year of 1896, the use of the Welsh Congregational church was secured to hold services in, but in the summer of 1897, as the congregation determined to rebuild their church, our congregation held their services at the house of Henry Schweinhart. The congregation adopted the constitution recommended by the General Council, during the pastorate of Rev. Weicksel. A very fine communion set was presented to the congregation by Mrs. Joseph Deppen, and a German Bible for the pulpit, by Henry Schweinhart. It is hoped that the congregation may be able to secure a church building of their own, and that then a permanent congregation and Sunday-school may be established.

Shamokin, Penn'a, October 21, 1897.

STONE VALLEY PARISH.

BY THE REV. W. H. GEIGER.

THE Stone Valley parish was formerly a part of the extensive Lykens Valley parish. As early as 1864 the increase of the work and the inability of the pastors serving the Lykens Valley parish to serve efficiently the congregation as such, together with Mission congregations which were organized in the course of time, it was suggested that a division be effected and the congregations lying on the north side of the Mahantongo mountain to form a separate parish. But on account of the long period in which they were connected with the Lykens Valley parish, the ties which had been formed were reluctantly broken. Not until the year 1870 was a division actually effected. The parish as it is now constituted consists of four congregations, to wit: Zion's (Stone Valley); Trinity, Georgetown; St. Luke's, Vera Cruz, and Zion's, (Pillow), the first three lying in Northumberland and the last one in Dauphin county, Pa. All of them are union churches with the exception of Zion's (Pillow).

PARSONAGE. The congregations, being accustomed to the advantages of a parsonage while connected with the Lykens Valley charge and owning a part share of the same, no sooner was a division effected and their share transferred that they utilized the money in addition to money raised in each individual congregation, in buying a property for the use of the pastor. After some hesitancy as to the proper location of the same for convenience both to pastor and people it was finally decided to locate the same at Pillow, Pa., each congregation owning an equal share.

ZION'S, STONE VALLEY. The organization of this congregation, which is looked upon and respected as the mother church of the other three, dates back prior to the year 1775. This organization was effected as far as is known by Rev. Wolf. There was occasional preaching

ZION CHURCH.

and administration of the Sacraments as early as 1750; probably by such men who had been sent by Rev. H. M. Muhlenberg, the patriarch of our Lutheran Zion in this western world. This supposition varies from the fact that this part of the country was mostly settled by families coming from the lower counties, such as Montgomery, Berks, etc. The first church edifice was probably built prior to the time of the organization of the congregation for church and school purposes. It was but a small building, probably 20x30 feet. It was built of logs and situated in the lower part of the old portion of the burial ground. In the year 1796 the erection of the second and present church edifice was commenced. Its completion was not effected until the year 1802 so that it is upon its centennial and expects to celebrate the same during the present year in connection with the 150th anniversary of the organization of the Ministerium of Penn'a. Among the names which stand connected with the erection of this second church edifice we note the following: Lenker, Emerich, Shaffer, Broscious, Kerstetter, etc. After an organization was effected and a house of worship erected the congregation took steps towards procuring an unoccupied track of land which lay close by. In the year 1808 an application was made to the Commonwealth of Pennsylvania and a grant given to Adam Lenker, Lutheran, and John Bigaman, Reformed trustee. The tract as now owned by the two congregations contains 65 acres and 93 perches and is used for burial purposes and for the support of the organist. The price paid for was $4.53.

PASTORS. The first pastor of whom anything positive is known was Rev. Wolf by whom it was organized. He was followed by Revs. Adams and Samsel. How long they served or whether they were merely supplies is not known. The Rev. J. C. Walter was pastor from 1805 or 1806 to 1809. The Rev. Daniel Ulrich from 1809 to 1811. The Rev. John P. Shindel from 1815 to 1830 or 1831. The Rev. J. N. Hemping from 1831 to 1850. The Rev. C. F. Welden from Sept., 1850, to Sept., 1851. The Rev. Nathan Yaeger from 1852 to 1853. The Rev.

F. Walz from Jan. 1, 1854, to Jan. 1, 1865. The Rev. Jeremiah Shindel from 1865 until the time of his death, in March, 1870. The Rev. J. W. Early from Nov., 1870, to May, 1875. The Rev. J. M. Uhrich from July, 1875, until the time of his death, in May, 1882. The Rev. C. N. Drumheller from April, 1883, to April, 1884. The Rev. W. H. Geiger from May, 1884, down to the present time.

This Zion's congregation of Stone Valley is looked upon as the mother of the other three congregations which are served with her. But although three daughters have grown up with and aside of her, she continues to hold her own strength unreservedly. Her present membership is 300, it being one-half of the total membership of the charge.

ZION'S, PILLOW. The organization of this congregation was effected about the year 1830 or 1831, by the Rev John P. Shindel. Immediately upon the organization of the same steps were taken towards the erection of a church edifice, the land for the building and the burial ground being donated by John Beck, a member of the congregation, its corner-stone having been laid in the year 1832 under the name of Christ church by the Rev. J. P. Shindel; the church having been built of logs, 30x40 feet. Before it had been brought to completion, it was demolished by a storm, but afterwards rebuilt and consecrated in the year 1833. During the forties it passed through a trying ordeal on account of the sensational move of "new measureism" passing over this section of country, diverting many from the faith once delivered unto the saints. In the year 1868 a sentiment arose to either remodel the old church edifice or to build a new one on a new site. The sentiment was strongly in favor of the former, especially among the members living in the country. A small faction of those living in town insisted upon the latter and so to say forced the majority to desist, which they did, severing at the same time their connection and joining churches next nearest to them. The erection of the second church building was commenced under great dissatisfaction, the corner-stone of which was laid in 1869 by the Rev. J. Shindel. The church was built of brick with a high steeple, 40x65, at a cost of about $14,000. The greater

ZION CHURCH.

part unpaid at the time of the dedication in 1870, great difficulty was experienced until the debt was canceled, which was not until 1882. In July of 1885 it was struck by lightning and destroyed, leaving nothing for the congregation to start with but the bare walls. On account of difficulties it was decided that a division should be effected and each congregation build for itself. The site of the first church together with the building having been sold, was bought back again by the Lutheran congregation to the great satisfaction of all; because of the attachment to the old site. Work upon the erection of another house of worship was commenced and on Oct. 11, 1885, the corner-stone was laid by the pastor under the name of Zion's, the pastor being assisted by the Revs. M. B. Lenker and S. S. Henry. It was consecrated Oct. 10, 1886, at which time the pastor was assisted by

TRINITY CHURCH.

the Revs. F. J. F. Schantz, D.D., M. B. Lenker, S. S. Henry, J. Hilpot, C. K. Drumheller. The church is built of brick in the form of an L, size 35x55, with a S. S. annex, at a cost of $4500. The congregation, notwithstanding the sore trials she experienced and the losses she sustained by removals and deaths is about holding her own, the present membership numbering 87.

From Rev. J. N. Hemping on the pastors have been the same as those of Zion's, Stone Valley.

TRINITY, GEORGETOWN. The organization of this

congregation was effected in the year 1845. Immediately upon its organization steps were taken in the erection of a house of worship upon land donated by George Broscious. For reasons unknown this congregation was organized on the part of the G. Synod branch of our church. Corner-stone laying and dedication the same year of its organization. It was organized by Rev. C. Martin who was succeeded by Revs. C. F. Stoever and

ST. LUKE'S CHURCH.

D. E. Reed. Members of Stone Valley congregation residing at Georgetown continued their connection with the mother church until the year 1870, when it was dismissed by the G. Synod and connected itself with the General Council. Since that time the pastors serving it have been the same as those of Stone Valley and Pillow. The church edifice is of frame, with cupola, size 32x42 feet. In the year 1887 it was greatly improved and made more inviting. The parish membership is 119.

St. Luke's, Vera Cruz. This congregation was organized under the pastorate of Rev. F. Walz. On account of the distance from the mother congregation the members living in and around Vera Cruz resolved to effect an organization among themselves. Rev. F. Walz being pastor of Stone Valley congregation at the time, supplied these people with preaching occasionally in the public school house. Aug. 12, 1860, the corner-stone of this church was laid by Rev. F. Walz; the church not being completed until the year 1862 when it was consecrated to the service of Almighty God June 8th of this year. The congregation has since been regularly supplied by the pastors of the Stone Valley congregation. The building is of brick, 40x50, with cupola. Its present membership is 110.

St LUKE'S, SUNBURY.

• BY REV. J. N. WETZLER, PH.D.

DURING a number of years the 5th district, now Danville Conference of the Ministerium of Pennsylvania, made a series of efforts to establish a congregation at Sunbury. The importance of having a church at this place was strongly felt. Hundreds of people have drifted away from our Church on failing to have a spiritual home here to receive them; some became identified with other bodies, while others lost their interest in Christianity altogether.

It became evident to accomplish something definite, more decided measures must be taken; and thus Conference, at its meeting held in Catawissa, April 17-18, 1894, after some interesting discussion, adopted the following resolutions, viz.: "That this Conference charge the President with the duty of securing a man to make a month's canvass of this field at once, at the expense of Conference, and that, if the result be favorable, to recommend the field to the Executive Committee for support. That this Conference pledge to pay for said exploration $50 for the month, and that each pastor send the amount he may be able to raise to the treasurer at the earliest date."

Rev. J. N. Wetzler was requested to undertake the work and see what can be done to the establishment of a congregation. After some consideration, he consented.

Not being acquainted in the place, he requested Rev. W. H. Geiger, of Pillow, Pa., to accompany him on the first trip and introduce him to some Lutheran people there. They went to Sunbury on the 1st of May, 1894, and met a few Lutherans and presented the matter. Rev. W. H. Geiger left in the afternoon. The work of canvassing was further proceeded with, and a few families were found who became interested and took a willing part in the work. The necessity of procuring a suitable property to locate a church was strongly felt, and the attention was directed in that line and various locations were considered.

ST. LUKE'S CHURCH.

The first meeting was held in the parlor of No. 802 Market street. Its purpose was the location of a place to erect a church. It was reported that the northwest corner of Catawissa and Reagan streets could be bought for $2,200. Also other properties were named.

After a lengthy talk on this subject, Rev. J. N. Wetzler

and Joseph Emerick were instructed to enter into an agreement for the said place, then owned and occupied by R. D. Shipe at as low a figure as possible. The following persons were present: Rev. J. N. Wetzler, Joseph Emerick, Rily Zerbe, Conrad Hoffman, Jacob Gessner, Peter and Jared Lenker, Isaac Snyder, and James Brosius. Nominations of officers were made; and it was decided to meet in some hall, if able to get one, on Sunday morning, May 13th, to hold religious services.

On May 13th (Pentecost), divine services were held in the P. O. S. of A. hall, on Market street, Rev. J. N. Wetzler preaching in the morning from Acts 1:4, and in the evening from Philip. 3:9-11. During the same services, election and installation of officers took place. A meeting was announced to be held the following evening at the home of Peter Lenker, No. 417 Catawissa street, East Sunbury.

At that meeting the entire General Council constitution for congregations was adopted. The congregation was named "St. Luke's Evangelical Lutheran Church, of E. Sunbury."

The committee went into an agreement with R. D. Shipe for said property (two lots, 60x150 feet) for $2,200. Soon a full purchase of the property was made.

The next action was directed toward the building of a church and parsonage. On the 2d of September, 1894, the corner-stone of the new church was laid. The weather was fair but warm. Divine services were held in the fore and afternoon, which were largely attended. The pastor was assisted by Rev. Wm. A. Schaeffer, Supt. of Missions, by the President of Conference, Rev. S. E. Ochsenford, Rev. J. F. Wampole and T. Zuber, all of whom excepting the latter delivered addresses.

On Sunday, Feb. 17th, 1895, the church was dedicated. Divine services were held on the day of dedication and on

Saturday evening previous. These services all were largely attended. The sermons were preached by Revs. J. F. Wampole, W. H. Geiger, O. E. Pflueger, and W. A. Schaeffer, Supt. of Missions, who also performed the dedicatory service. The amount raised at the occasion was $1,175. The cost of lot, church and parsonage is about $6,000.

On Sunday, March 3d, 1895, the first communion was held, when twenty-five communed. The Lord all along has blessed the work. The congregation uses the full English services of the Church. The present number of members is about 153. The number of baptisms performed since the starting of the church, is 114; marriages, 20; and funerals, 21.

Sunbury, Penn'a, Oct. 11, 1897.

THE TREVORTON PARISH.

BY REV. G. G. KUNKLE.

THIS parish consists, at present, of three congregations, all in Northumberland county. The combined membership is 513 communicants.

EMANUEL'S, NOW ZION'S.—The Evangelical Lutheran congregation of Trevorton, Pa., was organized in 1860. during the pastorate of the Rev. John Hornberger. The same year it was decided to build a church, the cornerstone of which was laid May 13, 1860. The church council at this time consisted of Gotthilf Crone and Michael Knapp, elders; Conrad Stein and Henry Shlimme, deacons; and Dr. Wm. Fritz, treasurer.

The church was dedicated June 30, 1861. There is no record of those who officiated on that occasion, but it is altogether likely that Rev. Hornberger and Rev. C. J. M. Neumann performed the interesting service, as both of them lived at Trevorton at the time. Rev. Hornberger closed his labors here in the fall of 1862.

From 1863 to 1864, Rev. G. C. Hasskarl served the congregation. In 1864 Rev. J. H. Schmidt became the pastor. In this same year a bell was purchased for the church, at a cost of $152.14, and promptly paid. In 1865 certain improvements were made, including the painting of the church building, at a total expense of $209.40, of which sum the Ladies' Aid Society of the congregation contributed $61.40.

Rev. Schmidt resigned in 1868, and during the two succeeding years Rev. L. G. Eggers was the pastor. From 1871 to 1874, the congregation was under the pastoral care of Rev. J. Albert, who has the honor of introducing English services in the evening. In 1874, a heater and chandalier and lamps were secured for the church, at a cost of $100.

From the spring of 1875 to Sept. 30, 1877, the Rev. A. Berg was the pastor. During his pastorate an organ was purchased, at a cost of $180.

The English Sunday School was organized Aug. 15, 1875, and has steadily grown and now numbers 180. The German Sunday School was organized in July, 1864, with Gotthilf Crone as superintendent. This school is still alive, under the superintendency of one of its founders, Tobias Binder.

After the resignation of Rev. Berg, the congregation had no regular pastor for nearly a year. It was visited, however, by Rev. J. W. Early, Rev. M. B. Lenker, Rev. S. S. Henry and others.

On the 22d of June, 1879, Rev. H. T. Clymer assumed the pastorate of this church, and was regularly installed Dec. 7, 1879, by Rev. J. W. Early. In the course of this year also, two pulpit Bibles and a sofa were bought for the church, at a cost of $36.25. Already in the seventies, this congregation began to pay the expenses of their pastors and lay delegates to Synod and Conference meetings. In August, 1882, Rev. Clymer was compelled by failing health to resign as pastor.

Revs. Early and Breinig served the congregation as per dates given under Emanuel's Church.

Rev. A. J. L. Breinig assumed the pastorate in July, 1887, and labored here until July, 1893.

THE NEW ZION'S CHURCH.—Feb. 18, 1889, at 7 o'clock, "working time," a congregational meeting was held in the old Emanuel's church, and was opened with prayer by the pastor, Rev. Breinig. It was resolved to build a new church, to be called Zion's Evangelical Lutheran Church, of Trevorton, Pa. Both the English and the German languages are to be used at the services. An impromptu subscription was so encouraging that it was decided to go on with the work on the new building. The present edifice is of brick, 36 by 60 feet. The cornerstone of the new church was laid with appropriate services in August, 1889, the pastor, Rev. Breinig, officiating. For a while the basement was used for divine ser-

ZION CHURCH.

vices; but on the 14th and 15th of October, 1893, the main auditorium was consecrated, the pastor, Rev. Theophilus Zuber, being assisted by Revs. D. M. Stettler, J. H. Raker, H. T. Clymer. The cost of the church as it now stands, is $5,500.

A Ladies' Aid Society, in some form or other, has existed in the congregation almost from its organization, and has often rendered valuable assistance. On New

Year's Day, 1897, a Luther League was organized, from which we hope for some good. This congregation has made commendable progress in practical beneficence.

Rev. Zuber was pastor of this church from September, 1893, to Oct. 1st, 1896. Rev. G. G. Kunkle assumed the pastorate on the first Sunday in Advent, 1896.

July 11, 1897, the congregation decided to build a parsonage alongside of the church, and to do it at once.

PARSONAGE.

EMANUEL'S, CROSS ROADS CHURCH.—This congregation originated in a defection from the Stone Church, as a protest against "New Measures" introduced and maintained there. In 1847, the first money was subscribed, and by Oct. 29, 1850, $997.14 had been realized.

The building was the joint property of the Lutherans and the Reformed. After the installation of both the Lutheran and the Reformed church councils, they met on the 8th of April, 1848, and adopted articles of agreement, called a constitution. In these articles, the Lutherans declared themselves unequivocally in favor of the Evangelical Lutheran Ministerium of Pennsylvania, and resolved to have no minister from any other body.

There are no records accessible of the time of its dedication, nor who officiated on that occasion. The first communion record shows eighty-one participants, ten of whom were confirmed at that time,—the spring of 1851.

From this time till 1856, the list varies from forty to eighty. About this time a number united with Elias' Church, in Lower Augusta township, which had been organized in 1851.

The list of communicants then ranged from forty to sixty. The membership continued to grow, and now, July, 1897, it has 230 names.

During 1869 or 1870, the Lutherans made an effort to organize and hold a Sunday School in this union church. To this the Reformed objected, and the good movement had to be abandoned. This Sunday School trouble led to a proposition by the Lutherans to the Reformed, looking to a peaceable separation between the two congregations. After waiting eight months for an answer and receiving none, the Lutherans proceeded to collect funds and gather materials for an exclusively Luthran church, at Wolf's Cross Roads, about a mile east of the union church. The ground, one and a fourth acres, was donated by Mr. Joel Wolf.

On May 24, 1885, the corner-stone of the Evangelical Lutheran Emanuel's Church was laid, with appropriate services. The pastor, the Rev. J. W. Early, was assisted on this occasion by Rev. M. B. Lenker, who preached the sermon. At these services the German liturgy of the Synod was used.

The consecration services continued for one week, from November 6 to 13, 1885, and were taken part in by the officers of the Fifth Conference of the Ministerium of Pennsylvania, Revs. J. H. Groff, President; S. S. Henry, Secretary; and J. F. Wampole, Treasurer, as well as by Revs. A. P. Pflueger and S. E. Ochsenford. The consecration proper took place on the afternoon of Sunday, November 8, on which occasion the Rev. L. Lindenstruth, of Mauch Chunk, Pa., preached the sermon, and assisted the pastor loci, the Rev. J. W. Early. The total cost of the church is $3,500.

RECORD OF PASTORS.

The following list of pastors and the length of their respective pastorates is as nearly correct as can well be ascertained:

From 1848 to 1851, no record.

Rev. C. J. M. Neumann, from beginning of 1851, or possibly the fall of 1850, till the close of 1859, or beginning of 1860.

Rev. J. F. Hornberger, from 1860 to 1864.

Rev. J. H. Schmidt, from fall of 1864 to spring of 1868.

Rev. L. G. Eggers, from May, 1869, to May, 1871.

Rev. J. Albert, from fall of 1871 to his death, January, 1875.

Rev. A. Berg, from spring of 1875 to September, 1877.

Rev. H. T. Clymer, from June 22d, 1879 to August, 1882.

Rev. J. W. Early, from Jan. 21st, 1883, to March, 1886.

Rev. A. J. L. Breinig, from October, 1887, to July 1st, 1893.

Rev. Theophilus Zuber, from September, 1893, to October, 1896.

Rev. Geo. G. Kunkle began his pastorate on the first Sunday in Advent, Nov. 29th, 1896.*

---

* NOTE.—This parish was resigned by the Rev. Kunkle, to take effect July 3, 1898, but Zion congregation at Trevorton, having unanimously resolved, May 1, 1898, to become a self-sustaining parish, re-elected the Rev Kunkle as its pastor, and he re-entered upon his pastoral labors in that congregation, July 10.—*Editor*.

A Sunday School has been held in this church since the new church was built.

ELIAS' CHURCH.—The first recorded meeting for the purpose of discussing the feasibility of organizing a congregation in Lower Augusta township, Northumberland county, Pa., was held December 26, 1850, at the house of Samuel Kaufman. This was a joint meeting of the Lutherans and the Reformed, and it was resolved to build a so-called union church. The church was built on land bought of Henry Reitz, who gave a clear title for the same to Samuel Kaufman and Daniel Schmeltzer, who had been appointed trustees.

It was also decided to build a frame church, the corner-stone of which was laid on the 20th of April, 1851, and the title Elias' Lutheran and Reformed Church engraved on it.

Of this occasion there is no official record within the reach of the writer, but from eye-witnesses, he was informed that Rev. C. F. M. Neuman officiated at that service. When and by whom the church was dedicated, cannot be definitely ascertained. But this also was attended to either late in fall of 1851 or in the spring of 1852.

The articles of agreement are simple and provide that there shall be preaching in English and German; services to be held in the latter language as long as there are four members who desire it. They are also particular to state that this church is a protest against the so-called "New Measures," and such will not be tolerated in this church.

The articles of agreement are signed by Christopher J. M. Neuman, Lutheran pastor, and R. A. Fisher, Reformed pastor.

The Lutheran council at the organization of the congregation, was Joseph Folk, trustee; Daniel Schmeltzer and Daniel Kaufman, elders; Jacob Kreler and Peter Ferster, deacons.

Henry Reitz donated one acre of ground for church and burying-ground. There is no record of the original membership. The congregation has had a steady growth, and now numbers 103 members.

A Sunday School has been in connection with this church since 1866. George Raker and Henry Drumm were among the originators. For a long time the school was kept only from April till some time in the fall of the year; but now it is open the year round.

The old frame church having become inadequate to the needs of the congregations, the Lutherans and the Reformed again decided to build a church together, on the same ground, but this to be a brick building. It was erected at a cost of about $2,500. The corner-stone was laid with appropriate services in the spring of 1880, the pastor, Rev. H. T. Clymer, officiating on the Lutheran side.

The new church was consecrated in May, 1881, on which occasion the cermony was conducted by Pastor Clymer, assisted by Rev. J. F. Bayer. In the fall of 1896, the church was unroofed by a severe storm; this, however, was promptly replaced.

For the record of pastors, see under Emanuel's Church. Trevorton, Pa., July 16, 1897.

TURBOTVILLE PARISH.

BY REV. E. H. EBERTS.

MANY years ago this parish consisted of Turbotville, Washingtonville, McEwensville, Paradise River Church and White Deer Valley.

After the lapse of time and a number of divisions and reconstructions, it now consists of Turbotville and Washingtonville, and is one of the most desirable country parishes on our Synodical territory.

TURBOTVILLE ZION'S EVANGELICAL LUTHERAN CHURCH.—The early history of this congregation is unwritten. If its early pastors kept any records, they are lost. There is now no record extant from which any data can be gathered prior to 1837. It is probable that records were kept. In the oldest record now on hand, there appears a page of "Baptism Records," the earliest of which is that of "Christiana Waleiser, 1807." This is followed by a number of others, at which "The Parents" were the sponsors.

The date of the organization of this congregation is not recorded. The first church was a union church. It was a log building, erected by the Lutheran and German Reformed people of this community on the site now occupied by the St. James (G. S.) Lutheran Church. It was a union church indeed. Rev. J. F. Engel, who preached here 1815-1817, was pastor for both Lutheran and Reformed congregations.

Services were held in this church till 1853, when it became necessary to put up a new building. This necessity involved the congregations in a bitter fight.

Rev. S. R. Boyer, the Lutheran pastor, and part of his congregation insisted on building a Lutheran church.

The Reformed minister and his people, together with some Lutherans, were equally determined to build a union church.

The union element having a majority, a union church was built by the side of the old log church. When almost completed, "it was set on fire" and completely destroyed, together with the old log church. The result of this unfortunate event, was an immediate separation of the Lutheran and Reformed congregations, and the erection of Trinity Reformed Church on the ground owned conjointly with the Lutherans.

Serious troubles arose among the Lutherans, which also resulted in a division. Part of the congregation built a large brick church on the spot where the union church burned down. This is St. James Lutheran Church, now in the hands of the General Synod, with a membership of about 250. Zion's, the mother congregation, under Rev. S. R. Boyer, built its present house of worship on Paradise street in 1856.

The above facts almost force upon us the conclusion that "church fights" are a good thing. When all was peace, these people felt too poor to build one church. When all was strife, they built four, and paid them cash. The records have been faithfully kept since 1851, and contain many interesting and important items, which cannot be presented in so brief a sketch.

The congregation has been served by the following pastors: Rev. J. F. Engel 1815-1817. Rev. J. Rebas, 1817-1826. Rev. F. Waage, April, 1826,-April, 1829. Rev. William German, 1829-1830, about nine months. Rev. C. P. Miller, 1831- about four years. Rev. C. F. Stoever, 1836-1845. Rev. S. R. Boyer, April, 1846,-1859. Rev. J. Albert, November, 1859,-November, 1866. Rev. J. F. Wampole, October, 1867,-November, 1876. Rev. A. P. Pflueger, 1876-1891. Rev. E. H. Eberts, as supply, November 8, 1891, to July 1, 1892; as pastor from July 1, 1892, to the present time.

In 1893, the church was completely remodelled. New furniture and two Sunday-school rooms were put in, and the walls and ceiling beautifully frescoed. In 1895, the congregation built a beautiful parsonage on the lot adjoining the church, making a pleasant and convenient home for the pastor. The wisdom manifested in the erection of this parsonage is commendable. It was erected and is owned by Zion's congregation. And to do its part towards procuring a home for the pastor, the Washingtonville congregation pays annually the interest on half the .cost. The congregation at present numbers 260 members.

WASHINGTONVILLE EVANGELICAL LUTHERAN CHURCH —According to a brief historical sketch prepared by Rev. S. R. Boyer, and recorded in one of the old church records, this congregation was organized in the year A. D. 1812. In this year, about 25 or 30 Lutherans, together with a small number of German Reformed people, met and resolved to erect a house of worship. Accordingly, a subscription of about $360 was taken, ground broken, and the corner-stone laid. On this occasion, Revs. Walter, Engel, Fries and Patterson officiated. For some now unknown reason, the completion of this new house of God was delayed till the year 1818, when, on the 4th day of October, it was dedicated to the service of the Triune God, and received the name Zion's Church. The ministers who officiated on this occasion, were Revs. Fries. Patterson, Rebas and Kessler. This church was not located at Washingtonville, but two miles north, on an elevation now called Strawberry Ridge.

The Lutherans continued to worship in this union church till the year 1850, when the usual "union troubles" arose. On October 15th of the same year, the pastor,

Rev. S. R. Boyer, "called a meeting of all the Lutheran members of the church for the purpose of taking into consideration the propriety and necessity of erecting another house of worship to be located at Washingtonville." The meeting was well attended.

The object of the meeting was stated by the pastor, together with some important reasons for building a church in Washingtonville, after which it was "Resolved that in humble reliance upon God, and by His blessing, we will take up a subscription and build a new church, 55 feet deep and 40 feet wide, with a basement story and a cupola." Jacob Wagner was elected treasurer of the church, and Peter Wagner and Jesse Gresh were appointed a building committee.

By the united efforts of the pastor, officers and members, sufficient money was raised to warrant the beginning of this important work. The corner-stone was laid on the 15th day of May, A. D. 1851, and the solemnities of the day attended by Revs. Henry Ziegler, P. Willard, J. M. Alleman, and the pastor, Rev. S. R. Boyer.

On the 21st day of September, 1851, the church was solemnly dedicated to God, and received the name Washingtonville Evangelical Lutheran Church. The officiating ministers were Revs. Henry Ziegler, P. Willard, J. M. Alleman, and the pastor.

On the day of dedication, the sum of $400 was raised. And this, with the sum formerly subscribed, $1,200, was sufficient to liquidate the entire cost of the church, $1,600.

The first communion was administered in the new church October 19, 1851, when 145 persons communed. On the same day, a class of 19 persons was confirmed. The same pastors who served the Turbotville congregation also served this congregation.

Although the number of members is now three times as large, the same old building, after being remodelled many times, still stands, a monument to the fathers' struggles and their children's indifference. It has served its purposes well, but is entirely inadequate to accommodate the present large congregation, and a larger and more modern building is sorely needed. By the will of the late Michael Hawk, this congregation received a bequest of $3,400, which, by a vote of the congregation, is to be applied towards erecting a new church. Like Rev. S. R. Boyer, the present pastor "called a meeting of the members, November 14, 1897, and gave some important reasons for erecting a new building." the result of which will be an election, in the near future, on whether a new church is to be built.

The congregation at present has a nominal membership of 450.

TURBOTVILLE, Nov. 23, 1897.

St. Mark's Church, Williamsport.

THE history of the Lutheran church, in Williamsport, dates back beyond the middle of the present century. The Lutherans from the Fatherland, at first, worshiped with the Reformed in a small one-story stone church on Third street. The first English Lutheran congregation was organized by the Rev. Dr. H. Ziegler, March 7, 1852, with twenty-seven members. At first they worshiped in the German church. The congregation was incorporated December 31, and a lot was purchased on Market street for the location of an English church, overtures to the German Lutherans for the erection of a common house of worship having failed. April 3, 1853, found the congregation still worshiping in the old German church, but without a pastor, the Rev. Dr. Ziegler having resigned.

July 5, 1853, the new pastor, the Rev. Joseph Welker, arrived from Clarion county and took up the heavy work, the congregation now numbering about thirty members. Realizing the necessity of a church of their own, he began the work of erecting a church building, the corner-stone of which was laid October 27, 1854, and the completed building, which cost $4,000, consecrated January 22, 1856.

The next pastor was the Rev. J. F. Fahs, who labored here for five years, and at the close of his pastorate the congregation had one hundred members. After his resignation, the Rev. F. C. H. Lampe became the pastor and served the German and English congregations, for a time worshiping in the English church on Market street, from May, 1863, to September, 1864. At the end of his pastorate, the English congregation had 120 and the German 130 members.

OLD ST. MARK'S CHURCH.

April 1, 1865, the Rev. A. R. Horne became the pastor, and from this date until April 1, 1868, services were held in both languages, when the German congregation,

NEW ST. MARK'S CHURCH.

having a membership of 230, separated again from the

English and built the German Immanuel church, on Basin street, with the Rev. Mr. Zentner, as its first pastor. In 1867, members of the congregation, living in South Williamsport, organized Messiah Lutheran congregation, and in 1871 St. Paul's congregation was organized by those members who preferred to unite with the General Synod. Although two new congregations had been organized by members formerly connected with the congregation, its membership had reached the number of 307 during Rev. Horne's pastorate. He resigned in 1872, and was succeeded by the Rev. W. H. Rickert, who served the congregation for a period of fourteen years, resigning January 15, 1886, and on December 18, the Rev. A. L. Yount assumed the duties of the pastorate.

During his pastorate numerous changes and improvements were made. A debt of $800 was cancelled, a parish paper was published, the name changed from Market Street church to that of St. Mark, and another new congregation helped in its organization,—the Church of the Redeemer. The flood of 1889 did great damage to the church building, which necessitated extensive repairs. The pastor resigned September 28, 1889, the congregation numbering 331 members, and after a long delay, he was succeeded by the Rev. Geo. G. Kunkle, who served the congregation for one year, 1891-92.

In 1883, the Rev. William Fr. Rick assumed the duties of the parish. He came from our Seminary at Philadelphia, was installed in August of the same year, and at once began his energetic labors, which have resulted in the erection of the handsome new church, the corner-stone of which was laid in September, 1895, and the building consecrated October 14, 1896. The building cost $25,000, and is one of the finest church edifices in Williamsport. The Rev. Mr. Rick is chaplain of the Twelfth Regiment of Penna. Volunteers.* His absence from home has prevented him from preparing this sketch, the material of which has been gathered from "A Brief History of St. Mark's Ev. Luth. Church," prepared by the pastor and published in 1896, from the closing pages of which the following extract is taken:

"We have a history of which we need not be ashamed. It should inspire us to great deeds. The Williamsport of today is ten times as large as the Williamsport of those days; but the English Lutheran church here is seventy-five times larger. Oh, ye little band of twenty-seven brave and stalwart souls, 'behold how great a fire a little spark enkindleth!' Is it strange, then, that our hearts should be filled with hopes for the future? Shall we tell of some that we entertain for St. Mark's? We believe through the agency of our Normal Class we shall have a corps of teachers in our Sunday-school not inferior in the art of teaching to the very best in our public schools. Our Deaconess institution, we hope ere long to contain a nurse who shall minister to the sick, free of all charge. . . Our Young People's Association and our Cotta Society shall be far-reaching arms for good and our new beautiful edifice too small a power-house for the great uplifting influence we shall exert in this city. . . The flood of '94 did not dishearten us like that of '89; for the following spring we began the erection of our new church, which has been successfully completed. Despite the cares of building and the discouragement of worshiping in the First Baptist church, most kindly loaned us by that congregation, but unfortunately out of the beat of our people, the proportionate increase in membership and attendance is greater than that of any

---

*With deep regret do we add that Brother Rick fell a victim to typhoid fever contracted in the army, and died at his home, August 21 1898.—*Editor.*

church in this city. Lutheranism everywhere is winning the admiration of the thoughtful. Her deep sympathy with American institutions, her truly liberal theological views, her churchliness, her many learned men, the sterling characteristics of her people, her rich heritage of history, her catechisation of the young, her philanthropic spirit, her high regard for God's Word—all unite to make her the Church of Future America. Ah, as a band in that great army of Christ, well may we believe we have a divine mission."

CHRIST GERMAN CHURCH, SOUTH WILLIAMSPORT.

BY THE REV. HANS MEYER.

THIS congregation was organized November 9, 1896, with 38 members, by the Rev. E. F. Steinhagen. Present were also the Rev. S. E. Ochsenford, D.D., president of the Danville Conference at that time, and Rev. L. Rosenberg, of Jersey Shore. Most of these members formerly went to the German Reformed church at Williamsport, one of the oldest congregations in that city, but which congregation ceased to exist early in the summer of 1896. Desirous of having German services on the South Side, so that they were not obliged to cross the river, when attending services, the Rev. E. F. Steinhagen, acquainted with most of those people started a Sunday-school with a small number of children in the middle of August, giving the people at the same time German services. The beginning of this work was humble. But as pastor and people worked faithfully, their labor was crowned with success, and soon they could step to the organization of Christ Lutheran church. The young congregation worshiped in the Baptist chapel, on Southern avenue.

Together with the organization of the church, a Ladies' Aid Society was organized with about 20 members. Soon after this an organization of a Young People's Society was effected. The attendance of the Sunday-school and services at this time were very encouraging, especially the evening services were well attended.

On Easter Sunday, for the first time, the Lord's Supper was administered, when 38 persons appeared at the

Lord's table. A handsome communion set was shortly before purchased.

The last of June Rev. E. F. Steinhagen laid down his pastorate, and two weeks after, Rev. Hans Meyer, from Philadelphia, Pa., accepted a call from the congregation, entering upon his labor as pastor, on Sunday, July the 25th. He was installed on the 25th of November, 1897, by the president of the Danville Conference, the Rev. O. E. Pflueger.

Up to the month of June the congregation was allowed to use the chapel both morning and evening, but then another party was granted the privilege of partially using the chapel for preaching purposes, our congregation occupying it in the morning, the other in the evening. But as it was a fact that our evening services had always showed the largest attendance, the congregation took the matter into consideration and finally the Church Council called a meeting in which it was decided to buy the chapel for $1,400. This was a most important step; morning and evening services could now be held without further interruption by other parties. Since this time much has been done to beautify the interior of the church. Chancel has been remodeled and now shows a more church-like appearance. The congregation, which is increasing slowly but steadily, counts at the present time about 70 members. The Sunday-school is visited by nearly 70 children and young people. On Palm Sunday confirmation was administered in this church for the first time, when eleven or twelve young Christians were added to the church.

A pipe organ was presented by the Trinity German Lutheran church at Camden, N. J. The date of dedication of this church has not been fixed.

PLATE IX.

S. E. OCHSENFORD.

N. SCHEFFER.

S. B. STUPP.

J. W. KLINGLER.

O. REBER.

J. H. RITTER.

III. Biographies.

BIOGRAPHIES.

ABELE, JOHN F., was licensed by the Ministerium of Pennsylvania, to serve congregations at Williamsport, White Deed, Jersey Shore and Pine Creek, Pa., 1822; had removed to Aaronsburg, Centre County, Pa., serving with it congregations at the Meeting House, Loop and Springfield, 1824; ordained, 1828; again moved to Williamsport, 1837-8; engaged in secular business and the practice of medicine against which Synod advised him; was honorably dismissed, 1845; received again and again dismissed, 1847. He ended his days in the New York Ministerium.   J. W. EARLY.

ALBERT, JOHN JACOB, was born near Elizabethtown, Lancaster County, Pa., in the year 1798. At an early age his attention was directed to the ministry, which he finally entered in the year 1820, after having pursued a course of theological studies under the Rev. Christian Endress, D.D., then of Lancaster City, Pa. He was first called to the charge of congregations at Berlin, Adams County, Pa., where he labored with commendable success for six years, when he removed to Manchester, Carroll County, Md. Here he remained from 1828 to 1837, cultivating his large and laborious field with great diligence and faithfulness. While at Manchester he received a call to Hanover, York County, Pa., which, after mature deliberation, he accepted, entering upon his labors there in the year 1837. His ministry at Hanover was characterized with unwearied interest in his work and was largely blessed to the good of souls. The accessions to the church were very numerous, adding materially to the strength and general welfare of the charge. After remaining at Hanover eleven years, he removed in 1848 to Bellefonte, Centre County, where, in connection with the service given to a part of the same charge at Salona, Clinton County, he remained until 1853, when he accepted a call to Millersville, Lancaster County, which charge he served but one year. From Millersville he was called to Centreville, Northampton County, laboring in that difficult field for six years, from whence he moved to Northumberland County, where he served successfully the congregations at Turbotville, Muncy Hills and Trevorton. It was while temporarily supplying the Trevorton charge, that he contracted the sickness, which ended his useful life on Sunday, January 3d, 1875. For nearly 54 years he was engaged in the active work of the ministry, crowning his life with good deeds to his Divine Master, and to his fellow-men. Blessed with a strong constitution and excellent health, he seemed never to tire in the work to which he had consecrated his life, strictly conscientious in the discharge of his duties, he was ever to be found at his post, undeterred by any exposure to the elements, or by any roughness of the way. He emphatically loved his calling, never wishing for a moment to change it for any other, however attractive to the outward eye, or lucrative in its rewards. The people among whom he labored, were ever dear to his heart, permitting nothing to alienate them from his Christian regard. Wherever he toiled he made hosts of friends, who ever welcomed his return among them, with gladsome hearts. A modest and unobtrusive man, he never mingled much in the active proceedings of Synods and Conferences, but was ever intensely interested in every measure looking towards the development of the Church and the extension of the Redeemer's kingdom. From an account kept of his labors in the ministry for the space of 50 years, we find among the items of interest the following: Baptized 3,052, confirmed 2,491, married 2,052, buried 2,653, and administered the communion to about 30,000 souls. He was twice married, having by his first wife twelve children, of whom five are living, two of whom are in the ministry, Rev. L. E. Albert, D.D., of Germantown, Pa., and Rev. Charles S. Albert, D.D., of Philadelphia, Pa. To him might truly be applied that beautiful passage of Scripture: "They that be wise shall shine as the brightness of the firmament: and they that turn many to righteousness as the stars forever and ever."

C. S. ALBERT.

ALLEMAN, MONROE J., pastor at Danville, Pa., 1847-8, was born at Maytown, Lancaster County, Pa., August 18, 1820. He attended the preparatory department of Pennsylvania College, Gettysburg, Pa., 1841-3, and received his theological training in the Seminary at the same place, being licensed by the West Pennsylvania Synod, 1845, and ordained, 1846. He was pastor at Northumberland, Pa., adding Lewisburg to his parish, 1850; Aaronsburg, Centre County, Pa., with three connected congregations, 1852-56; Hanover in connection with St. Paul's and St. Jacob's, 1857-65; Littlestown, Spring Grove, York, 1882. He was at one time President of the West Pennsylvania Synod, and had conferred upon him the degree of D.D. He married, October 15, 1846, Catharine E. Shellman, and died December, 1897.

ALTPETER, PETER, pastor of St. John's, Catawissa, Pa., since April 1898, a son of Peter and Martha Elizabeth Altpeter, was born at Rochester, N. Y., May 7, 1868. He entered the Sophomore class at Thiel College, Greenville, Pa., having prepared under the direction of his pastor, the Rev. J. E. Whitteker, graduating June, 1892, the salutatorian of his class. He graduated from the Theological Seminary at Philadelphia, 1895, and was ordained the same year by the Ministerium of New York. He also took a two years' course in Philosophy at the University of Pennsylvania. He was pastor of Trinity congregation, Rochester, N. Y., 1895-8. He married Rozetta Julia Hogue, January 15, 1896, of Greenville, Pa.

* ANSPACH, JOHN MELANCHTHON, D.D., pastor of Trinity, Danville, Pa., 1868-72, son of the Rev. John George, and Susan Wolf Anspach, was born in Mifflinburg, Union County, Pa., January 13, 1841. He prepared for college in the Academy at Mifflinburg, and graduated with honor from Wittenberg College, Springfield, O., in 1861; received his theological training in Missionary Institute, now Susquehanna University, Selinsgrove, Pa., and was ordained in 1863. His first pastoral service was as the assistant of his father, and his pastorates after that at Danville were: St. Matthew's, Reading, Pa., 1872-7; Christ, Easton, Pa., 1877-92; St. Paul's, Williamsport, Pa., since 1892. He was Secretary of the Central Synod of Pennsylvania, of the Second Conference of the Ministerium of Pennsylvania, 1883-7, and of the Ministerium itself the English Secretary, 1888-92. He married, June 27, 1865, Lydia Catharine, daughter of the Rev. J. C. Bucher, D.D., of the German Reformed Church, at Pottsville, Pa. In 1890 he received the degree of D.D. from the Missionary Institute, Selinsgrove, Pa.

ANSTADT, PETER, D.D., pastor of the First Lutheran church, Selinsgrove, Pa., 1860-3, son of Peter and Elizabeth (Altman) Anstadt, was born November 19, 1819, in Germany. He came with his parents to America and settled at Muncy, Pa., 1830; graduated from Pennsylvania College, Gettysburg, Pa., 1844, and from the Theological Seminary in 1846. His pastorates were: Hollidaysburg, Pa., 1846-8; Luther Chapel (now Third church), Baltimore, Md., 1848-51; St. James', Gettysburg, Pa., 1851-60; Selinsgrove, Pa., 1860-70; York, Pa., since 1870. For eleven years he published "Der Lutherische Kirchenbote," and its English successor, "The American Lutheran," for thirteen years. He publishes Sunday-school lesson helps, and is the author of a number of books. In 1889 he received the degree of D.D. from his Alma Mater. He married Miss E. A. Benson, December 22, 1853.

BAHL, ISAIAH, pastor of the territory of what are now the Berwick and Mainville parishes, 1830-62, was born in Berks County, Pa., February 6, 1803. He was licensed by the Ministerium in 1825, and ordained in 1828. He labored at Newport, 1825-8; Wilkes-Barre, Pa., 1828-30, and is reported to have had a wide but secular influence. He died March 6, 1862, at Berwick, where, in 1832, he had been married to a Miss Snyder.

BARNITZ, FREDERICK AUGUSTUS, son of John E. and Elizabeth Barnitz, was born September 4, 1821, in York, Pa. He graduated from Pennsylvania College, Gettysburg, Pa., 1842, studied theology in the Seminary at the same place, and was licensed in 1844. He was pastor at Jersey Shore, Pa., 1845-9; Bloody Run (Everett), Pa., 1849-52; Smicksburg, Pa., 1852-5; Lairdsville, Pa., 1855-61; Ashland, Pa., 1861-3. Owing to impaired health he retired from the active ministry, at Middletown, Pa., where he died, August 19, 1889. He was twice married: March 9, 1846, to Sarah J. Babb, Jersey Shore; November 13, 1866, to Dora Reimsnyder, Hummelstown, Pa.

BARR, WILLIAM PENN, son of Francis A. and Lizzie

Anna Barr, was born at Mauch Chunk, Pa., February 16, 1867. He graduated from Muhlenberg College, Allentown, Pa., 1896, and is now a member of the Senior class at the Theological Seminary at Philadelphia. He married Laura Mary Swab, Elizabethville, Pa., March 25, 1890.

BAYER, JOHN FREDERICK, pastor of the Mahanoy parish, 1869-70, and again 1881-6, was born in Germany, December 20, 1826. In the spring of 1852 he emigrated to America and settled at Orwigsburg, Pa., where he held the position of teacher and organist, and where he married Johanne Brandle, August 11, 1852. He became a colporteur of the American Tract Society, and while thus engaged prepared for the ministry, and was ordained by the East Pennsylvania Synod, 1856. He was called to the Middleport parish, and in 1861 was received into the Ministerium, together with his congregation at Tamaqua, Pa., with which congregation he continued till 1868. After spending about a year in the Mahanoy parish he returned to Tamaqua, and at the end of his second pastorate at Mahanoy, he retired from the active ministry, at Philadelphia, where he died early in 1887.

BEILHARZ, JOHN J., a traveling missionary in Lycoming and Tioga Counties, 1825-6, was licensed by the Ministerium in 1824. In 1827 he went to Seneca County, New York, and in 1842 he was dismissed to the Ohio Synod.

BERG, ANDREW, pastor of the Trevorton parish, with residence at Sunbury, Pa., 1874-7, was born in the Palatinate, Germany, and received his education in Pennsyvania College and Theological Seminary at Gettysburg, Pa., being licensed in 1842. He served congregations at Liverpool, 1842-3; Shrewsbury, 1843-73; and from Sunbury he went to Leacock, Lancaster County, Pa., where he died, February 7, 1884. He was married in 1842, to Eliza Williams, of York County, Pa.

BERGNER, JOHN G. CHR. AUGUST, was born March 28, 1806, in Thaldorf, Principality Schwarzburg Rudelstadt, Germany. He emigrated to America in 1837, teaching school for a number of years, and studying theology under the Rev. A. T. Geissenhainer, being licensed by the President of Synod *ad interim*, November 17, 1843. He was ordained at Orwigsburg, Pa., June 10, 1846, and served the congregations now constituting the Line Mountain and Mahanoy parishes from that time till his death, October 26, 1860. From 1850 till his end he also served Simeon's at Gratz. Six new churches were built in his parish during his pastorate, viz., St. Paul's, another St. Paul's (formerly Mahanoy school house), St. Peter's, in Northumberland County; St. John's, Artz's at Sacramento, and St. Matthew's, in Dauphin County. At his birthplace he was married, May 26,1834, to Maria Amelia Augusta Feldtroppe. His remains are buried at Himmel's (Schwoben Creek) church.

BINNINGER, JOHN JACOB (or Benninger), pastor on the territory of the Numidia and Mainville parishes, 1827-46, with his residence at Nescopeck before 1831, and after that time at Conyngham, Luzerne County. At least some of his former congregations were retained on his removal to Conyngham, where he died about 1846-7.

BRAUNWARTH, W., having come to us from the Ohio Synod, was pastor of Zion congregation, Jersey Shore, Pa., 1878-9, while he was pastor of the German Immanuel's church, Williamsport, Pa., from which congregation he led away some members and organized a new congregation in the same city.

• BREINIG, ALFRED LEWIS, pastor of the Trevorton parish, 1887-93, son of Edwin L. and Catharine Breinig, was born at Egypt, Lehigh County, Pa., April 25, 1860. He was a student at the Keystone State Normal School, Kutztown, Pa., 1878-80, graduated from Muhlenberg College, Allentown, Pa., 1884, and from the Theological Seminary at Philadelphia, 1887, being ordained by the Ministerium the same year. Since 1893 he serves the Bowmanstown parish, Carbon County, Pa. He was married in 1888 to Annie S. Keefer.

BREININGER, H., was pastor in Snyder County, Pa., his name appearing at Christ (Hassinger's) as well as at St. Peter's congregations, Freeburg, about 1866-74.

. BRUNING, HERMAN HENRY, pastor of the First church, Selinsgrove, Pa., 1872-4, son of Herman Henry Bruning and Margaret Sophia, nee Daunettel, was born at Baltimore, Md., May 17, 1835. He graduated from the Baltimore City College, 1851; engaged in teaching German, French, Spanish and Greek, preparing students for the Junior class at various colleges, 1851-65; eighteen months were spent as book-keeper on a large slave farm; founded and conducted Conestogo Collegiate Institute for Young Ladies in Lancaster, Pa., 1865-70; studied theology privately and was ordained to the ministry at Frederick, Md., October, 1860; served missions in Baltimore and supplied vacant congregations till 1865; Strasburg, 1866-71, and Millersville, both in Lancaster County, Pa., 1868-72; First English church (now Luther Memorial), Erie, Pa., 1874-80; St. Paul's, White Haven, Pa., since 1881. He was Secretary of the Fifth (now Danville) Conference, 1874-5; Trustee of Thiel College, Greenville, Pa., and President of the Northern Conference of the Pittsburg Synod, both between 1877-80; Secretary of the old Second Conference of the Ministerium and first President of the Wilkes-Barre Conference, 1894-5. He married Frances, daughter of Jacob Gable, of Lancaster, Pa., September 23, 1873.

BOCKSTAHLER was pastor at Jersey Shore, Pa., 1867-9, after which he went to New York State.

BOYER, SIMON R., was pastor of the Turbotville parish, 1846-59, when he removed to Lancaster County, Pa., serving the congregations at Leacock, Bergstrass, Muddy Creek, Centre. Voganville and Reamstown, where, through his efforts, a parsonage was procured at Hinkletown. In 1860 he resigned Leacock, serving the remainder of the congregations till 1868, when he assumed charge of the Lyons parish, Berks County, which he served till suspended for misbehavior, 1873. He was restored 1874, and died in Philadelphia about 1878-9.

CLYMER, HENRY TREICHLER, pastor Trevorton parish, 1879-82, son of Henry S. Clymer and Lavina, nee Treichler, was born in Milford Township, Bucks County, Pa., April 6, 1853. He attended the Quakertown Academy, 1870-1, taught school several terms, and graduated from Muhlenberg College, Allentown, Pa., 1876, sharing second honor with Charles F. Camp. He graduated from the Theological Seminary at Philadelphia, 1879, and the same year was ordained by the Ministerium. At the conclusion of his pastorate at Trevorton he spent a year regaining his lost health, after which he was pastor at Sand Cut, Wayne County, Pa., 1883-5; Seven Valley parish, York County, Pa., 1885-90; Frackville, Pa., since 1890. November 11, 1886, he married Kate Idella Springer, of Phoenixville, Pa.

CORNMAN, WILLIAM O., son of Jonathan and Anna M. (Embich) Cornman, was born February 1, 1841, at Carlisle, Pa. He graduated from Dickinson College, Carlisle, Pa., 1862, and the following August enlisted in the army, serving in Company A, 130th Pennsylvania Volunteers, was wounded at Fredericksburg, Va., and honorably discharged May 21, 1863. He studied theology in the Seminary at Gettysburg, Pa., 1863, and later in the Seminary at Philadelphia, from which he graduated in 1866, being ordained the same year by the Ministerium. His parishes were: Trinity, Danville, Pa., 1867-8; Lunenberg, Nova Scotia, 1868-9; Grace church, Phillipsburg, N. J., 1872-3. While being assistant pastor of Christ church, Easton, Pa., laboring particularly among the colored people, he also engaged in teaching in Trach's Academy. Principal of the Eclectic Academy, Phillipsburg, N. J., 1879-81. He now lives in retirement in Reading, Pa., where he married Mary A. Monyer, June 20, 1867.

DARMSTETTER, JACOB, pastor First Lutheran church, Lock Haven, Pa., 1885-93, son of the Rev. J. A. and Mary A. Darmstetter, was born at Lancaster, Pa., March 27, 1863. He graduated from Concordia College, Springfield, Ill., 1882, and from the Theological Seminary at Philadelphia, 1885. Since 1893 he is the pastor of Paradise Lutheran church, York County, Pa., since 1896, also the assistant to his father as pastor of St. Paul's, Columbia, Pa., and of Concordia, near Columbia, and since 1897 also pastor of Salem, Rohrerstown, Pa. He married Mary E. Fabel, of Lock Haven, Pa., March 4, 1886.

DIETSCH, L., (also written Ditsch and Dietsche), for three months traveling missionary in the vicinity of Pine

Valley and Klingerstown, Schuylkill County, Pa., with residence at the Block House, Tioga County, 1833-5, came to this country from Germany, an ordained minister, 1832, but was not received into the Ministerium till 1834. He moved to New Hanover, Montgomery County, Pa., in the year 1835-6, where he seems to have had no congregations, and in 1842 resumed work in Tioga County, serving Peace, Salem and Zion congregations, apparently the Block House charge, formerly served by the Rev. Peixoto. He died in the year 1843, at the age of 46 years.   J. W. EARLY.

DIMM, JONATHAN ROSE, D.D., pastor German Danville parish, 1862-4, was born in Lycoming County, Pa., August 28, 1830. He graduated from Pennsylvania College, Gettysburg, Pa., 1857; studied theology privately; was licensed, 1859; pastor at Bloomsburg, Pa., 1859-67; Barren Hill, Pa., 1867-71; Corresponding Secretary Board of Publication, 1871-2; pastor Messiah church, Philadelphia, 1872-4; Principal Lutherville Female Seminary, 1874-80; Principal Pickering Institute, Kimberton, Pa., and now the President of Susquehanna University, Selinsgrove, Pa. Married Mary C. Hill, Hughesville, Pa., May 31, 1859.

DRUCKENMILLER, GEORGE D., son of Enos and Elizabeth (Desh) Druckenmiller, was born at Hereford, Berks County, Pa., February 26, 1864. He graduated from Muhlenberg College in 1894, having received his preparatory training in the Academic Department of the same institution, studied theology in the Theological Seminary at Philadelphia, graduating in 1897, and being ordained the same year by the Ministerium of Pennsylvania. He at once assumed charge of the Freeburg parish, which he serves to the present. He married Ella J. Lerch, of Allentown, Pa., September 8, 1897.

DRUMHELLER, CLAYTON KULP, pastor at Pillow, Pa., 1883-4; Danville English parish, 1887-90, son of George M. and Elizabeth (Kulp) Drumheller, was born at East Coventry, Chester County, Pa., May 8, 1855. He attended the Kallenian Academy, Boyertown, Pa., 1870-77, graduated from the Theological Seminary at Philadelphia, 1880, and was ordained the same year by the Ministerium. Pastor at Hamburg, Pa., 1880-3; Tamaqua, Pa., English, 1884-7; Ringtown, Pa., 1890-93; Mulberry and Fair Haven, Ind., 1893-6; Roseville, O., 1896. In 1896 he received the degree of M.D. from the Illinois University, and in 1897 that of Ph.D. from the same institution. He now holds the position of Medical Examiner of the Medical Congress, Chicago, Ill. June 1, 1882, he married Etta A. Wagner, of Hamburg, Pa.

DRY, CHARLES FUNK, pastor of the Mainville parish since 1890, son of John K. and Hannah (Funk) Dry, was born in Rockland Township, Berks County, Pa., June 2, 1851. He graduated in the Elementary Course at the Keystone State Normal School, Kutztown, Pa., 1874, after which he devoted himself to teaching for a period of eleven years, ten in his native county. He held the position of Superintendent of the Model School in the Keystone State Normal, 1884-90. He took the regular course in theology in the Seminary at Philadelphia, graduating in 1890. November 14, 1874, he married Mary Ann Mast.

EARLY, JOHN WILLIAM, pastor at Selinsgrove, Pa., 1868-70; Pillow, Pa., 1870-5; Danville, Pa., German, 1875-83; Trevorton, Pa., 1883-7; Jersey Shore, Pa., 1889-93, is a son of William and Leah (Dutweiler) Early, and was born near Palmyra, Lebanon County, Pa., September 3, 1835. He entered the Preparatory Department of Pennsylvania College, Gettysburg, Pa., 1852, graduated from the College, 1857, and, after spending a year in regaining lost health, he entered the Theological Seminary at the same place, 1858, and was ordained by the Ministerium of Pennsylvania, 1860. His pastorates, besides those on the territory of the Danville Conference, were at Leacock, 1860-6; Elizabethtown, 1866-8; Millersville, 1887-9, all in Lancaster County, Pa. From Jersey Shore he removed, in 1893, to Reading, Pa., where he still resides, active, though not serving any parish. He married Jane M., daughter of the Rev. L. G. Eggers, of Stouchsburg, Pa., January 8, 1861. He was Secretary of the Lancaster Conference, 1861-8, and of the Fifth (now Danville) Conference of the Ministerium of Pennsylvania, 1869-74. Of the latter he was the President, 1874-7 and 1880-3, and of the Ministerium itself he was the English Secretary, 1886-8. He also filled the offices of Member of the Board of Trustees of Muhlenberg College, Allentown, Pa., 1877-86; Director of the Theological Seminary, Philadelphia, 1886-9; Delegate to General Council, 1886, '88. He is a regular contributor to "The Lutheran" since its establishment, as well as to the other periodicals of our branch of the Lutheran Church. He published a Map and Chart of the Fifth (now Danville) Conference of the Ministerium of Pennsylvania, 1894, and is a contributor to the new series of Sunday School Literature of the General Council.

EBERTS, EDWIN H., since 1892 pastor of the Turbotville parish, son of Charles and Hetty Eberts, was born in Monroe Township, Northampton County, Pa., October 5, 1861. He was a student of Muhlenberg College, Allentown, Pa., relinquishing his studies at the end of the

Sophomore year. He held the office of Justice of the Peace, 1888-91, during which time he studied theology under the direction of the Rev. Prof. William Wackernagel, D.D., Allentown, Pa., which studies he finished in the Theological Seminary at Philadelphia, being ordained by the Ministerium in 1892. He married Eva D. Appel, Bingen, Pa.

EGGERS, LEWIS GUSTAVUS, son of Henry Eggers and wife Charlotte, nee Lambrecht, was born at Luten, Hanover, Germany, February 14, 1805. He attended the parochial school until between 13 and 14 years of age, when he was confirmed. He was then apprenticed to a bookbinder, but before his apprenticeship was completed, his parents emigrated to America, in the Spring of 1822. His mother died soon after their arrival at New York and lies buried there. For a time he worked at his trade at Hagerstown, Md. Subsequently he carried on the trade in his own name. Seeing that there was a great want of ministers in our Church, he determined to devote his life to the preaching of the Gospel. In 1829 he entered the Gymnasium at Gettysburg. At the end of two years he entered the Seminary and spent three years there. June 19, 1835, he was licensed by the "German Ev. Luth. Ministerium of Penna. and Adjacent States" to serve the Lutheran congregations in the Nittany and Sugar Valleys, Centre County, Pa., Rev. J. P. Hecht, President, and Rev. B. Keller, Secretary. As he could more conveniently attend the meetings of the West Pennsylvania Synod, he had his license renewed by the officers of that body, President, J. G. Schmucker and Secretary, Rev. G. A. Reichart, until first Sunday in October, 1836. December 4 of the same year he was ordained by a special Conference of that body, Rev. W. Yeager, President, and G. A. Reichert, Secretary, at Water

Street, Huntingdon County. The writer has the documents in his possession, the former German, and the latter English. He continued to serve this field for twelve years. He had previously received a call to Mifflinville, Columbia County, but could not see his way clear to accept. He preached at Loganton, Brumchord's, and possibly at Tylersville, in Sugar Valley; at Salona, Snydertown, Zion, and Bellefonte in Nittany Valley, at the "Loop" Church, and, if we mistake not, at Balsburg in Penn's Valley,—a territory more than thirty miles in length and from ten to twenty in width. The church at Bellefonte was organized by him, and a lot purchased from Mr. McConnel, for the erection of a Union church.

Frequently he left home between 4 and 5 a. m., riding eighteen to twenty miles before reaching his appointment at the "Loop," eating his breakfast, which he carried in the saddle-bag, as he rode along, reaching home between 9 and 10 p. m., having spent the entire day, except during the hours of service, in the saddle. He also preached regularly in a number of school houses.

In the Fall of 1846 he received a call to the newly organized Palmyra parish, which he accepted. In April, 1847, he removed thither. While there he served the Palmyra, Campbellstown, Bindnagel's, and Shell's churches, which composed the charge. He also organized the congregation at Union Deposit and supplied Sandy Hollow. During his pastorate the parsonage at Palmyra was also built.

In the Fall of 1851, the Stouchsburg charge, lately served by Rev. D. Ulrich, consisting of Christ or Tulpehocken and Rehrersburg in Berks County, and Newmanstown and Muehlbach (Millcreek) in Lebanon County, extended him a call, which he accepted. He also served Myerstown during the greater part of his stay here. Under him the present church was erected. He also served Womelsdorf for several years, and the Zion's or Reed's church for a year or two.

Having now spent sixteen years in this laborious field, in April, 1867, he retired from the active ministry and removed to his old home in Centre County to enjoy much needed rest, although the Rehrersburg congregation urged him to remain and serve that congregation alone. He had resided here but a short time when his beloved wife Lydia, nee Schaeffer, whom he had married February 6, 1838, died suddenly, October 16, 1868, being ill but four days.

Being thus left alone, and his residence here being made very unpleasant by the pernicious activity of some so-called New Lutherans, apparently endorsed and encouraged by the pastor in charge, he determined to resume the active duties of the ministry. Having received and accepted a call to the Trevorton charge, he entered upon his duties in the Spring of 1869. He took up his residence about three miles east of Sunbury and served the three congregations,—Emanuel's at Lantz, now transferred to Wolf's Cross Road, Elias, at Hallan Run, and Emanuel's at Trevorton. He served these people faithfully for two years and was beloved by them. In the Spring of 1871 he received an urgent call to return to his former field at Palmyra, and accepted it. He continued to serve this field nearly four years, when he retired permanently from active service as a regular pastor, still preaching occasionally. He supplied Walmer's, a part of the Lickdale charge, for a time. In 1872 he contracted a second marriage with Mrs. Elizabeth B. Kettering, nee Harper.

During the month of October, 1882, he set out to visit his former people of the Trevorton charge. But owing to delay of trains at Harrisburg, he was compelled to turn back. It worried him greatly. A few weeks afterward, he made the trip, and although afflicted with serious heart troubles, he preached in two of the churches,— Lantz's and Hallan Run. On Monday morning Miss S. Kaufman, confirmed by him during his pastorate, conveyed him to a point about 300 to 400 yards from Selinsgrove Junction. The exertion of the walk, coupled with the labors of the previous day, and the incident excitement proved too much. Having purchased a ticket, he sat down and expired instantly, closing a long career of activity and useful labors. His remains repose in the cemetery at Palmyra, with many of those to whom he administered the consolations of the Gospel.

J. W. EARLY.

EGGERS, H., pastor of the congregations at Jersey Shore and Cogan Station, Pa., 1874-8, had for a time been professor in Hagerstown Female Seminary, and was received into the Ministerium in 1872. He was pastor of the German Church, Carlisle, Pa., 1872-4, and of the German Church at Phillipsburg, N. J., from 1878 till his death in the Winter of 1879-80.

EISTER, G., was recommended to Synod by the Rev. J. N. Hemping for licensure, 1822, which was, however, not granted for want of efficiency in literary attainments, till 1824, after which he served congregations at Deep Creek, Roaring Creek and Bolich's, adding two other congregations. In 1827 he is found at Conyngham, Pa., and in 1828 his request for a dismissal from the Ministerium was granted, and trace of him is lost.

J. W. EARLY.

ENGEL, JOHN FREDERICK, was licensed in 1810, and was pastor from that date to 1818, of St. James' congregation, Mahoning, Pa., now a part of the Danville German parish, together with five other congregations, with his residence at Bloomsburg. Of the Turbotville parish he was also pastor, 1815-17. In 1811 the Ministerium, by resolution, expressed doubt as to the propriety of his renewal of license, still, on June 12, 1816, he was ordained a Deacon (an inferior order of ministers), and in 1819-20 he lived at Hamburg, Pa., pastor of seven congregations, apparently influential and honored, having under his instruction the catechete Gottlieb Jaeger. He died at New Holland, Pa., where he had been pastor, April to August, 1823.

• ENTERLINE, JOHN MICHAEL, was born in Bavaria, Germany, 1726. He was educated in the University at Leipzig. He married, November 1, 1760; came to America, 1768; was pastor at Indianfield, etc., 1768-70; we find him at Hummelstown, 1771, where he remained several years; he took up two hundred and fifty acres of land in Lykens Valley, October 6, 1773, but was driven back by the Indians. He served St. John's, Lykens Valley, 1773-93, and most probably organized the congregation. He also served Hassinger's (Christ), 1785-90; Botschaft's about as long; Rau's (Salem), as an occasional supply; Himmel's (Schwaben Creek), 1773-87. It is altogether probable that he also served Werth's, Fetterhoff's, Dreisbach's, etc., as he was the only Lutheran pastor in that section, and these were nearly all organized about that time. Some claim that he came as an ordained minister, but Muhlenberg calls him a catechist, and the Synod always records him among candidates. He died March 6, 1800, and is buried at St. John's church in Lykens Valley.   J. W. EARLY.

ERLE, CARL LUDWIG, was born March 10, 1805, at

Muenden, Hanover, Germany. On Easter, 1819, he was confirmed. He arrived at New York, May 24, 1824. After spending some time in teaching, he was licensed by the Evangelical Lutheran Ministerium of Pennsylvania, June 17, 1840, at Sunbury, and ordained, May 21, 1845, at Reading. September 8, 1840, he was joined in matrimony to Miss Esther Huntzinger. They had nine children, eight sons and one daughter. He died August 10, 1891, survived by four of the sons, the daughter, and their mother.

It was while engaged as a school teacher in the charge of Rev. Binninger, then located at Conyngham, that his attention was directed to the ministry by his pastor. Under his direction, he seems to have preached about a year before he applied for a license. That portion of Sullivan County, then Lycoming, in which he commenced his labors, and where he spent his entire ministry, nearly thirty-four years in active service and nineteen in retirement, was an almost trackless wilderness, here and there a clearing or a few cultivated fields, when he entered upon his work.

Occasional services had been held at intervals for probably fifteen to twenty years prior to his arrival. Rev. Beilharz had traversed the field and ministered to our scattered members as a travelling missionary in 1826. Rev. Dietsch had labored in Cherry, or the Loyalsock, from 1833-1835, and the Synod had made an appropriation from its funds towards the completion of the church. Even prior to this, Revs. Kessler, of Bloomsburg, and Miller, apparently C. P., of Milton, had visited the field, and some one, probably Rev. Binninger, had confirmed a class of twelve catechumens in 1836.

Although licensed in the Summer of 1840, Rev. Erle evidently came among those people and preached a year earlier, May, 1839. As soon as he was licensed, steps were taken to have the old Friedens (Peace) church restored. The first service was held by Rev. Erle, May 26, 1839, in Hollacher's school house, about one mile south of the old Zion's Church. The following Sunday he preached at Bahr's school house, one mile south of Dushore. Two years later he commenced preaching at Heverly's settlement, now Overton, about eight miles northwest of Dushore. This afterwards passed into the hands of the Reformed. November, 1845, he commenced preaching at a point on the North Mountain, Fairmount, and about the same time, or a short time prior, at Ballatemer, between Lopez and the present Bella Sylva. When the German colony, known as "Deutsch Columbia," was founded, the place of worship was transferred to that point. St. Matthew's Church, at Bella Sylva, is still standing, but without a congregation. He continued to serve this part of the field—ten to fifteen miles southeast of Dushore—from fifteen to eighteen years. He organized St. John's, Wilmot Township, Bradford County, about 1844. It is about six miles northeast of Dushore, and between eight and nine miles from the original Peace Church. It was rebuilt, 1873. 1852-1853 he organized Zion's, about midway between Peace and St. John's on the State road from Dushore to Wyalusing. After laboring in this hard field in a territory larger than the whole of Lebanon County, about 34 years, travelling to many of his appointments, we think we could safely say to most of them, afoot, he retired from the active ministry. After spending the remaining eighteen years in retirement, in obscurity and in poverty, after a life of toil and of privation, being maintained in great part by a widowed sister, during his retirement, he calmly fell asleep on Monday, August 10, 1891, at the

ripe age of 86 years and three months. On Wednesday, the 12th, his remains were committed to the tomb, addresses being delivered by Revs. S. Wenrich and J. W. Early.
J. W. EARLY.

ERLENMEYER, CHARLES GUSTAVUS, or "Father Erlenmeyer" as he is still affectionately spoken of by a host of friends in the community in which he spent nearly the whole of his long and useful ministerial life, was born at Boensheim, Leonburg County, Kingdom of Wuertemberg, Germany, February 18, 1808. He was a son of Balthasar and Dorotha Sophia Erlenmeyer, baptized in early infancy and confirmed as a member of the Lutheran Church, at the age of fourteen, by the Rev. Geo. Roessler. He received his educational training at Stuttgart, where he remained four years, and at the University of Tuebingen, where he studied Theology. After nine years of special and patient study, he entered the holy ministry. He left his native country in 1832, and, after a stormy voyage, landed at Baltimore, October 9, 1832. During the following Summer (1833) he began his labors in the Liverpool, New Buffalo, Wild Cat and St. Michael's congregations, in Perry County, and at McAlisterville, in Juniata County. In the Fall of the same year he was licensed to preach by the West Pennsylvania Synod, at Mifflinburg, Pa., and ordained by the same Synod, in 1835, at Mechanicsburg. In 1836 he also became the pastor of the congregation at Fremont, in Snyder County. He became pastor of the Freeburg parish in 1857, which at that time embraced the larger part of the present Snyder County. He remained in connection with synods of the General Synod until 1869, when he was dismissed by the Central Pennsylvania Synod to unite with the Ministerium of Pennsylvania. He entered the latter in 1870, at the convention at Pottsville, with his entire parish. He was pastor of the Freeburg parish for thirty-four years, until the end of his life. He preached his last sermon on Sunday, February 20, 1876, on the text Luke 8: 4-15, "The Parable of the Sower." He died at Freeburg, March 6, 1876, at the age of 68 years and 16 days. "His death caused the profoundest sorrow in the community where he lived, and among the members of his congregations. He was a faithful pastor, a courteous gentleman, an earnest, sincere minister, a man of amiable disposition, and suavity of manners. His peaceable disposition was proverbial, and he seemed to realize to the fullest extent, 'Blessed are the peacemakers, for they shall be called the children of God.'" His funeral service was held at Freeburg and his body interred in the cemetery near the church. At least fifteen hundred people attended the service, Revs. J. G. Anspach, J. W. Early, E. L. Reed and P. Born, Lutheran clergymen, and Revs. W. A. Haas and L. G. Edmonds, of the Reformed Church, officiating. Funeral services were held, and discourses delivered, in all the churches connected with the Freeburg parish, subsequent to his burial, by the pastors on the Reformed side, in charge of the same. A beautiful monument of Italian marble was erected over his grave by the members of his congregations and his numerous friends.

"His was indeed a busy pastorate. His careful and neatly kept diary showed the following record of his ministry: Infant baptisms, 5273; adults, 185; confirmations, 2013; weddings, 1395; funeral sermons preached, 2228. The last record in his diary is February 22, recording a visit to a sick member of his congregation. He was assiduous in his visitations of the sick. At all hours, in all kinds of weather, he responded to the calls of his sacred office. His fervent prayers, the hymns he sang, and his selections from God's Word, were always appropriate for the sick room. He was passionately fond of church music, and he had a strong voice, which could be distinctly heard above all the rest, especially when he led the congregation in German hymns. He was a ripe scholar and a man of excellent literary taste, of refined sentiments and cultivated mind, carefully and classically educated, yet modest and unassuming. He manifested an interest in the cause of education, and he was president of the Freeburg Academy a number of years. The poor and needy found in him a devoted friend. Trouble and distress always enlisted his warmest sympathy and generous aid. His benefactions often brightened the homes of the poor and needy." He was married to Catharine Steel, of New Buffalo, Pa., who survives him, and resides at Freeburg.

ESPIG, CHRISTIAN, (also Espich and Espith), was licensed by the Ministerium of Pennsylvania, 1791, on his renunciation of the ordination received from Inspector Goetz in Germany, being placed under the supervision of the Revs. Weinland and Roeller; 1793 the license was renewed by Synod, and again in 1794, but for the congregations at Sunbury, Pa., Penn's Hill (Penny Hill probably), and Buffalo, Northumberland County; 1795 he was serving in addition, Aaronsburg, Brush Valley, Beaver Creek and Mahanoy. From this time on he no longer attended Synod. Subsequently he went to Fayette County, Pa., and ultimately to Ohio.

J. W. EARLY.

EYER, WILLIAM J. The parents of Rev Eyer came from Germany, and settled for a time in Lebanon County, Pa., where Rev. Eyer was born, January 4, 1803.

Some time after this, his parents moved to Snyder County, Pa., a short distance below Selins Grove, on a farm, where W. J. Eyer was raised, and became acquainted with farm life. But this was not to his taste, and he could not think of becoming a farmer. His inclinations were to become a minister, but how to procure the required education was a difficulty; for at that time colleges and theological seminaries in our own Church were but few in this country. But this did not prevent our young man from making an effort. He attended the best schools available, after which he put himself for further instruction in literature, and more especially in Theology, under the instruction of Rev. Dr. Frederick W. Geisenheiner, then pastor of congregations in East Vincent, Chester County, Pa. Here Mr. Eyer remained (not known how long) until Dr. Geisenheiner moved to New York City, whither Mr. Eyer accompanied him to further his studies, which came to a close, September, 1825, when he was received as a minister into the Evangelical Lutheran Ministerium of New York.

Whilst a student in New York City, our young pastor became acquainted with Miss Charlotte, daughter of F. C. Havemeyer, Sr., who established in company with his brother William, the first sugar refinery in New York, which is now conducted on a large scale by F. C. Havemeyer's grand children, at the head of which stands Mr. H. O. Havemeyer. This acquaintance with Miss Charlotte ended in marriage, which took place on May 7, 1829, after which they moved to Rhinebeck, Dutchess County, N. Y., where Rev. Eyer had four years before taken charge of St. Paul's Lutheran Church, in which he successfully labored for twelve years. In the Fall of 1837 he received and accepted a call from several congregations in and about Catawissa, Columbia County, Pa. At one time he served in this charge as many as six congregations, preaching in most of them in both languages, German and English. He established a flourishing German Church in Danville, Montour County, Pa. He also organized the second, or St. Matthew's English Church in Catawissa in 1845, which he served until 1862, and then resigned. The territory over which Rev. Eyer traveled and the number of congregations (6) he served, are now traversed and served by five pastors, and the German language is but little used in any of them save the Danville congregation. Rev. Eyer in his long pastorate of nearly fifty years, had but two charges,—first, Rhinebeck, for twelve years, and Catawissa thirty-seven years. This was the best evidence both of his ability and popularity as a Gospel minister. When St. John's congregation (Catawissa) erected, a few years since, their new church, they had the name of their old pastor, Rev. W. J. Eyer, inscribed on the large front window in his memory. So also did St. Matthew's (Catawissa) when that church was remodeled, place his name in the large front window. This shows that his memory is yet in the hearts of his many friends. As we are all probationers here below, so was our brother, whose end came in a sad and painful manner, through injuries inflicted by his horse in the stable. Just how is not known. It occurred on the 6th of February, 1874, and he died on the 9th of the same month, aged 71 years, 1 month and 4 days. The news of his sad death soon spread over the whole community, far and near, which brought a large concourse of his parishioners, as well as others, to look upon the face of their beloved pastor for the last time. His funeral took place on Thursday, the 12th of February, 1874, conducted by Revs. Horine and A. T. Geisenheiner. After service at the house, his body was taken to Bloomsburg, where a funeral sermon was delivered by Rev. A. T. Geisenheiner, after which his remains were buried in Bloomsburg cemetery. Well can we say of the departed, "The memory of the just is blessed," and "Blessed are the dead which die in the Lord from henceforth; yea, saith the Spirit, that they may rest from their labors: and their works do follow them." D. M. HENKEL.

· FAHS, JOSEPH FREDERICK, pastor of St. Mark's, Williamsport, Pa., 1857-62, son of Samuel and Catharine Fahs, was born at York, Pa., January 18, 1825. He studied theology under the Rev. Joseph A. Seiss, D.D., LL.D.; was ordained by the Maryland Synod, 1852; served pastorates at Hancock, Md., 1852-5; Newtown, Va., 1857; St. John's, Allentown, Pa., 1862-72; Akron, O., 1872-82; Canton, O., since 1882. He was professor of History in Muhlenberg College, Allentown, Pa., 1867-70. May 9, 1854, he married Emma, daughter of the Rev. Henry S. Miller.

· FELTY, J., hailed from the vicinity of Klingerstown, Pa., and was brought to the notice of the Ministerium for licensure as early as 1831, by the Rev. J. N. Hemping, which was at first refused, but after a number of years, was granted. He served congregations in Schuylkill County, Pa., and ended his days in the vicinity of Pine Grove, Pa.

· FOGLEMAN, DAVID LAUCKS, pastor of the German Danville parish, since April, 1888, son of Mahlon and Elizabeth (Laucks) Fogleman, was born at Womelsdorf, Pa., November 14, 1861. He studied in Palatinate College, Myerstown, Pa., and Ursinus College, Collegeville, Pa., from which latter institution he graduated, 1884. He studied theology in the Seminary at Philadelphia, graduating in 1887, and was ordained the same year.

Before assuming his present field of labor, he engaged in missionary work for a short period, in Minneapolis, Minn. He married Ella A. Keiser, of Womelsdorf, Pa., April 21, 1892.

Fox, WILLIAM BEITERMAN, pastor of what are now the Berwick and Mainville parishes, 1862-8, son of Jonas and Susanna (Beiterman) Fox, was born at Congo, Montgomery County, Pa., October 21, 1837. He pursued preparatory studies at Freeland Seminary (now Ursinus College), and Frederick Seminary, 1856-8, and graduated from the Theological Seminary, Gettysburg, Pa., 1862. Since his removal from the territory of the Danville Conference in 1868, he has been pastor of the Sumneytown parish, Montgomery County, Pa. He married Lizzie F. Mack, June 5, 1864.

FRIDRICI, M. CARL SOLOMON, appears as the pastor of the congregations of the Berwick parish about 1807, his signature having been found by the present pastor in an old record. Since all search for facts as to his life and work are fruitless, it is doubtful whether he was really a minister.

FUCHS, AUGUSTUS, pastor at Mifflinville, Columbia County, Pa., 1833-6, was born in Germany, May 6, 1803. He emigrated to America in 1831, intending to become a missionary among the American Indians. He went to acquire the English language in the institutions at Gettysburg, Pa., was licensed by the Ministerium in 1833, and ordained in 1836. He was called to Columbia County as the assistant to the Rev. Jeremiah Schindel, and during the year 1835-6 he removed to Bath, Northampton County, Pa., where he remained till his death, December 20, 1879.

GEIGER, WILLIAM HENRY, pastor of the Stone Valley parish since June, 1884, son of Joel P. and Hannah (Miller) Geiger, was born at Saegersville, Lehigh County, Pa., September 7, 1854. After preparatory training in various Academies, he entered the Sophomore class in the North Western University, Watertown, Wis., and in the Fall of 1876, the Practical Seminary, Springfield, Ill. A year later he entered the Theological Seminary at Philadelphia, graduating from the latter institution in 1880, and was ordained by the Ministerium in the same year. He was pastor of the Ringtown parish, Schuylkill County, Pa., 1880-4. He married Louisa L. C. Harter, September 3, 1876.

GERMAN, JONAS PETER, pastor of the Berwick parish, Columbia County, Pa., 1880-92, son of Daniel and Rebecca (Werly) German, was born at Germansville, Lehigh County, Pa., September 25, 1849. He attended the Keystone State Normal School, Kutztown, Pa., 1870, the Academic Department of Muhlenberg College, Allentown, Pa., 1871, and graduated from the College in 1875. He graduated from the Theological Seminary at Philadelphia in 1878, was ordained by the Ministerium the same year, and served the Ringtown parish from that time till 1880. Since 1892 he is pastor at Minersville, Pa. He married Ida L. Miller, of Pottsville, Pa.

GERMAN, WILLIAM, was born at Womelsdorf, Berks County, Pa., March 6, 1806, and spent the earlier years of his life at that place. He studied, for a time, under the Rev. William Baetis, and then entered the Theological Seminary at Gettysburg, in 1827. He was ordained, in 1830, by the Ministerium of Pennsylvania, at its meeting in Lancaster. His first parish was in Lycoming and Northumberland counties, in the vicinity of Muncy and

Turbotville, where he labored only a short time. He became the pastor of the Middleburg parish, October 10, 1830, serving all the churches formerly served by the Rev. J. G. Walter, except at Salem and Selinsgrove. He resigned at Fremont in 1836, but continued to serve the Freeburg and Grubb's congregations until the beginning of November, 1839, when he accepted a call to a parish near York, Pa. In 1848 he became pastor of congregations near Allentown, and resided at Emaus, where he died, January 28, 1851, at the age of 54 years, 9 months and 12 days. He was "an able and earnest preacher, and magnified his office by a truly Christian character and life. Whilst he was always kind and sympathizing, he feared not the face of man, and always had the courage of his honest convictions, and never feared nor failed to rebuke and reprove." He was married to a Miss Baum, of New Berlin, Pa., who was a sister of the wives of the Revs. John Kohler, D.D., and S. R. Boyer.

GREYMILLER, GEORGE, preached at Christ (Hassinger's) Church of the Beavertown parish, about 1850.

GROFF, JOHNSON R., pastor of Trinity, Danville, Pa., 1881-6, and of the German parish at the same place, 1883-8, is a son of Rudolph and Mary A. Groff, and was born at Lebanon, Pa., February 7, 1832. He graduated from Pennsylvania College, Gettysburg, Pa., 1860, and studied theology in the Seminary at the same place. He was licensed in 1861, and was pastor of Trinity, Mechanicsburg, Pa., 1861-2; St. John's, Mechanicsburg, Pa., 1862-72; First Church, Erie, Pa., 1872-4; St. John's, Easton, Pa., 1874-81; Mt. Pleasant, Westmoreland Co., Pa., 1888-90; St. Paul's, Doylestown, Pa., since 1890. He was president of what is now the Danville Conference, 1883-6. He married S. Gertrude Riegel of New York, January 18, 1865.

GROTHE, EDWARD, pastor of the First Lutheran Church, Lock Haven, Pa., 1862-70, was born, January 22, 1830, in Stadthagen, Principality Schaumburg-Lippe. He studied theology at the Missionary Institute, Selinsgrove, Pa., was licensed by the Central Pennsylvania Synod, 1862, and ordained by the same, 1863. Because of extreme views held by him, his congregation at Lock Haven became divided, the pastor with some followers erecting another church which was relinquished when he left, most of the members returning to the mother church. He is now a member of the Wisconsin Synod, stationed at Reeseville, Dodge County, Wis.

· GUENSCH, G. F. W., pastor at Germania, Potter County, Pa., 1868-9, and Jersey Shore, Pa., September 1869 to September, 1871, hailed from Williamsburg, New York, and was ordained by the Ministerium in 1863. At White Haven, Pa., he was pastor of the Carbon and Luzerne County Mission, serving five congregations, 1865-8; at Germania the congregation erected the church during his pastorate, and his supply of this congregation continued even while pastor at Jersey Shore, though 50 miles away. He was pastor at Minersville, Pa., 1872-92. In 1894 he was for a time suspended from the functions of the ministerial office.

GUENSEL, MATTHIAS, was pastor of the Lutheran Church at Selinsgrove, Pa., as well as at Kratzerville, prior to the year 1800. He is also known to have served Botschaft's of the Freeburg parish, and Christ (or Hassinger's) of the Beavertown parish. His name seems to be unknown in the minutes of Synod.

HAAL, PETER, (also spelled Hall, and believed to be the same as the J. K. Haal, of the history of the Berwick parish), was licensed in 1817, and accepted a call from six congregations of Columbia County, with residence at Catawissa, Pa. In 1820 he reports five congregations as pastor at Newville, most likely in Cumberland County. He was ordained a deacon by the Ministerium, June 21, 1821, and served eight congregations, which number was afterwards reduced to five. In 1826 his name disappears from the roll of Synod, which is a fair indication that he became one of the organizers of the West Pennsylvania Synod.

HASSKARL, WILLIAM R. C., son of Rudolph, Professor at the Rostock University, Mecklenburg, Germany, was born in Doveran, 1809. He graduated from the famous Gymnasium at Halle, after which he studied theology at the University of Muenchen, where he received the title of Ph.D. at the conclusion of his course. In 1832 he entered the University of Berlin and read law, receiving the degree of LL.D. He was ordained in 1851, emigrated to America in 1853 and was received into the Ministerium in 1857. He served congregations at Conyngham and vicinity, 1857-9; Wilmington, Del., 1859-60; parts of the present Line Mountain, Mahanoy, Pine Valley and Lykens Valley parishes, 1861-4; Christ church, Hazleton, Pa., 1864-72; Roxboro, Philadelphia, from 1872 till his death, March, 1875. In 1854 he was married to Elizabeth Lang. Two sons are in the Lutheran ministry, and one is the first lieutenant in the regular United States Navy.

HEIM, GEORGE, pastor at Selinsgrove and Kratzerville, 1809, serving the latter congregation for a period of possibly 20 years, is not to be confused with William, who was ordained in 1819 and served congregations in the vicinity of Lewistown, Pa. He was licensed in 1809; ordained a deacon in 1816; his name appears in the list of full pastors in 1824. His general location is given as Union County, 1809-12; Buffalo, 1812-20; Jungmanstown (Mifflinville), 1820-8; Northumberland after 1828; after the latter date he failed to attend the meetings of Synod and his name was dropped, 1834-5.

• HEMPING, JOHN NICHOLAS, pastor of the Lykens Valley parish, Dauphin County, Pa., at that time also including Stone Valley, Mahanoy and Line Mountain, 1812-50, with residence two miles southwest of Berrysburg, was born July 4, 1778, at Schoenberg, Grand Duchy Mecklenburg, Strelitz-Natzeburg. He received his classical training in the Gymnasium at Jetzeburg, afterwards studying pharmacy at Hamburg. The war-like movements of the times caused him to emigrate to America in 1802. After teaching for a time at Nazareth, Pa., he accepted a position as teacher in the high school then established by St. Michael's and Zion congregations, Philadelphia. Having studied theology under Revs. Dr. Helmuth and F. Smith, he was licensed at Carlisle, Pa., May 27, 1812, with 12 others, among them being J. C. Becker, Abraham Reck, J. P. Schindel, Sr., and John Herbst, and accepted the call to his immense parish as above mentioned, where he had been preaching, as is generally accepted, already the year before. June 12, 1816, at Philadelphia, he was ordained a deacon, with George Heim, W. Baetis, J. P. Schindel, Becker, Herbst and others, and June 1, 1820, he was voted a full pastor. In 1845 his field was divided, the Rev. J. G. C. A. Bergner succeeding him in what are now the Mahanoy and Line Mountain parishes, with a few other congregations. In 1850 he retired from the active ministry, on his farm near Halifax, Dauphin County, Pa., where he died, March 12, 1855, aged 76 years, 8 months and 8 days. Burial took place at St. Peter's (Fetterhoff's) church, the Rev. F. Walz officiating. He always manifested a deep interest in the promotion of Christ's kingdom, and was a thorough linguist, being master of six or seven languages. J. W. EARLY.

HENKEL, D. M., D.D. A mere sketch of the work and life of myself is hereby given, as a more extended work is in preparation for publication at some future time.

If permitted I will say, I come from a long line of Lutheran ministers, both in Germany and in this country. After graduating in the Theological Seminary at Columbus, Ohio, I took my first charge (1849) in the wilds of Northern Indiana, Goshen, Elkhart County. Here I did not accomplish much in consequence of fever and ague, which took such hold on me as to unfit me for all ministerial duties. In this condition, after a short stay of 18 months, with wife and child, we returned to New Market, Va., for repairs, which took in my case some three or four years to accomplish. In 1855, I received a unanimous call from the Stewartsville congregation in New Jersey, which I accepted. I was the first resident pastor of the congregation. Here I found an unfinished church with a small but intelligent and active membership. But in consequence of the limited material I had to work upon, I remained but four years, and in May, 1859, I moved to Danville, Montour County, Pa. Here I organized a congregation of 45 members under the name of Trinity Lutheran church. This was an offshoot of the First English Lutheran church of Danville, from which I received much opposition, yet it prospered. We had a large majority of the community with us, which greatly assisted us when we came to the building of our church. After this was completed our congregation grew rapidly, so much so that, today Trinity congregation is much larger than the First church. Here I remained until 1867, when urgent appeals came to me from a number of Lutheran families in and about Stroudsburg, Monroe County, Pa., to become their pastor by organizing them into a congregation, with which I complied. This organization consisted of twelve male members (but two now living, 1897) which took place in the Court House. This was our place of worship for two years until our church was completed. In the meantime I served two congregations in the country which had wandered off from the old Pennsylvania Synod, but returned as per agreement, and are still in the old Synod. But for the organization of a Lutheran church in Stroudsburg, it is very doubtful whether Gettysburg and Mt. Airy Seminaries ever would have received each $54,000 from any source in Stroudsburg. Thus it is seen that missions sometimes do pay.

And now through the earnest solicitations of Revs. Drs. C. F. and C. W. Schaeffer, I was induced to move to Richmond, Va., to take charge of a little broken-down mission. In the spring of 1871 I moved and commenced work, meeting the little congregation for worship in the third story of a city building, not at all suited to our work. We did not remain in this long, but rented a Universalist church, which gave us better accommodations and larger audiences. Soon the congregation began to grow both in interest and in accessions, so much so that I commenced taking subscriptions for the building of a chapel. In this I would have succeeded but for the prevalence of malaria in and about the city, which I did not escape, and which prevented me from going on with my work, and at last necessitated me, after 18 months' trial, to resign the charge. But before this I received two invitations from North Carolina, one from the congregation in Concord, the other from St. John's and Mt. Pleasant, all in Cabarrus County. I accepted the latter on account of the college being located in Mt. Pleasant. Here I found a half-finished church which we soon completed In this charge I remained until the spring of 1876, when I received and accepted a call to Nokomis, Illinois, without having seen the place or the congregation. This call and acceptance I never regretted, and in all probability would be there yet could I have kept my health. But with no prospect of recovery so long as I remained there, I concluded to leave. Fortunately for me, my wife owned a good home in Catawissa, Pa., into which we moved, July, 1882. Here I had nothing to do but try to regain my health, which in a measure I did in about two years' time, when I was called upon to supply vacant charges, one in Catawissa, and others elsewhere. My last regular charge was the English church of Catasauqua, Pa., for two years, from 1887 to 1889. Here I found a little band of but 34 members, with a heavy debt of $2,000 resting upon them. The little congregation felt very much discouraged, and ready to sell out and disband. To this I strenuously objected, because of the fine material which composed the congregation. We all went to work, and not only did the audience but the congregation grow, and within two years' time $1,500 of the debt was paid, and the membership increased to 75, and the wealth of the congregation doubled. The congregation long since is out of debt, and spent $1,000 or more in repairing and beautifying the church. Here I received but $400 salary, while now they pay, unaided, $1,000 salary. Here my work was not in vain. Nearly all my work in the Church has been missionary, never having had but one old congregation.

And now my work is done. Being in the 79th year of my age, I am now awaiting my last call.

Catawissa, Pa.   AUTOBIOGRAPHY.

HENNICKE, F. F., pastor at Lock Haven, 1880-5, was ordained in 1858 and came to Pennsylvania from the Michigan Synod in 1873, assuming charge of three congregations at Weisport, Carbon County, where he remained till 1876. He was pastor of St. John's, Tamaqua, Pa., 1876-80; Frostburg, Md., retaining connection with the Ministerium, 1885, and thence removed to Chambersburg. He is now at Hagerstown, Md.

J. W. EARLY.

HENRY, SAMUEL STRICKHOUSER, pastor at Berwick, Pa., 1869-73; Jersey Shore, Pa., 1882-5; Pine Creek parish, in Dauphin and Schuylkill Counties, Pa., 1885-9, is a son of George M. Henry and his wife, Lydia C., and was born at Shrewsbury, York County, Pa., March 12, 1838. He prepared for College in the Preparatory Department of Pennsylvania College, Gettysburg, Pa., and graduated from that College, 1865, also from the Theological Seminary at Philadelphia, 1868. In addition to the above parishes, he served at Hinkletown, Lancaster County, Pa., 1873-82, and his present parish is at Smallwood, Carroll County, Md. He was Secretary of the Fifth (now Danville) Conference, 1885-6. He married Maggie A. Ruhl, of Shrewsbury, Pa., December 13, 1866.

HERBST, JOHN, pastor in Snyder County, Pa., including the Freeburg and Salem parishes, Christ (Hassinger's), of the Beavertown parish, Selinsgrove, and Wert's church, Lykens Valley, Dauphin County, Pa., 1801-4, was licensed at York, 1796, to serve Shierman's Valley, Great Spring, Trendel's, Carlisle, etc. In June, 1801, he received permission to serve Christ, Rau's, Selinsgrove, Mohr's and Bauman's churches. For some reason Derstown and Dreisbach were excepted. He moved to Middleburgh, serving seven congregations. In 1805 we find him serving Fissel's (or Fistel's) and other congregations in York County. He was ordained at Germantown, 1805; removed to Manchester, possibly change of residence only, 1811; his name disappears from the minutes, 1821, and probably in 1824 he died.

J. W. EARLY.

HILLPOT, JOSEPH, pastor at Cogan Station, 1867-71, and of the Lykens Valley parish, 1881-9, was a son of Samuel S. T. and Eva (Trauger) Hillpot, born at Tinicum, Bucks County, Pa., December 27, 1835. He attended the Normal and Classical School at Quakertown, Pa., and graduated from Pennsylvania College, Gettysburg, Pa., 1865. After studying theology at the Philadelphia Seminary, he was ordained in 1867 by the Susquehanna Synod. He served parishes at Richland Centre, Pa., 1871-81; Lickdale, Pa., 1889-90; Girardville, Pa., 1890-1. In 1866 he was married to E. A. B. Wambold, of Philadelphia, and after her death to Sarah E. Dubbs, of Allentown, Pa. He died at Quakertown, Pa., October 30, 1896.

HINTZE, FREDERIC, appears to have been pastor at an early unknown date, at Botschaft's congregation of the Freeburg parish.

HINZE, E., is reported to have been pastor in Lykens Valley from 1795 to 1797, and is similarly mentioned in connection with the Freeburg parish. His identity is however unknown, and it is even suspected that he may have been no more than a school teacher.

HORINE, MAHLON CARLETON, D.D., pastor of Trinity, Danville, Pa., 1872-81, a son of John and Catharine Horine, was born near Myersville, Md., July 14, 1838. He received his classical and theological training in the institutions at Gettysburg, Pa., graduating from Pennsylvania College in 1861 with the first honor and the valedictory, and from the Seminary in 1864, being ordained the following year. He was pastor at Smithburg, Md., 1865-9; Dayton, O., 1869-70; Zanesville, O., 1870-3; St. James', Reading, Pa., since 1881. He was President of what is now the Danville Conference, 1877-80; President of the Reading Conference, 1894-7; Trustee of Muhlenberg College, 1888-96; Trustee of the Theological Seminary since 1891; Delegate to the General Council, 1887, '89, '91, '95. During his pastorate at Danville he served as superintendent of public schools of Montour County, and in 1892 he published "Practical Reflections on the Book of Ruth." He married Emma F Winebrenner, of Gettysburg, Pa., May 16, 1865.

HORNBERGER, JOHN FREDERICK, pastor in Columbia County, serving St. James' and St. Peter's, of the Danville German parish, 1858-60, and of the Trevorton parish, then also including St. John's and St. Paul's, of the Line Mountain parish, and Emanuel's, of Mahanoy, 1860-2; was born in Germany, August 29, 1812, and came to America in 1846. He engaged in teaching school and studied theology under the Rev. Jeremiah Schindel, was licensed, 1851, and ordained in 1853. He served three congregations in Monroe County, Pa., 1851-8, and in 1862 removed to Randolph County, Ill.

HORNE, ABRAHAM REASER, son of David L. and Mary, nee Reaser, was born in Springfield, Bucks County, Pa., March 24, 1834. Having followed farming and teaching, he prepared himself by attending private schools, for Pennsylvania College, Gettysburg, Pa., from which institution he graduated in 1858. He studied theology privately, was licensed by the East Pennsylvania Synod in 1859, and ordained in 1860. He was Principal of Bucks County Normal and Classical School, Quakertown, Pa., 1858-63; pastor of Paradise parish, Turbotville, Pa., 1863-65; pastor of St. Mark's congregation, Williamsport, Pa., 1865-72, and superintendent of the public schools of that city, 1867-72; Principal Keystone State Normal School, Kutztown, Pa., 1872-77; Principal Normal and Academic Department of Muhlenberg College, Allentown, Pa., 1877-82; President Texas University, 1882. In 1885 he succeeded the Rev. Father Joshua Jaeger in his parish, consisting of Friedensville, Schoenersville, Rittersville and Lehigh Church, all in Lehigh County, Pa., which position he holds to the present, residing at Allentown, Pa. In the summers of 1881-83 he engaged in institute work in Texas and Louisiana, and in 1887-88 did similar work in New Jersey. In 1860 he founded the "National Educator," of which paper he still continues the editor and publisher. Since 1883 he has been the Secretary of the Keystone Mutual Benefit Association, Allentown, Pa., served on the Allentown School Board, was President of the Second Conference of the Ministerium of Pennsylvania, 1892-3, and in 1881 received the degree of D.D. from Lebanon Valley College. Among his publications may be mentioned: "The Pennsylvania German," 1875; "Manual of Botany," 1875; "Pennsylvania German Manual," 1876 and 1898; "Memoirs of the Rev. Joshua Jaeger," 1886; "Horne's Health Notes," 1894. He married Jemima E. Yerkes, Bethlehem, Pa., in 1857.

Hursh, Stephen, a native of Mayberry Township, Montour County, Pa., was licensed on the high recommendation of his teachers, Dr. S. S. Schmucker and others, with C. W. Schaeffer and L. G. Eggers, 1835. He never had a parish and died early. J. W. Early,

ILGEN, L. A. W. The following is a translation of the German inscription on a tombstone, about 50 feet from the northwest corner of the Lutheran church at Aaronsburg, Centre County, Pa.: "Lewis Albert William Ilgen, former pastor of this Evangelical Lutheran congregation, born October 15, 1759, at Heebsingen, Margraviate Anspach, Germany. In the year 1800 he was called to the pastorate of this church and the congregations connected with it. This office he filled nearly 23 years. He died August 20, 1823, having attained the age of 63 years, 10 months and 5 days." At the meeting of Synod at McAlister (Hanover), June 9, 1800, a paper offering a salary of 140 pounds, from Penn's Valley and five other congregations, was presented. At the same meeting Mr. Ilgen, a teacher, applied for license and secured it. He proceeded to Centre County and took charge of the congregations there. Aaronsburg and Rebersburg are known. The others cannot be positively located now. He organized a congregation at Penn Hall, five miles west of Aaronsburg, in 1801, and that at the Loop, then known as Early's church, about the same time. He also served the congregation at Penn's Creek. As his address in 1802 is given as Northumberland County, it is altogether probable that his field extended eastward to the Susquehanna, including all of Buffalo Valley. He was ordained at Easton, 1804. This year he reported 893 communicants and 110 confirmed. In 1806 he was serving Aaronsburg, Brush Valley, Early's (Loop), Jungmanstown (Mifflinburg), Langstown (New Berlin), Dreisbach and Meeting House, seven congregations, and seems to have continued as pastor until his death. He did much pioneer work and seems to have been not only faithful, but very successful in his work.

J. W. EARLY.

PLATE X.

G. J. SCHAEFFER.

O. E. PFLUEGER.

D. L. FOGELMAN.

O. S. SCHEIRER.

W. E. RONEY.

W. WEICKSEL.

JASINSKY, FREDERICK WILLIAM, was refused admission to the Ministerium of Pennsylvania, 1789 and 1792, notwithstanding which he served the congregations at Freeburg, Snyder County, Pa., 1790-8; Salem (Rau's), 1790-6 or 8; and probably other congregations. Having spent some time at Jonestown, Lebanon County, Pa., he moved to Chambersburg, 1798 or 9, and was licensed by our Synod on his submitting to an examination and his renunciation of a previous irregular ordination, 1799; he went to Shepherdstown, Va., 1802, and to Frederick, Md., 1803; was ordained, 1804, and in 1807 was elected pastor of Zion and St. Peter's (Pikeland), Chester County, Pa., where he died in 1817, being buried at St. Peter's. J. W. EARLY.

JAEGER, NATHAN, was born in Bucks County, Pa., March 7, 1820. He attended the preparatory department of Pennsylvania College, Gettysburg, Pa., 1839-41, studied theology under the Rev. J. O. Herbst, and was licensed in 1845. He served parishes at Orwigsburg, Pa., Lykens Valley, Pa., including what is now the Stone Valley parish, 1852-3, New Hanover, Bethlehem, Pa., Upper Mount Bethel and Riegelsville, and died January 2, 1864

KEMPFER, D. O., pastor of congregations now connected with the Beavertown parish, for a short time, prior to 1867. He was not a member of the Ministerium, nor of our Conference.

KESSLER, JOHN PETER, one of our pioneer ministers in Columbia and Montour counties, and for some time the only Lutheran minister in that part of our territory. He served congregations at Danville, Catawissa, Mahoning and numerous others, now connected with the Berwick parish, 1820-30. He was licensed by the Ministerium at York, Pa., June 5, 1817, and ordained at Chambersburg,

Pa., in 1821. In 1819 he resided at Bloomsburg, Pa., and in 1826 he served eight congregations. Six parishes have since been formed on the territory for which he cared during his ministry of about twelve years.

KLINE, SAMUEL S., pastor of Beaver Valley, Conyngham and other congregations in Columbia and Luzerne counties, 1867-75, was licensed by the Ministerium at Lancaster, Pa., in 1830, and shortly afterwards removed to New York State and labored there more than thirty years. Late in the fifties he returned to this State and took charge of congregations in connection with the East Pennsylvania Synod, at Hamilton, 1858-60. In 1861 he took charge of six congregations in Berks and Lehigh counties. His next parish was in our territory, where he remained until 1875, when he assumed the duties of the Ringtown parish. Here he died suddenly in July, 1877.

• KLINGLER, JOHN W., son of J. L. Klingler, was born March 19, 1858, educated at Palatinate College, Myerstown, Pa., 1874-76; Muhlenberg College, 1876-80, and the Philadelphia Seminary, 1880-83; ordained by our Ministerium, May 22, 1883. He was pastor in Northampton county, 1883-87; Principal of Stouchsburg schools, 1887-90; Principal of schools in Delaware County, 1891, and Hamburg, 1891-92; pastor of St. Michael's, Cogan Station, 1892-94; and of the Dushore parish since 1894.

• KOHLER, JOHN, D.D., son of Andrew and Anna Kohler, was born in Juniata County, Pa., May 27, 1820, died suddenly at New Holland, Pa., April 11, 1898. He was educated in Pennsylvania College, Gettysburg, graduating in 1842, and in Gettysburg Theological Seminary, and was ordained in 1844. He was born on the territory of our Conference and his first parish was the Lutheran congregation at Williamsport, Pa., 1845-49. He was pastor at New Holland, 1850-64; Trappe, 1864-73; Stroudsburg, 1873-82; Principal of the Academic Department of Muhlenberg College, 1882-84; pastor at Mechanicsburg, 1884-85; Leacock, 1885-93; member of the Board of Trustees of College, 1869-76, and for many years a Director of the Philadelphia Seminary. He was President of the Lancaster Conference for a number of years. He was a busy and useful man to the day of his death.

KOPENHAVER, WILLIAM MILTON, was born at Elizabethville, Pa., March 20, 1866. He engaged in teaching school for six years, and prepared in Greensburg Seminary for Muhlenberg College, Allentown, Pa., from which he graduated in 1897. He is now a student of the Theological Seminary at Philadelphia, from which he expects to graduate in 1900.

KRAMER, J. P. F., one of the pioneer ministers on our territory, who cared for our scattered people amid many self-denials and under adverse circumstances. He was pastor of St. James' congregation (Mahoning), three miles east of Danville, besides many others, 1803-05; and St. James' (Howetter's), Upper Mahanoy Township, Mahanoy and Lykens Valley parishes, 1805-06.

KUNKLE, GEORGE G., son of John and Sarah Kunkle, was born September 7, 1847, educated at Wyoming Seminary, 1865; Millersville Normal School, 1866; Keystone State Normal School at Kutztown, 1867-69; Muhlenberg College, 1869-73, and the Philadelphia Seminary, 1875, finishing his theological course under private instruction; engaged in teaching, 1875-87; ordained by our Ministerium in June, 1887; pastor at Weatherly, 1887-

91; St. Luke's, Easton, 1891-92; St. Mark's, Williamsport, 1892-93; Berwick parish, 1894-96, and Trevorton parish since the fall of 1896.

, KUNTZ, WILLIAM H., pastor at Jersey Shore and Cogan Station, 1873-74. He is a son of Samuel and Sara Kuntz, was born at Treichler's, Pa., September 5, 1845, educated at Freeland Seminary, 1862; Allentown Collegiate Institute, 1864; Pennsylvania College, 1866; Muhlenberg College, 1867-70, and the Philadelphia Seminary, 1870-73; ordained by our Ministerium in 1873, and immediately afterwards became pastor of the Cogan Station parish. He was pastor at Schuylkill Haven, 1874-86; then took a course in medicine and is now located at New Castle, Del.

¦LAITZLE, WILLIAM G., pastor of the Catawissa parish, 1874-78, was a son of Christopher F. and Catharina Laitzle, and was born at Canstadt, Würtemberg, Germany, October 1, 1814. He came to America in 1816, was educated at Gettysburg, was ordained by the East Pennsylvania Synod in 1840, and in 1841 united with the Ministerium. He labored in Dauphin County, Pa., until December 1843; in Blair County, Pa., 1843-48; in Huntingdon County, 1848-50; as missionary of the American Home Missionary Society in Indiana, 1850-52; in Lebanon and Dauphin counties, 1852-54; Elizabethtown, 1854-65; Pottstown, 1866-74; Lehighton, 1877-82, and then retired, residing at Lebanon, where he died, July 13, 1894.

, LAMPE, F. C. H., pastor of the English and German congregations at Williamsport, May, 1863, to September, 1864. He was ordained by the Ministerium in 1860, was pastor at Pottsville, Pa., 1860-63; Reading, 1865-67, when he was dismissed to the Pittsburg Synod. He died at Williamsport, Pa., in 1884, at the age of 53 years.

LAZARUS, R., pastor of Sieber's congregation at Globe Mills, some time about the year 1866, and of congregations now connected with the Beavertown parish, 1867-68.

LENKER, MICHAEL B., son of John and Mary Lenker, was born near Pillow, Pa., May 22, 1835, died at Lykens, Pa., March 19, 1897. He was educated at Freeburg Academy and Capital University, Columbus, O., and was ordained in 1865. He labored for some time in Ohio, and in 1873 was called to the newly-organized St. John's congregation at Lykens, Pa., which he served until his death. The first church was built in 1874, but was destroyed by fire, probably of incendiary origin; and the second, a frame structure, was erected in 1877-79, the corner-stone of which was laid July 27, 1877, and the building consecrated, October 19, 1879.

LENTZ, ANDREW P., son of Augustus and Rebecca Lentz, was born near Paxton, Pa., February 25, 1869, educated in Muhlenberg College, 1890-95, and the Mt. Airy Seminary, 1895-98, ordained by our Ministerium in 1898.

LINDENSTRUTH, LOUIS, pastor of the Catawissa parish, 1878-81, is the son of Louis and Elizabeth Lindenstruth, was born in Philadelphia, June 18, 1853, educated in Philadelphia parochial schools, Seidensticker's Classical Academy, University of Pennsylvania, 1870-74, and the Philadelphia Seminary, 1874-77; ordained by our Ministerium, May 30, 1877. Since 1881 he has been pastor of St. John's congregation, Mauch Chunk, and for some time also of East Mauch Chunk; German Secretary of the Second Conference, 1882-87; German Secretary of the Ministerium, 1886-90, and President of the Wilkes-Barre Conference since the fall of 1895.

LINSZ, AUGUSTUS, pastor at Lock Haven, 1870-80, and from 1879-80 also serving the congregation at Jersey Shore, Pa., was received into the Ministerium from the Central Synod of Pennsylvania in 1879, and since 1880 has been pastor of Trinity German church at Tioga, Philadelphia.

*MEYER, HANS ERNST WILLIE ROBERT, pastor of Christ church, South Williamsport, Pa., since July, 1897, is a son of the Rev. George and Marie Meyer, and was born in Muender, Province of Hannover, Germany, Jan. 17, 1872. He received his preparatory training in the Gymnasium Adolfinum, Bueckeburg, and the Koengl. Kaiser Wilhelm Gymnasium, Hannover, Germany, from the latter of which he graduated in 1892; served in the German army, 1892-3; and took the full theological course in the Seminary at Mt. Airy, graduating and being ordained by the Pennsylvania Ministerium in 1896. He was pastor of Salem church, Philadelphia, 1896-7. April 21, 1898, he was married to Martha Rudiger of Philadelphia.

MILLER, C. P., pastor of the Turbotville parish, 1831-35, residing at Milton, Pa. His labors began about 1827, as a licentiate, when he served Belmont from about this time until 1830. After his resignation at Milton, he served the following parishes: Warwick, Lancaster County, Pa., 1836-37; Brickerville, Pa., 1838-42; Bucksville, Pa., 1843-66, including the congregations at Nockamixon, Durham, Springfield and Tinicum. In the latter year he resigned and resided at Kintnersville, Bucks County, Pa.; in 1868 he had removed to Upper Eddy, Bucks County; in 1871, to Holland, N. J., and died at Milford, N. J., January 17, 1880, at the age of 74 years, 4 months and 21 days.

PLATE XI.

H. G. SNABLE.

G. D. DRUCKENMILLER.

C. D. ZWEIER.

P. ALTPETER.

F. A. WEICKSEL.

H. E. C. WAHRMANN.

MILLER, HARRY PHILIP, son of Martin Luther and Esther Lydia Miller, was born in Selinsgrove, Pa., April 22, 1873. He is a member of the First Evangelical Lutheran church of Selinsgrove, Rev. S. E. Ochsenford. D.D., pastor. After completing a preparatory course in the public schools and graduating from Missionary Institute, now Susquehanna University, he was admitted to the Junior class of Muhlenberg College in the fall of 1893, and graduated from that institution June 20, 1895. He continued his studies at the Lutheran Theological Seminary, Mt. Airy, Pa., and graduated May 31, 1898. He was ordained by the Ministerium of Pennsylvania and accepted a call to the pastorate of the English Evangelical Lutheran Church of the Reformation of Brooklyn, N. Y., took charge of the work on June 26 and is at present laboring in that field.

MOELLER, HEINRICH, one of the pioneer laborers on our territory, serving numerous congregations in Lykens Valley, during his pastorate at Harrisburg, 1797-1801, was born at Hamburg, Germany, in 1749, and came to this country, landing at Philadelphia in 1763. He met Patriarch Muhlenberg, was taken into his family, and studied theology under his direction, and in due time was licensed by the Ministerium. He was pastor at Reading, Pa., 1775-77; served a number of congregations in New Jersey and was assistant teacher in Dr. Kunze's Academy in Philadelphia, 1778-84; was pastor at Albany and Athens, N. Y., 1784-90; at New Holland, Pa., 1790-95; Harrisburg and surrounding country, including Lykens Valley, 1795-1802; Albany, N. Y., 1802-08; Sharon and New Rhinebeck, N. Y., after 1808, where he labored until physical infirmities compelled him to relinquish the active duties of the ministry. The last six years of his life he spent in retirement, and died at Sharon, N. Y., September 16, 1829.

NEIMAN, JACOB H., pastor of the Catawissa parish, 1881-92. He is the son of George and Catharine Neiman, was born at Limerick, Pa., July 31, 1844, educated at Washington Hall, Trappe, 1866-68; Muhlenberg College, 1868-71, and Philadelphia Seminary, 1871-74, and ordained by our Ministerium, 1874. He was pastor of the Conyngham parish, 1874-81, and after his resignation at Catawissa, in 1892, he accepted a call to Royersford, where he still labors. When he became pastor of the Catawissa parish, he served three congregations, but succeeded in effecting divisions, so that when he left there were two parishes. He built St. Paul's Lutheran church at Numidia, the corner-stone of which was laid March 31, 1889, and the church consecrated, January 19, 1890. He succeeded in separating the Lutheran and Reformed interests at Catawissa, remodelled the old church, erected in 1852, and reconsecrated it in 1881. On June 13, 1891, the corner-stone of the new brick church was laid and the chapel consecrated January 1, 1892.

NEUMAN, E. J., pastor of Emmanuel (Lantz) church, four miles southeast of Sunbury, in 1851.

OCHSENFORD, SOLOMON ERB, D. D., pastor of the Selinsgrove parish since 1879, is a son of Jesse N. and Mary Anna, nee Erb, and was born in Douglass Township, Montgomery County, Pa., November 8, 1855. He prepared for college in Mount Pleasant Seminary, Boyertown, Pa., 1871-3, graduated from Muhlenberg College, Allentown, Pa., 1876, and from the Theological Seminary, Philadelphia, 1879, being ordained by the Ministerium of Pennsylvania the same year. He took a special course in Hebrew under Dr. W. R. Harper, 1886-7.

He was Secretary of the Fifth (now Danville) Conference of the Ministerium of Pennsylvania, 1883-4, as well as its President, 1889-98. Of the Ministerium itself he has been the English Secretary since 1895, and was also Secretary of its Board of Presidents, 1897-8, and Secretary of its Executive Board since 1897. He has also filled the offices of Trustee of Muhlenberg College, since 1889; Delegate to General Council, 1891, '93, '95, '97; President Alumni Association of Muhlenberg College, 1891-3; Secretary and Treasurer of Historical Academy of the Lutheran Church, since 1895; news editor of "The Lutheran" for a number of years prior to 1896. He married Sallie C. Boyer, of Selinsgrove, Pa., June 5, 1881. He has published the following books: "My First Book in the Sunday-school," Reading, 1883, fourth edition, 1898; "Lutheran Church in Selinsgrove," Selinsgrove, 1884; "Passion Story," Philadelphia, 1889; "Muhlenberg College Quarter Centennial Memorial Volume," Allentown, 1892; and he is one of the editors of the "Jubilee Memorial Volume of the Danville Conference of the Ministerium of Pennsylvania," 1898. He is the editor of the "Church Almanac" since 1883, an annual contributor to "Appleton's Cyclopedia" since 1884; a contributor to the new "Lutheran Cyclopedia," and to the present series of "Sunday-school Literature" of the General Council. He continues a frequent contributor to all the periodicals of our branch of the Lutheran Church, and has under way of preparation works on Church and Biblical History, Church Polity, Exegesis, Homiletics and Catechetics. In 1896 he received the degree of D.D. from his Alma Mater.

ORWIG, pastor of Beavertown parish in 1866, and of Sieber's congregation for some time between the years 1866 and 1874.

OEFFINGER, C., pastor of St. Paul's, Wilkes-Barre, and St. John's, Pittston, Pa., 1862-68, and St. Peter's, Hampton, 1865, came to our Ministerium in 1862, was Secretary of the Sixth Conference, 1865-67, and died at Wilkes-Barre, Pa., September 9, 1868, in the prime of life. He was known for his laborious zeal and ready self-sacrifice in his work.

•PFLUEGER, ASHER P., pastor of the Turbotville parish, 1876-91. He is a son of James L. and Elizabeth Pflueger, was born in East Allen Township, Northampton County, Pa., April 1, 1850, educated in Polytechnic College, Philadelphia, 1868, privately, under Prof. R. K. Buehrle, Allentown, 1868-69; Quakertown Academy, 1869; Muhlenberg College, 1869-73, and Philadelphia Seminary, 1873-76; ordained by our Ministerium June 14, 1876, and immediately afterwards became pastor of the Turbotville parish. He was pastor at West Newton, Pa., 1891-3, and is at present pastor of the Ringtown parish. He was Secretary of the Fifth (now Danville) Conference, 1880-83, and President of the same, 1886-90. He married Valeria Elizabeth Appel in 1877.

•PFLUEGER, OSCAR E., son of James L. and Elizabeth Pflueger, was born March 11, 1861, educated in Muhlenberg College, 1880-84, and Philadelphia Seminary, 1884-87; ordained by our Ministerium in 1887. He was pastor of the Beavertown parish, 1887-89; Lykens Valley parish, consisting of five congregations, 1889-94. In the latter year, he succeeded in dividing his large parish, St. John's congregation, near Berrysburg, becoming self-sustaining, whilst he retained the four other congregations, which now constitute the Lykens Valley parish. He has been the pastor of this parish since 1894. He was Secretary of the Fifth (now Danville) Conference, 1890-96, and is now its honored President, having been elected in the fall of 1897. He is the Chairman of the Conference Jubilee Committee, and the leading factor in the preparation of this Memorial Volume. He married Ella C., daughter of the Rev. O. Leopold, Allentown, Pa., June 14, 1887.

PLITT, J. FREDERICK, pastor at Catawissa, 1808. How long he served is not known. He was a brother of the Rev. John Plitt, and an uncle of the Rev. J. K. Plitt, for many years the Treasurer of Synod.

•RAKER, JOHN HENRY, son of Conrad Hoffman and Susan (Dornsife) Raker, was born at Raker, Pa., January 1, 1863. He graduated from Muhlenberg College, Allentown, Pa., 1889, and from the Theological Seminary at Philadelphia, 1892. He also graduated at the National School of Elocution and Oratory, Philadelphia. Since his ordination he has been pastor of St. John's, Pen Argyl, Pa., but has lately accepted a call to Trinity, Lebanon, Pa. After extensive travel in Italy and the Land of Luther, he has prepared and delivers a number of lectures which are well received by the public.

•REBER, OWEN, pastor of St. Michael's congregation at Cogan Station, Pa., since October, 1896, is the son of Jeremiah Reber, was born at Shoemakersville, Pa., October 3, 1858. He received his preparatory training in the Scientific Academy, Reading, Pa., and the Academic Department of Muhlenberg College, 1879-80. He graduated from the Philadelphia Seminary in 1888, and was ordained in the same year. He was pastor at Unionville, Ontario, Can., 1888-90; Annapolis, O., 1890-93; Middle Point, O., 1893-96. He was Vice Principal of the Scientific Academy, Reading, 1879-80; and has held offices in the Conferences to which he belonged. He is taking a post graduate course in the Chicago Seminary. He married Ida M. Jackson, of Reading, Pa., November 30, 1890.

REED, DAVID E., pastor of the congregations at Jersey Shore and Cogan Station, Pa., 1885-89. He died at the latter place, February 15, 1889, at the age of 52 years, and was buried in the graveyard of St. Michael's church. He was pastor at Georgetown and Vera Cruz some time before 1854; Line Mountain parish, 1868-70; Richfield, 1870-72, and again, 1881-85, and of Sieber's church, Globe Mills, Pa., at the same time, having his residence at Middleburg, Pa.

REED, EZRA L., pastor of the Selinsgrove parish, 1875-78, and of St. John's church, Catawissa, Pa., 1892-98. During his pastorate St. John's church was completed, and consecrated, Nov. 5, 1893. He is the son of John G. and Mary Reed, was born at Stouchsburg, Pa., November 7, 1842. He was educated in Pennsylvania College, Gettysburg, Pa., 1861-63; Franklin and Marshall, Lancaster, Pa., 1863-65; the Philadelphia Theological Seminary, 1865-68, and was ordained in the latter year by the Ministerium of Pennsylvania. Besides the parishes already indicated, he was pastor at North Wales, Pa., 1868-73, during which time a new church was erected; Trenton, N. J., 1873-75; Millersville, Pa., 1879-80; assistant pastor of Trinity church and pastor of Christ church, a mission of Trinity, 1881-92, when he became pastor at Catawissa. During his pastorate at Lancaster, Christ church was erected. Since November 28, 1897, he is pastor at West Newton, Pa. He married Annie Linley, of Norristown, Pa., August 20, 1868. Their only son is the Rev. Luther D. Reed, of Allegheny, Pa.

RENNINGER, JOSIAH S., at one time pastor of St. Peter's congregation, Beaver Valley, Pa., is a son of Peter and Anna Maria Renninger, was born in Montgomery County, March 7, 1838, was educated in Frederick Institute, Freeland Seminary, Mt. Pleasant and Dickinson Seminaries, Gettysburg Theological Seminary, and was licensed by the Allegheny Synod. He was ordained by our Ministerium in 1864, was pastor of the Ringtown parish, 1863-67; Schnecksville parish, 1867-88, since which time he has been engaged in doing mission work in Allentown. He married Mattie M. Kull, of New Alexandria, Pa., during his labors at Ringtown, Pa.

REPASS, J., pastor at Turbotville, 1817-26.

RICK, WILLIAM FREDERICK, pastor of St. Mark's congregation, Williamsport, Pa., since 1893, is a son of Frederick and Rosina Rick, was born in Utica, N. Y., May 27, 1868, educated at Utica Academy; Thiel College, Greenville, Pa., 1886-90; Philadelphia Theological Seminary, 1890-93, at the same time also taking a course in philosophy at the University of Pennsylvania, and in oratory in Neff's College, Philadelphia. He was ordained by the New York Ministerium in 1893, and at once assumed the duties of his parish. He married Edith Stanton Clarke, May 14, 1894. He is chaplain of the Twelfth Regiment, National Guards of Pennsylvania.* During his pastorate, the present handsome St. Mark's church has been erected, the corner-stone of which was laid in 1895, and the building consecrated October 14, 1896.

RICKERT, WILLIAM H., pastor of St. Mark's church, Williamsport, Pa., 1871-86, is the son of Joseph and Hannah Rickert, was born at Coopersburg, Pa., June 4, 1844, educated in Allentown Seminary, Pennsylvania College, 1865-67; Muhlenberg College, 1867-68; and the Philadelphia Seminary, 1868-71, and was ordained by our

---

* Rev. Rick died at his home at Williamsport, Pa., August 21, 1898, of fever contracted in the service.

Ministerium in 1871. He married Lizzie V. McKinstry, April 11, 1872. In 1886 he retired from the active duties of the ministry and now resides in Philadelphia.

• RITTER, JEREMIAH H., pastor of St. John's congregation, near Berrysburg, Pa., 1895-98, is a son of Martin K. and Rebecca Ritter, was born near Allentown, August 27, 1858; educated in South Bethlehem High School, 1874-75, Lehigh University, 1875-76; Muhlenberg College, 1879-83, and the Philadelphia Seminary, 1883-86, and was ordained by our Ministerium in the latter year. He has been pastor at Masontown, Pa., 1886-88; Venango, Pa., 1888-89; Shannondale, Pa., 1889-95. He resigned his last parish, May 1, 1898. August 1, 1898, he assumed charge of St. John's congregation, Bath, Pa. He married Emma M. Geissinger.

• RIZER, PETER, pastor of the Freeburg parish, 1853-55. He died at Bellview, Md., April 25, 1886, at the age of 74 years.

• RONEY, WILLIAM ERNEST, pastor of Trinity congregation, Danville, Pa., since March 1, 1890, is a son of Joseph and Rebecca Roney (Ronge), was born at South Easton, Pa., January 16, 1863; educated in Trach's Academy, Easton, graduating June 23, 1882; Lafayette College, Easton, 1882-86, and Philadelphia Seminary, 1886-89, and was ordained by our Ministerium in the latter year. He was organist of St. Paul's church, South Easton, Pa., 1881-86. He married Clara A. Richards, June 12, 1890.

• ROSENBERG, LUDWIG, pastor of St. Michael's congregation, Cogan Station, Pa., 1894-95, and at Jersey Shore, Pa., since 1895, was born in Germany, was educated in the universities in Vienna and Berlin, came to this country in 1891, and studied theology in the Philadelphia

Seminary, graduating in 1894, and was ordained by our Ministerium in the same year.

RUTHRAUFF, FREDERICK, pastor of St. John's German congregation, Danville, Pa., and St. James (Mahoning) for a short time in 1846, residing at Milton, Pa., where he labored for nearly six years, and pastor of the Freeburg parish, 1855-57, was a son of the Rev. John and Ann Maria Ruthrauff, was born at Greencastle, Pa., October 25, 1796, and died at Worthington, Pa., September 18, 1859. He spent two years at Washington College, 1818-20, and then studied theology under the direction of the Rev. Dr. J. G. Lochman, and was licensed by the Maryland and Virginia Synod in 1822, and served successively the parishes at Williamsport, Md., 1822-26; Hagerstown, Md., 1826-27; Lancaster County,—Maytown, Marietta, Elizabethtown and Mt. Joy.—1827-32; Gettysburg, Pa., 1832-36; Chester County, 1836-43; Manchester, Md., 1843-45; Milton, Pa., 1845-50; and then successively at Loysville, Centreville, Mifflinburg, Wrightsville, Littlestown and Worthington, Pa., where he died.

SALLMAN, CARL FR. FERD., came as an ordained minister from the Electorate Hesse and located at Conyngham, Luzerne County, Pa., being received into the Ministerium in 1845. In 1854 he removed to Wilkes-Barre, apparently one of his congregations, for he requested an assistant. He was Secretary of the Sixth (now Danville) Conference, 1846-55. He died November 20, 1855, aged about 50 years.

-SANDER, JOHN, son of Jacob Michael Sander and his wife, Sophia, nee Aderhold, was born at Perryville, Lycoming County, Pa., November 3, 1850. He engaged in teaching public school, 1869-73; attended Normal

Schools at Montoursville and Kutztown, Pa., 1871-73; graduated from Muhlenberg College, Allentown, Pa., 1877, and from the Theological Seminary at Philadelphia, 1880; pastor First Evangelical Lutheran church, Ridgeway, Pa., 1880-5; Professor of Latin and German in Gustavus Adolphus College, St. Peter, Minn., 1885 to date, excepting a few months in the summer of 1889, when he was connected with Doctor Martin Luther College, New Ulm, Minn.; also pastor of the First English Lutheran church of St. Peter since 1892, and President Nicollet County, Minn., Bible Society, 1896-8. Married Lydia Anna Whitman, Lycoming County, Pa., May 24, 1881.

SCHAEFFER, GEORGE J., pastor of the Richfield parish, 1887-97, is a son of James and Maria Schaeffer, was born at Emaus, Pa , January 22, 1858, educated in Keystone State Normal School, Kutztown, Pa., 1876-79; Muhlenberg College, 1879-84, and the Philadelphia Seminary, 1884-87, and in the latter year ordained by our Ministerium. Immediately after his ordination he became pastor of the Richfield parish. He organized St. Peter's congregation March 5, 1888, and built a frame church about four miles south of Richfield, which was consecrated October 19, 1890. He also organized St. John's congregation, about six miles west of Richfield, September 16, 1888. He married Ella Burns, of Richfield, Pa., November 1, 1888, the writer performing the ceremony. In 1897 he accepted a call to the Line Mountain parish, and now resides at Hepler, Pa.

‘SCHEFFER, NATHANIEL, pastor of the Berwick parish since 1897, is a son of William and Priscilla Scheffer, was born at Salem, Clarion County, Pa., March 15, 1856, was educated at Tablean Seminary, Emlenton, Pa., 1872-73; Thiel College, Greenville, Pa., 1875-80, and the Philadelphia Seminary, 1882-85, and in the latter year was ordained by the Pittsburg Synod. He has been pastor of the Sarversville parish, 1885-89; Prospect, 1889-95; St. John, Mercer County, 1895-96, and for some time supplied a mission at Newcastle, Pa. He taught public school 1877 and 1878, and in Salem Academy, 1880-82.

SCHEIRER, OSCAR S., pastor of the Beavertown parish, 1894-96, is a son of Adam and Caroline Scheirer, was born at Egypt, Pa., May 17, 1862, was educated in Keystone State Normal School, Kutztown, Pa., prior to 1884, Muhlenberg College, 1884-88, and the Philadelphia Seminary, 1888-91. He was ordained by our Ministerium May 26, 1891, and immediately afterwards became pastor of the Lickdale parish, which he served 1891-94; labored two years on our territory, and in the latter part of 1896 accepted a call to the Grimsville parish in Berks County. He married Annie L. Kuhns, of Chapman Station, Pa., May 28, 1891.

SCHINDEL, JEREMIAH was the oldest son and child of Rev. J. P. Schindel, Sr., and was born in the town of Lebanon, May 15, 1807. When five years old he moved with his parents to Sunbury, Northumberland County, Pa., where his father labored as one of the pioneer Lutheran ministers of Northern Central Pennsylvania. He was baptized in infancy by Rev. George Lochman, D.D., then pastor of Salem Lutheran church, Lebanon, Pa., and confirmed by his father in Sunbury. He attended the public schools of Sunbury and when seventeen years old went to Harrisburg to engage in the printing and newspaper business. He served, as usual, his apprenticeship and had for his associates the late Hon. Simon Cameron and the Hons. John and William Bigler, respectively the Governors of California and Pennsylvania.

During his employment in this capacity his mind was directed to the ministry. By this time also, the Rev. Dr. Lochman, the preceptor of his father and intimate friend of the family, was living in Harrisburg and was pastor of the Lutheran church there. He at once came under the guiding moulding hand of that gifted and learned divine and thus laid the foundation of his course for the ministry. He later abandoned his calling as printer and completed his studies for the ministry under his father, in Sunbury. He was licensed to preach by the Ministerium of Pennsylvania, June 10, 1830, at Lancaster, Rev. J. Miller, D.D., being President and Rev. J. P. Hecht. Secretary. The following year, 1831, on June 1st, he was ordained by the same Synod, at Harrisburg, Rev. C. R. Demme, D.D., being President, and his father, Rev. J. P. Schindel, Secretary. On May 13, 1828, he was married to Elizabeth A. Masser, of Sunbury, who departed this life in Allentown, Pa., on January 22, 1892, nearly 87 years old. The family born to them consisted of nine children, four sons and five daughters, two sons and three daughters yet living. One of his sons is in the Lutheran ministry now over thirty years, and a grandson bearing his name, Jeremiah, is attending the Lutheran Seminary at Mt. Airy, in Philadelphia, preparing for the same ministry.

The first charge which the subject of our sketch served consisted of congregations at Bloomsburg, Mifflinburg, Catawissa, Danville, Mahoning and Chilisquaque. To these were added Roaring Creek, Briar Creek, Berwick. Conyngham and other places. He lived with his family part of the time at Bloomsburg and then at Mifflinburg. Besides the regular congregations, he had numerous stations and school houses where he preached, mostly during the week. His pastoral duties required much exposure and compelled him often to drive in his sulky over mountains, at all hours of the night, with the wolves howling to the right and to the left of him. His life was constantly in danger. He served these congregations about seven years and, in 1837, went to Lehigh County, as the successor of Revs. Doering and Wartman. He lived at first at Siegersville and later on he moved into the parsonage of Jordan Lutheran Church, where the family resided until 1861, and then moved to Allentown, where both parents died. The congregations of which he took charge on coming to Lehigh County, were Jordan, Union, Heidelberg, Lowhill, Weisenberg, Trexlertown, and Lehigh. The Lehigh church he served but a few years. He also later served Ziegel, Fogelsville, Macungie, Tripoli, Long Swamp, Frieden's, near Slatington, Mickley's, Catasauqua, Morgenland, and Cedar Creek. Of the last four congregations he was the first pastor, and assisted in organizing them. Some of these congregations he served but a short time and had the assistance of the young men who prepared under him for the ministry. From 1859 to 1861 the charge was cut down to Jordan, Weisenberg, Morgenland and Cedar Creek. During this time he served as State Senator, at Harrisburg, representing Lehigh and Northampton counties. In 1861 he resigned this charge and moved to Allentown, and in the Fall of the same year he entered the U. S. Army, as chaplain of the 110th Regt. Pa. Vols., serving under Generals Banks and Shields. He saw a great many hardships during his service in the army. At the second battle of Bull Run, while caring for the wounded, his own son, Captain Jer. P. Schindel, whom he had not seen since leaving for the army, fell into his hands and required his nursing, having been wounded by a minnie ball. Eighteen miles, through mud and rain, they had to walk until they found a place to dress the wound and refresh the wearied bodies.

In the Summer of 1864, he returned home from the army, and in the latter part of the year, accepted a call to congregations in Lykens Valley. He preached his introductory sermon on New Year's day of 1865. The charge he then served consisted of St John's, Elizabethville, Huber's, Miller's, Fetterhoff's, Pillow and Stone Valley. On Ascension day, 1865, he preached for the first time at Gratz, and soon after the congregation united with those already mentioned. He also occasionally preached at a place called Vera Cruz. He lived in the old parsonage not far from St. John's Church. He labored in these congregations until March, 1870. About this time his aged mother died at Sunbury. Whilst attending her funeral he was taken ill with asthma and made the remark that he would be the next to follow his dear mother. His prophecy came true. After a few weeks of suffering, his oldest daughter, Mrs. Mary Eisenhart, went to Lykens Valley and tenderly brought him to his home in Allentown. He lingered there, suffering from asthma and dropsy, until July 2, 1870, when, on Saturday night, he suddenly and peacefully breathed his last. His last words, to his youngest daughter by his side, were, "It is all right, my child." His age was 63 years, 1 month and 17 days. His remains repose in the family plot in Union cemetery, of Allentown. His life-long friend, the late Dr. C. W. Schaeffer, wrote of him in "The Lutheran," "A man of commanding presence, such as is rarely seen, of singular urbanity, endowed with rich oratorical gifts, of sound faith, of pure heart and of upright life. The record of his life will show, that his talents were faithfully employed in the Master's service, and that, as the diligent pastor, indeed the bishop of extensive charges, he did not live in vain." J. D. SCHINDEL.

PLATE XII

W. F. RICK.

T. ZUBER.

HANS MEYER.

J. H. RAKER.

J. H. STETLER.

EUGENE STETLER.

SCHINDEL, JOHN PETER, JR., was the third son of Rev. J. P. Schindel, Sr. He was born at Lebanon, Lebanon County, Pa., July 25, 1810, and went to Northumberland County with his parents when two years old. He was baptized by Rev. George Lochman, D.D., in Lebanon, and confirmed by his father in Sunbury. The advantages for education were somewhat limited, yet Sunbury and Northumberland in those days, as small inland towns, had schools, scholars and private instructors, considerably in advance of many places in the State that were much larger. Of these schools the young man took advantage to the best of his ability. For a number of years he assisted his father, who gave him his special instruction and preparation for the ministry. He also devoted a number of years to teaching school. Quite a while he was thus occupied, in the vicinity of Gratztown, where at that time his brother, Solomon Schindel, was engaged in the mercantile business. During this time he was engaged in studying theology, and a number of times filled the pulpit for his father, who had over thirty miles to come to his appointments, and was sometimes prevented from coming by sickness and other causes.

It is claimed that he preached his first sermon at Little Mahanoy, on November 11, 1832, where he also preached regularly from 1834 to 1838. At the meeting of the Ministerium of Pennsylvania, in Philadelphia, 1838, he was licensed to preach, and at the next annual meeting of that Synod, in Allentown, Pa., May 22, 1839, he was regularly ordained. Previous to 1838, he had preached as a student, and under the supervision of his father. Before he was ordained he preached for a small congregation at Hollowing Run or Conrad's school house. In June, 1835, he commenced preaching at Kratzerville, and also collected a small congregation at Shamokin Dam, which he served in connection with Kratzerville. After his ordination in 1839, he accepted a call from three congregations, viz.: Black Oak Ridge, Beaver Dam and Hassinger, which then formed a charge with Kratzerville. Later on he took charge of the congregations at Laurelton, Union County, and at Centreville. When, in 1840, St. Peter's Church, at Globe Mills was built, he organized the congregation and preached for them until 1853. On June 21, 1856, he was recalled and served them a second time until 1866. He also organized and served congregations at Samuel's Church, in Decatur Township, Mifflin County, at Beavertown, and at Troxelville. In most of these congregations he labored with a great deal of self-denial, sacrifices and sincere devotion until December, 1868, when he retired from the ministry, having preached, in all, over thirty-six years. The summary of his ministerial labors, which he kept very accurately, shows the following: Sermons preached, 2650; lectures delivered, 1031; children baptized, 3229; funerals, 636; marriages, 1044; communion services, 162; catechumens confirmed, 2097; miles traveled in the charge, 49,116, and to Synod, 2688.

He was married, the first time, to Miss Sophia Young, of Sunbury, on September, 1833, by his brother, Rev. Jeremiah Schindel. This wife died in or near Middleburg, March 14, 1852. They had six children, of whom two are living at this time, viz., M. Louisa, the widow of J. P. Cronemiller, esq., of Mifflinburg, and Lizzie B., the widow of Thomas J. Smith, esq., of Middleburg. The late John Y. Schindel, M.D., who had a drug store at Middleburg, and was an assistant surgeon during the rebellion, in 47th Regt., Pa. Vols., was his son. On January 18, 1855, he was married to Miss Sallie Gobin, of Sunbury, with whom he had two children, a son and a daughter, who, with the widow, still live. On August 30, 1838, he moved with his family to near the town of Middleburg, where he resided for a long time. Later on, he moved with his family into the town and lived there until his death, which occurred on March 16, 1888, at the age of 77 years, 7 months and 22 days. His remains are buried where he lived so long and labored so faithfully. He was of a modest, unassuming disposition, had an exceedingly mechanical, inventive turn of mind, was very skillful with tools, and was frugal, careful and regular in his habits. His memory is sacred and dear to all those who knew him. J. D. SCHINDEL.

SCHINDEL, JOHN PETER, SR., was the son of John Peter Schindel, esq., and wife, Anna Maria Menges, and a grandson of the original ancestor of the Lebanon branch of the Schindel family. This ancestor was also named John Peter Schindel, and came to America from Euerlebach, Grafschaft Erbach, Odenwald, in Germany, in 1751, making his home at once at Lebanon. Both the ancestor and his son, John Peter, esq., are buried in the old grave yard of Salem Lutheran Church, of Lebanon.

Rev. J. P. Schindel, Sr., the subject of this sketch, was born in Lebanon, October 3, 1787. He was baptized and confirmed by Rev. George Lochman, D.D., pastor of Salem Lutheran Church, of Lebanon, who took a special interest in the young man, guided him in his education, and later on prepared him for the ministry. The family was always much attached to Rev. Lochman, who after he was pastor at Harrisburg, also, in part, prepared the oldest son of this family, the Rev. Jeremiah Schindel, for the ministry, and the late Judge Schindel, of Selinsgrove, was named Jacob George Lochman, in honor of Rev. Lochman. Rev. J. P. Schindel, Sr., was married to Susanna McCulloch, of Lebanon, who died, March 14, 1870, in Sunbury, over 82 years old. They had twelve children, eight sons and four daughters. Of the sons, three entered the ministry, viz., Jeremiah, the oldest, John Peter, the third, and M. Luther, the second youngest, who is now the only one of the family living, and is pastor of Pine Street Lutheran Church, at Danville, Pa. He entered the ministry in 1861, and had previously practiced law at Sunbury. There are also three of the grandsons now in the ministry of the Lutheran Church, viz., Rev. J. D. Schindel, of Allentown, Rev. E. H. Leisenring, of Chambersburg, Pa., and Rev. James C. Schindel, of Circleville, Ohio. Another grandson, Alter Y., the son of Rev. M. L. Schindel, of Danville, a talented, promising young man, was about entering the ministry, having completed his College Course at Gettysburg, and being a senior in the Seminary there, when his life was sadly ended by drowning in a small lake near the Seminary building. There is also a great grandson now preparing for the ministry in the Lutheran Church, viz., Jeremiah J. Schindel, the son of Rev. J. D. Schindel, of Allentown. The young man is attending Mt. Airy Theological Seminary, in Philadelphia.

After Rev. Lochman had prepared the subject of our sketch for the ministry, he was examined and licensed to preach, by the Ministerium of Pennsylvania, at Carlisle, May 24, 1812. On June 4, of the same year, he moved with his wife and four children to Sunbury, Northumberland County, Pa., where he took charge of a large and laborious field of labor and where he remained until his end in 1853. It would be a difficult task to describe definitely the field he served with Word and sacraments. It includes Northumberland, Lycoming, Dauphin, Schuylkill, Union and Snyder counties. In many places he had to preach during the week, not being able to supply them on the Lord's Day. He went south as far as Lykens Valley and beyond it, where he labored for some twenty-eight years. The present church building at Gratz was erected during his ministry, as also the one in the village of Berrysburg. North he went as far as Muncy, and preached in the old brick church between Muncy and Hughesville. He served the towns of Sunbury and Northumberland, as well as the whole territory from Sunbury to Shamokin and down to Trevorton. On the west side of the Susquehanna he preached at Selinsgrove, from 1819 to 1843, and at Salem, or Row's Church, until 1843. A number of other places, in this neighborhood, were supplied by him with the assistance of young men who were preparing for the ministry under his care. He prepared quite a number of such for the ministry, as was the custom in those days. Besides his own sons, Jeremiah and John Peter, may be mentioned Rev. Peter Kessler and Rev. Jacob W. Smith.

The subject of our sketch was a regular member of the Ministerium of Pennsylvania, from the time of his reception in 1812 until 1842. In that year, May 3, the Synod of East Pennsylvania was organized in the city of Lancaster. He united with that body then and served as its President during the years 1843, 1844 and 1845, so that he was really the first regular President of the same. His last report, in manuscript, dated September 24, 1846, is in the possession of his grandson and is an interesting document. Whilst he was a member of the Ministerium of Pennsylvania, over thirty years, he was strongly attached to the same, served on the examining committee, and also as secretary of Synod. He was honored by the mother synod, by being selected to serve on the committee of 1839, appointed at the meeting in Allentown, "to prepare a new edition of our Church Liturgy, in an improved and more complete form." The committee consisted of Drs. Demme, Baker, J. Miller, and Revs. J. P Hecht and J. P. Schindel, Sr. During the excitement in connection with the introduction of so-called "New Measures," he allowed himself to be captivated thereby and passed through many sad experiences in consequence thereof, especially so in Selinsgrove and in Lykens Valley. He however never lost his interest in and his fondness for catechising the young and receiving them regularly and properly into Church connection. From the sad experiences which he had made, he frequently cautioned his two sons, then in the ministry, to guard against such a course, and both sons wisely heeded the father's advice. He had talent in the line of hymnology and composed a number of hymns for his catechumens, which hymns, together with some others he had composed for funeral occasions, were collected and published, some years ago, by Rev. P. Anstadt, D.D., then of Selinsgrove.

Towards the close of his life, which shows a service in the Master's vineyard of over forty years, he confined himself to a few country congregations where he served until a year before his end. When he began to give out he declined rapidly, and the good Lord called him to his rest and reward, October 23, 1853, aged 66 years and 23 days. Rev. P. Born, D.D., became his successor at Sunbury and Northumberland, and a full dozen of others now labor on the field occupied by him. He had but this one field of labor,—here he began and here he ended. He rests from his labors, and his works do follow him. His remains are buried at Sunbury, and quietly sleep, awaiting the resurrection of the dead.

J. D. SCHINDEL.

• SCHMIDT, J. C., pastor of St. Peter's congregation, Mahanoy, Pa., since 1887. He is one of the older pastors who has been laboring in the territory of our Conference for thirty-five years. He served the congregations which now form Trevorton, Line Mountain and Mahanoy parishes, 1863-69; St. John's, Upper Mahanoy Township, 1870-73; Mahanoy parish, 1870-81, when he retired from the active duties of the ministry. When the Mahanoy parish was divided and St. Peter's congregation undertook to support its own pastor, he accepted a call as its pastor and continues in that position.

SCHUETZ, JARED, (also Schitz), was licensed as a catechist by our Ministerium in 1825, and began serving congregations in the northern part of Northumberland County. In 1828 he was serving the White Deer, Black Hole, St. John's and Paradise congregations. In 1831. at the earnest request and appeal of six congregations, he received full license, and in 1833 he was ordained at Pottstown, Pa. In 1836 he resided at Milton and in 1839 he notified Synod that he was about to move. From this time his name does not appear on the records of Synod.

SCHULTZE, GUSTAV, was pastor at Cogan Station, Pa., 1847-67, and during the years 1851-55 also at Lock Haven. He organized St. Michael's congregation, Cogan Station, in 1847, with twenty-five members, built a frame church two miles northwest of Cogan Station, the cornerstone of which was laid in the Summer of 1862, and the building consecrated, December 25, 1863. He was, at different times, president of Conference, and also its secretary. He lived in retirement at Bahl's Mills, Lycoming County, Pa., after 1867, where he died in 1874.

SCHWARTZ, ELIAS, pastor of St. John's German congregation, Danville, Pa., 1843-46, and St. James, Mahoning, 1843-44. He was sent to Danville by the Home Missionary Society of our Ministerium and at first ministered to about twenty members. In 1844 he began the erection of a church building, the corner-stone of which was laid during that year, and the building consecrated in June, 1845.

•SELL, D., pastor at Lock Haven, Pa., 1861-62, was born in Cumberland County, Pa., August 18, 1819, and died at East Berlin, Pa., May 30, 1888. He was educated at Gettysburg College and Seminary, 1845-51, and labored in the ministry, 1851-88, as pastor at Rosville, Berrysburg, Lock Haven, Aaronsburg, Pinegrove Mills, Loysville, Dillsburg and others.

.SMITH, JACOB W., pastor at Freeburg, Pa., 1821-31, and during the years 1823-30 also at Fremont; Beavertown parish some time about the year 1843; and St. James, Mahoning, for a short time about the year 1846.

• SMITH, LEWIS, pastor of the Dushore parish, 1877-79, and of Cogan Station, 1879-83, was born in Germany, November 5, 1845, graduated at our Philadelphia Seminary in 1877, and ordained by our Ministerium the same year, was pastor at Ellenville, N. Y., 1889-96, and Weatherly, Pa., 1883-89. Died Apr. 21, 1899. Read

•SNABLE, HARVEY G., pastor of the Freeburg parish, consisting of six congregations, 1892-96, and since January 1, 1897, of the Salem parish, consisting of three congregations, formerly a part of the Freeburg parish, was born in Northampton County, Pa., educated at Lafayette College, Easton, 1885-89, and our Philadelphia Seminary, 1889-92, was ordained by the Ministerium in the latter year and has since then been laboring in the territory of our Conference. He married Mary A. Miller, of Salem, Pa., April 28, 1898. On Sunday, April 24, 1898, the Lutherans and Reformed of Salem consecrated a handsome (union) church, erected during the pastorate of the subject of this sketch.

STECK, THOMAS, pastor of the Lykens Valley parish, 1870-73, and of the Berwick parish, including the congregation at Mifflinville and others in Luzerne County, 1874-86, was born at Manchester, Pa., January 1, 1822, ordained in 1851, entered the Ministerium in 1857, and, besides those already mentioned, served the following parishes: Wilmington, Del., 1857-58; Schnecksville, Pa., 1859-67; Bernville, Pa., 1867-68; agent of Orphans' Home, Germantown, Pa., 1868-70; Germantown, Pa., 1870-71; Phillipsburg, N. J., 1880-82; Bridgeport, N. J., 1883-89, after which he lived in retirement at Dover, Del., and died at Catawissa, Pa., November 21, 1892.

STEINHAGEN, E. F., was pastor at Jersey Shore, Pa., 1893-96. After his retirement from this pastorate, he preached for some Germans in Williamsport, for a short time during the year 1896, and in the latter part of the year organized Christ German congregation in South Williamsport, which he served until the summer of 1897.

STETLER, DANIEL M., pastor of the Beavertown parish, 1874-87, and of the Mahanoy parish since 1887, is a son of Isaac S. and Sarah Stetler, was born in Montgomery County, Pa., November 17, 1843, educated at Frederick Institute; a Classical School in Philadelphia and the Philadelphia Seminary, 1871-74, and was ordained by our Ministerium in the latter year. His entire ministerial life has been spent in the service of the Church on our territory. He was very successful in his labors in the Beavertown parish. He re-organized St. Paul's congregation, Beavertown, January 28, 1878; organized St. Matthew's, McClure, January 28, 1877, with 24 members; re-organized St. James, Troxelville, in 1878, erect ed a frame church, the corner-stone of which was laid, June 13, 1880, and the church consecrated, July 3, 1881; organized St. Mark's, near Dormantown, October 1. 1885. He also served Sieber's congregation, Globe Mills. Pa., 1876-81. He has for many years been the Conference Treasurer. He served in the Civil War, in 1862 as Corporal of Company G, 11th Regt., Pa. Vols. He married Barbara Anna Shetler, of Frederick, Pa., December 1, 1866.

, STETLER, EUGENE, son of the Rev. Daniel M. Stetler and his wife Barbara Anna, was born in Frederick Township, Montgomery County, Pa., September 29, 1870. He graduated from Muhlenberg College, Allentown, Pa., 1893, and from the Theological Seminary at Philadelphia, 1896. Until lately he was pastor of the Mission congregation at Gouldsboro, Wayne County, Pa. He married Ursula Benner, Allentown, Pa.

, STETLER, ISAAC HENRY, son of the Rev. Daniel M. Stetler and his wife Barbara Anna, was born at Philadelphia, March 14, 1869. He graduated from Muhlenberg College, Allentown, Pa., 1892, and from the Theological Seminary at Philadelphia, 1895. He was pastor at the Falls of the Schuylkill, North East and Coudersport, Pa. He married Lillian Wilkes, June, 1897, North East, Pa.

STOCK, CARL V. G., of Picket Mountain, Va., was licensed by the Ministerium of Pennsylvania, 1796, after a number of futile applications, but he seems never to have been ordained. He spent a short time at Huntingdon, Pa., 1800; came to Sunbury, Pa., 1801, where the following year he also served Muncy and Catawissa, residing at the latter place, on which general territory he continued to serve. He made frequent appeals to Synod for financial assistance, 1811-35, till finally Synod absolutely refused, and he was entirely dropped.   J. W. EARLY.

STOEVER, CHARLES F., pastor of the Turbotville parish, 1836-45, and part of the Lykens Valley parish, 1845-50, was born at Lebanon, Pa., February 28, 1811, graduated at Pennsylvania College, Gettysburg, Pa., 1833, licensed by the West Pennsylvania Synod, 1836, and ordained by our Ministerium in 1838. Until 1845 he served Milton, Paradise, Follmer's Turbotville and Strawberry Ridge congregations. After this date he removed to Berrysburg, Pa., and until 1850 served Salem, Killinger, Gratz, Paul's, Dauphin and Schitz congregations. Later he served the Trindel Spring, Friedens, Peter's and Mt. Zion's congregations, residing at Mechanicsburg, Pa., where he died, February 17, 1880.

STOVER, MARTIN J., pastor of St. James, Mahoning, Pa., in 1859, was born at Pittston, N. Y., February 1, 1807, and died at Amsterdam, N. Y., November 26, 1893. He was educated in Hartwick Seminary, was licensed by the Hartwick Synod in 1834 and subsequently ordained by the same Synod, within whose bounds nearly the whole of his ministerial life was spent.

STRAUSS, ABRAHAM M., pastor of St. Michael's, Cogan Station, Pa., 1889-91, was born at Nockamixon, Pa., September 27, 1834, was educated at the Classical Institute, Trappe, Pa., Collegiate Institute, Allentown, Pa., and Missionary Institute, Selinsgrove, Pa., being the first theological student received into the latter institution, was licensed in 1861, and ordained in 1864, and since then labored at Freeburg, Wellersburg, Berlin, Gilberts, Cogan Station, Pa., Liberty, Ill., Tuscarawas, O., and Avonmore, Pa.

STRODACH, HENRY B., pastor of the Dushore parish, 1874-75, was born at Landau, Bavaria, Germany, September 26, 1847, educated at Gettysburg, 1865-67, Muhlenberg College, 1867-71, and the Philadelphia Seminary, 1871-74, and was ordained by our Ministerium in the latter year. After leaving Dushore, he served the following parishes: Norristown, Pa., 1875-82; Centre Square, Pa., 1882-83; Brooklyn, N. Y., 1883-95; and later, for a short time, at Jamestown, N. Y., and Lansford, Pa. At present he resides in Reading, Pa. He married Mary L. Zeller, of Reading. Died Jan. 1900.

STUPP, SOLOMON B., pastor of the Berwick parish, 1892-94, is a son of William and Rebecca Stupp, was born in Berks County, Pa., February 21, 1857, educated in Keystone State Normal School, Kutztown, Pa., an Academy at Jonestown, Muhlenberg College, 1877-80, and the Philadelphia Seminary, 1880-83, and was ordained by our Ministerium in the latter year. Besides the parish already mentioned, he has served the following: St. John's, Phillipsburg, N. J., 1883-85; Walmer's in Lebanon County, 1885-88; St. John's, Phoenixville, Pa., 1888-89; Pleasant Valley, 1889-92; Line Mountain, 1894-97; and since then the Mercer County parish in the Pittsburg Synod. He organized St. John's congregation, at Berwick, December 12, 1892, and erected a chapel in 1893.

UHRICH, JOHN M., pastor of the Stone Valley parish, 1875-82, was a son of Michael and Sarah Uhrich, was born at Myerstown, Pa., August 14, 1848, educated at Palatinate College, Myerstown, Muhlenberg College, 1868-72, and Philadelphia Seminary, 1872-75, and ordained in the latter year by our Ministerium. He was Secretary of Conference, 1877-79. He died at Pillow, Pa., April 10, 1882, having served his first and only parish until his death.

ULRICH, L. DOMER, a member of the First Evangelical Lutheran congregation at Selinsgrove, Pa., is the son of Lot and Margareth Ulrich, and was born at Selinsgrove, May 6, 1874. He received his classical training at Tressler's Orphans' Home, Loysville, Pa., 1883-90; Missionary Institute, Selinsgrove, 1890-94; and Muhlenberg College, Allentown, entering the Junior Class, 1894-96. He entered the Theological Seminary at Mt. Airy in the Fall of 1896, and expects to graduate in 1899.

ULRICH, SAMUEL JAMES, son of Benjamin and Angeline Ulrich, was born at Selinsgrove, Pa., January 11, 1868. After attending Missionary Institute at his native place, he studied at Muhlenberg College, Allentown, Pa., graduating in 1890. He studied theology at the Seminary at Philadelphia, and is now pastor at Wellersburg, Pa.

ULRICH, WILLIAM S., a member of the First Evangelical Lutheran congregation, Selinsgrove, Pa., is a son of Fred. B. and Annie M. Ulrich, and was born at Selinsgrove, February 10, 1873. He received his classical training in Missionary Institute, now Susquehanna University, Selinsgrove, entering the former in 1889 and graduating from the latter in 1896. He entered the Theological Seminary in the Fall of 1896, and expects to graduate in 1899.

ULRICH, DANIEL, one of the pioneers in our territory, and pastor of numerous congregations in Northumberland and Dauphin counties, which now constitute the Line Mountain, Mahanoy, Stone Valley and Lykens Valley parishes, 1809-11. He died at Pittsburg, in 1855, at the age of 66 years.

UNGERER, J. J., pastor of St. James, Mahoning, Pa., 1829-30. As his name cannot be found in our Synodical records, it is doubtful if he was a Lutheran clergyman.

Voss, Julius Hermann, for many years the missionary of the Ministerium in Potter and Tioga counties, was a son of Christian F. and Anna Dorothea Voss, was born in Commin, West Prussia, April 12, 1822. He was a missionary in East India (Gossnor Mission), 1842-50; travelling missionary in Germany, 1850-58; licensed by the New York Ministerium, December 22, 1859, ordained by the same, September 6, 1864, he labored at various places in the State of New York; later he was dismissed to the Michigan Synod, in whose bounds he labored some time; pastor at Germania, Pa., and doing missionary work at numerous places, 1872-85. In the latter year he removed to Ansonia, Pa., and from this place, as a centre, moved about from place to place doing such missionary work as his enfeebled health permitted. He died September 16, 1895, at Stokesdale, Pa., his remains were interred at Wellsboro, Pa., the Ministerium paying the expenses connected with his sickness and burial, and with the help of a few friends a small stone was erected over his grave.

Waage, Frederick, pastor of the Turbotville parish, 1826-29, a son of Claus Heinrich and Catherine Dorothea Waage, was born at Itzehoe, Holstein, Denmark, August 17, 1797, was educated in various classical schools and the University at Kiel, spending six years in the latter, and came to America in 1819. He studied theology under the direction of the Rev. F. W. Geissenhainer, was licensed by the Ministerium in 1822, and ordained at Reading, Pa., June 10, 1828. He served the following parishes, first, as licentiate, the congregations at Trumbauersville and Richlandtown, in Bucks County. After his ordination, he served an extensive parish in Northumberland, Columbia and Lycoming counties, embracing Milton, Follmers, Muncy, Williamsport, Paradise, St. John's, St. James, Black Hole Valley and others, including what is now our Turbotville parish. In 1829 he became pastor of the Goshenhoppen parish, including a number of congregations, and labored here until his death, August 23, 1884, at Pennsburg, Pa. In 1840 he severed his connection with the Ministerium and during the remainder of his life, together with his congregations occupied an independent position.

WAGNER, REUBEN S., pastor of the Berwick parish, 1861-62; Lykens Valley, 1874-81; and Dushore, 1881-84, was a son of John and Sophia Wagner, was born at Emaus, Pa., May 11, 1817, licensed by the Ministerium in 1846, pastor at Millersville, 1846-49; Norristown, 1849-50; congregations in the vicinity of Reading, 1850-59; Conyngham and Hazelton, 1859-64; Nazareth, 1864-69; Hinkletown, 1869-73; Doylestown, 1873-74; Lykens Valley and Dushore as stated above. He died at the latter place, May 19, 1884, and was buried at Zion's Church, two miles northwest of Dushore.

WAHRMANN, HERMAN ERNST CHRISTIAN, pastor of St. John's Church, Lykens, Pa., since August 8, 1897, is a son of John Christian and Wilhelmina Wahrmann, nee Rahn, was born at New Ruppin, Province Brandenburg, Kingdom of Prussia, Germany, December 2, 1869, came to America with his father in 1874, was educated at Wagner College, Rochester, N. Y., 1890-94, and Philadelphia Seminary, 1894-97, and was ordained by the New York Ministerium, June 27, 1897.

WALTER, JOHN CONRAD, was born in Germany, November 30, 1775, came with his parents to this country, when he was three years old, and settled in the Tulpehocken region, near Womelsdorf. His father being a shoemaker by trade, he learned the same trade; but afterwards entered the ministry. This change in his life was brought about in the following manner, as related by Dr. Harbaugh: "When a young man, while attending preaching, under Rev. William Hendel, D.D., a Reformed minister, of Womelsdorf, who, like his father, had a wonderful gift of prayer, being so fluent, full of unction, and peculiarly impressive, he was so deeply impressed under one of his prayers, and drawn so near to the Saviour, that he afterwards had no peace of mind, until he decided to devote himself to the work of the ministry." He placed himself under the instruction of some minister, either at Lebanon or Reading, and must have taken a thorough course of study in theology, for we find that during his pastorate he prepared the brothers, John George and John William Heim, for the ministry, the latter being under his instruction for five years. From the manuscripts found in the possession of the latter, referring to the instruction which he had received in theology, in which the Latin, Greek and even Hebrew are freely used, in definitions of terms and quotations from Scripture, forming a complete system of theology, we may learn something of the high theological attainments of the man, as well as of the sound and thorough training and instruction he was enabled to impart to his students.*

He was about thirty years of age when he completed his studies. He became pastor of numerous congregations on the territory now embraced in Snyder County. In 1804 he began his labors at Selinsgrove, Salem, Freeburg, Grubb's, Liverpool (Perry County) and St. Michael's in Pfoutz's Valley; in 1805 at Hassinger's Church; in 1807 at Adamsburg and Musser's Valley Churches; and in 1810 at Fremont, and continued his labors until his death, in 1819. It is stated, that his parents

---
* History of the Freeburg charge by Rev. J. F. Wampole.

moved up from Tulpehocken when he took charge of these congregations, and resided in Fire Stone Valley, not far from Freeburg.

He was married to Catharine Ulch, of Pfoutz's Valley, October 27, 1807. They had five children, of whom two died quite young. During the last years of his pastorate, he resided at Middleburg, where he died, August 10, 1819, and was buried at Hassinger's Church. His grave is marked: "John Conrad Walter (Preacher) born, November 30, 1775, in Germany, died August 10, 1819." The Rev. J. P. Schindel, Sr., preached the funeral sermon, on Heb. 13:7, to a congregation of 1500 people, who had come from the eight congregations, he had been serving, to attend the service. His age was 43 years, 9 months and 13 days. He belongs to the pioneer workers in the territory which now has numerous congregations and well equipped church properties. His activity was of short duration and he died in the prime of life and in the midst of his usefulness; but in that time he had become widely known as a faithful pastor and a man of excellent character.

WALZ, GEORGE FREDERICK, the youngest son of Michael and Katharine Walz, was born in Bretten, Germany, on the 12th day of January, 1822. After attending the public schools of his native home, he learned his father's trade. When about 18 years of age he was stricken twice with severe sicknesses. Attributing his unexpected recovery to the mercy of God, he now consecrated himself to His service, and finally resolved to study for a missionary. With this end in view he entered the Seminary at Basel, Switzerland, in 1843, where he applied himself to his studies so assiduously for five years, that he was graduated a year before his class. On his way to Illinois as a missionary, he made the acquaintance of Drs.

Demme and Mann at Philadelphia, who, recognizing his sterling qualities, insisted on his remaining in the East, where they were greatly in need of ministers at that time. Heeding their summons, he took charge of the newly organized mission at Wilmington, Del., in the Fall of 1848.

A more extensive mission field, with Pottsville, Pa., as its center, was committed to his charge from 1851 to 1853, where he succeeded in making the Pottsville Church self-supporting and in organizing a number of new churches in the vicinity. Receiving a call to the Lykens Valley parish, he entered, in January, 1854, upon the manifold duties of this new field, which comprised the following seven congregations: Miller's and Federhoff's in Armstrong Valley; Huber's, Bender's and St. John's in Lykens Valley; Uniontown and Steinthal in Mahantongo Valley. It goes without saying that this was a rather large charge for one minister.

But, in the prime of his life, naturally industrious and energetic, supported by an iron constitution, with highly developed vocal organs—nothing short of a large parish could have formed a fitting counterpart for his activity. He was now in his element. Pastor and people were congenial. They soon loved and cherished each other, while the blessing of God rested on the work.

However, new demands were ere long made on the minister, to which he responded, perhaps too readily. From 1856 to 1857 he served a small congregation, 16 miles distant, in the mountains of Schuylkill County. Then for nine consecutive years he preached every fourth Sunday evening in a school-house at Steinthal. In the last three years of his pastorate he preached every Saturday in a school-house at Vera Cruz, and at the same time every second Sunday evening at Lykens. This with all the funerals, catechetical classes, sick visits, etc., was a burden too heavy to carry for one man. Nature, overtaxed too long, gave a timely warning. The work must be diminished, or life may be shortened. The only course to pursue was to propose to the churches a division of the territory into two parishes. This would not only relieve the minister but would also ensure a better service to all the churches. This plan, however, was not favorably received, and the pastor was again left to get along as best he could. Seeing no hope of a better adjustment of the work, he accepted a call to the Old Goshenhoppen parish in Montgomery County, where there was but one service a Sunday. Today this large territory is divided into five parishes.

In his new field of labor, he served three congregations from January 1st, 1865, to January 1st, 1892, when on account of defective hearing, he retired from active ministry at the age of 70 years.

Beside his pastoral work he devoted much time to literary work. From 1870 to 1873 he served as German Secretary of the Ministerium, also serving at various times on many important committees of that body.

From 1880 to 1887 he wrote the weekly editorials for "Herold and Zeitschrift." These editorials soon gained for themselves a wide reputation, and were frequently reprinted in the religious papers of America and Europe.

Father Walz is noted for his sound judgment, his retentive memory, and no less, for his comprehensive knowledge. Always a diligent student and an extensive reader, a close observer of secular and ecclesiastical affairs, a clear and logical thinker, his judgment seldom leads him astray, while his wise counsel is continually sought by his brethren in the ministry. He was married to Charlotte Stuemmler in 1850. This union was blessed with nine children, of whom one son and five daughters are still living.

In company with his wife, surrounded by children and grand children, he is at present enjoying the fruition of a long and useful life, at his pleasant home in Sellersville, Pa., and though 76 years of age, his mental and physical faculties remain almost unimpaired.

ADOLPH F. WALZ.

WAMPOLE, JACOB FREDERICK, pastor of Grace Church, Shamokin, Pa., since 1891, is a son of the Rev. Jacob and Susanna Clementine Wampole, nee Fisher, was born near Spring City, Pa., June 6, 1833, was educated at Washington Hall, Trappe, Pa.; Pennsylvania College, Gettysburg, Pa., 1851-54; and Gettysburg Theological Seminary, 1854-56, licensed by the West Pennsylvania Synod in the same year, and ordained at Carlisle, Pa., in 1857. He has successively served the following parishes: Shamokin, consisting of five congregations, 1857-67; Turbotville, 1867-76; Freeburg, 1876-91. He has been President, Secretary and Treasurer of Conference; has served as Director of the Philadelphia Seminary and Trustee of Muhlenberg College; and Principal of the Elysburg Academy, 1860-66. He married Margaret Krick, of Paxinos, Pa., November 13, 1862.

WEBER, CARL F. C., pastor at Jersey Shore, Pa., 1872. He was received into Synod in 1870, as pastor of congregations at New Germany, Fruitland and Williamstown, N. J.; was pastor of St. Peter's, Scranton, Pa., 1871; Zion's, Jersey Shore, and St. Paul's and St. John's, 1872, and of Gilbert's parish in Monroe County, serving numerous congregations, 1873-74, and in the latter year was dismissed to the Western District of the Missouri Synod.

PLATE XIII

A. P. LENTZ.

H. P. MILLER.

W. S. ULRICH.

L. D. ULRICH.

W. P. BARR.

W. M. KOPENHAVER.

WEIAND, W. H., pastor of the congregation at Troxelville, some time prior to 1873.

•WEICKSEL, FREDERICK A., pastor of St. Paul's Church, Numidia, Pa., since 1893, is a son of the Rev. Henry and Angelina Weicksel, was born in Wilmington, Del., January 6, 1867, educated in Muhlenberg College, 1881-83 and Missionary Institute, Selinsgrove, Pa., 1891-93, and was ordained by our Ministerium in the latter year. On November 5, 1893, he organized St. Peter's congregatino at Montana, Pa., which he supplies in connection with his other work. He married Elizabeth Wolfgang, March 8, 1887.

WEICKSEL, HENRY. The firmness of purpose, unselfish devotion, and heroic fidelity of the unrecognized rank and file of Lutheran pastors which, under God, have made our beloved Church what she is today in this country, are conspicuously illustrated in the subject of this sketch.

Rev. Henry Weicksel was of the sturdy, sterling stock of intelligent, pious German peasantry. He was born to Nicholas and Kunigunde Weicksel at Pilmersreuth, Bavaria, Germany, September 22, 1817, the year of the great famine in that country; and was the youngest of a family of four sons and five daughters. Baptized, according to the good German custom, when eight days old, he was raised under rigorous but wholesome family discipline. He attended parochial school; was confirmed in his fourteenth year; served an apprenticeship at cabinet making and wood carving; and travelled as "Handwerksbursch." His life was seriously endangered on account of his pronounced and vigorous Protestant faith; and as a penance for befriending him a Roman Catholic companion was commanded to eat two pounds of hay.

Emigrated to America in 1838, arriving in Baltimore Md., in May, after a voyage of six weeks and three days. His fellow voyagers were greatly alarmed at the appearance of the negro stevedores, especially when told that they were cannibals; and a travelling companion returned to Germany at once, because told by a darkey that it was the climate in this country that had made him black. He worked at his trade in Baltimore, Md., Carlisle and Chambersburg, Pa. As there was no Lutheran church in Chambersburg a number of associates, religiously inclined like himself, met with him regularly for mutual edification in the study of the Word, and prayer. Showing marked ability in apprehending and expounding the Truth, his companions greatly encouraged and urged him to carry out a long cherished purpose, to prepare for and enter the Gospel ministry. Removing to Waynesboro, he married Miss Elizabeth Macdole, May 3, 1840 In order to raise money to enable him to study, he made a very remunerative trip as a scissor grinder to Easton Pa. His wife died January 5, 1842, leaving him the father of a very young daughter. The child was given a most excellent home, and raised by Mrs. Mary Gordon, nee Dettero. In the Autumn of 1842 he went to Gettysburg, where he studied for nearly two years, being married again meanwhile at Hanover, Pa., to Miss Angelina Creager. He read theology under Rev. Henry Ziegler, D.D., and helped him do mission work. Was licensed to preach by the Pittsburg Synod in 1848, and ordained to the ministry by the same body at Prospect, Pa., in 1851. From 1848 to 1858 he served the Venango mission, embracing points in Venango, Mercer, and Crawford counties. It was an extremely difficult and laborious field, and afforded but a very meagre support. The trials, hardships, and privations of that pioneer work are instanced by the facts that he was often away from his family a month or more at a time, and that for weeks in succession the family lived on potatoes and salt with a little butter in Summer, and in Winter on buckwheat cakes and molasses with black coffee. Subsequently he served the following charges: Warren, Pa., from 1858 to 1863; Wilmington, Del., 1864-67; teaching parochial school, beside his pastoral work in both of these places; Ringtown, Pa., from 1867-73; Line Mountain, Pa., January 1874 to January, 1894, twenty years. In the Autumn of 1895 he removed to Shamokin, Pa., where he lived in retirement until his death on December 18, 1896, attaining an age of 79 years, 2 months and 26 days.

In September, 1893, he had the pleasure of gathering his family around him, and celebrating his golden wedding. During his ministry he built six churches, and saw three of his sons follow him into his sacred calling, and a grand son preparing for it. He went to his longed for rest and reward full of years, rich in the love and honor of many friends, his great wish to see his children established in life gratified, and leaving to them the incalculable legacy of honor, integrity, and godliness. He is survived by his widow, four sons, two daughters, and seventeen grand children. His preëminent characteristics were the most absolute trust in God, confirmed by many remarkable providences, the most conscientious and faithful discharge of duty, deep personal piety, and an absorbing love for the Church and his family. He saw the Church of his love and labors grow in this country from a membership of 135,628 to 1,441,486. He was a type that is rapidly passing away, especially here in the east, the result of whose life and labors is our richest inheritance. L. M. C. WEICKSEL.

•WEICKSEL, WILLIAM, pastor of Grace congregation, Shamokin, Pa., 1888-91, is a son of the Rev. Henry and Angelina Weicksel, was born at Warren, Pa., March 29, 1863, was educated in Thiel College, Greenville, Pa., 1879-80; Muhlenberg College, 1880-85; and Philadelphia Seminary, 1885-88, and was ordained by our Ministerium. He organized Zion's congregation at Mt. Carmel, Pa., June 9, 1889, and served St. Paul's and St. Peter's congregations in Cameron Township, Northumberland County, Pa. He was pastor at Coudersport, Pa., 1891-96, and at North Lima, O., since 1896.

WELDEN, CHRISTIAN, D.D., pastor of the Lykens Valley parish, 1850-51, was born September 30, 1812, was ordained by the New York Ministerium in 1833, entered the Ministerium in 1835, and served in the following parishes: New Holland, Pa., 1834-38; Bucksville, Pa., 1839-42; Kimberton, Pa., 1842-50; Bethlehem, Pa., 1852-72; St. Peter's, Philadelphia, 1872-83; pastor emeritus of the same, 1883-97. He was President of the Ministerium, 1857-60, and Missionary Superintendent, 1868-72. He died in Philadelphia, October 2, 1898.

WELKER, JOSEPH, pastor of St. Mark's (Market Street) congregation, Williamsport, Pa., 1851-56. During his pastorate the brick church was erected, the corner-stone of which was laid in 1854 and the building consecrated, January 22, 1856.

• WENRICH, SAMUEL, pastor of the Dushore parish, 1884-93, is a son of John and Anna Wenrich, was born at Reinhold Station, Pa., April 1, 1844, was educated at Muhlenberg College, 1878-81, and the Philadelphia Seminary, 1881-84, and was ordained by our Ministerium in the latter year. During his pastorate at Dushore, he also preached for the Lutherans at Lopez and Ricketts. Since

1893, he has been pastor of St. John's congregation, Phillipsburg, N. J. He married Antonia Irene Yorkes, Bethlehem, Pa., July 2, 1881.

ᛌWETZLER, JOHN N., Ph.D., pastor of St. Luke's congregation, Sunbury, Pa., since 1894, is a son of John and Lydia Ann Wetzler, was born at Curtin, Pa., July 8, 1853, was educated at Berrysburg Seminary; Muhlenberg College, 1875-79; and Philadelphia Seminary, 1879-82, and was ordained by our Ministerium in the latter year. He has served the following parishes: Ringgold, Pa., 1882-90; Beavertown, Pa., 1890-94. In 1894 he organized St. Luke's congregation, erected a chapel, the corner-stone of which was laid, September 2, 1894, and the building consecrated, February 17, 1895. He has been Secretary of Conference since 1897. He married Clara N. Walz, daughter of the Rev. F. Walz, Sellersville, Pa.

WILLARD, PETER, pastor of St. John's German congregation, Danville, Pa., 1850-56, a son of George and Susanna Willard, was born at Jefferson, Md., September 29, 1809, died at Mexico, Pa., July 26, 1893. He was educated at Gettysburg, Pa., 1834-39, and was licensed by the West Pennsylvania Synod, in 1841, and labored at Boalsburg, Pa., 1841-42; Westminster, 1842-45; Lovettsville, 1845-48. Later he served at Loysville, Mifflintown, Schuylkill Haven, and as Superintendent of the Loysville Orphans' Home, 1868-89.

ᛌWITMER, CHARLES, son of George and Catharine Witmer, was born near Vera Cruz, Northumberland County, Pa., September 1, 1820. He was educated in the institutions at Gettysburg, Pa., graduating from the College in 1841. He was licensed in 1844. Between 1840 and 1845 he supplied the congregations of Rev. Eyer at Catawissa,

Pa.; served several parishes in the General Synod; was Superintendent of the Orphans' Homes at Germantown and McAlisterville, Pa., engaged in secular business; was received into the Ministerium in 1863; died at Des Moines, Iowa, July 22, 1884.

WOERNER, G. F., pastor of Immanuel's German congregation, Williamsport, Pa., 1870-76, came from Wuertemburg, Germany, as an ordained minister, and was admitted to the Ministerium in 1868. His parishes were Schuylkill Haven, 1868-70; Roxboro, 1876-80; Honesdale, Pa., which was an independent congregation, and he also severed his connection with Synod. He afterwards returned to Philadelphia, where he died.

J. W. EARLY.

YOUNT, A. L., D.D., pastor of St. Mark's Church, Williamsport, Pa., 1886-91, is a son of Noah and Elizabeth Yount, was born in Catawba County, N. C., July 28, 1851, was educated in Newton High School, Newton, N. C.; a similar institution at Hickory, N. C.; North Carolina College, Mt. Pleasant, N. C., graduating in 1876; and Philadelphia Seminary, 1876-77, and was ordained by the Synod of Southern Illinois, September 30, 1877. He has served the following parishes: First Church, Murphysboro, Ill., 1877-79; Bridgewater, Nova Scotia, 1879-86; and the First Church, Greensburg, Pa., since June 1, 1891. He is President of the Pittsburg Synod, member of the Board of Ministerial Relief of the same, member of the Board of Trustees of Thiel College, of the Greensburg Seminary and of the Executive Committee of his Synod. He has published numerous pamphlets and books, among which are "Lost and Found," a series of discourses based on the parable of the Prodigal Son; "Christian Missions," 1889; "Compulsory Attendance and Free Text-books in Our Public Schools;" "Christ Weeping Over Jerusalem;" "Clean Cut Views;" Kappf's "Holy Communion Book," translated; John Arndt's "Sermons on the Catechism," translated. He was honored with the title of Doctor of Divinity by his Alma Mater in 1895. He is married to the daughter of the Rev. D. M. Henkel, D.D., of Catawissa, Pa.

ZELLER, —, pastor at Lock Haven, Pa., 1859.

ZIEGLER, HENRY, D.D., pastor of St. Mark's (Market street) congregation, Williamsport, Pa., for a short time in 1850; Lock Haven, Pa., 1855; and supplied Kratzerville for a short time about 1858, is a son of Jacob Ziegler, was born near the Old Fort, Center County, Pa., August 19, 1816, was educated at Gettysburg, Pa., licensed by the West Pennsylvania Synod in 1843 and ordained by the Pittsburg Synod in 1846. He labored in numerous congregations in Pennsylvania, organized the first English congregation in Williamsport, was agent for the Parent Education Society of the General Synod, and for twenty-three years was Professor of Theology in Missionary Institute, Selinsgrove, and now lives in retirement at the latter place.

ZUBER, THEOPHILUS, pastor of the Trevorton parish, 1893-96, is a son of the Rev. Ludwig and Caroline Zuber, was born at Pittston, Pa., January 7, 1872, educated at Wagner College, Rochester, N. Y., 1885-90, and Philadelphia Seminary, 1890-93, and ordained by our Ministerium in the latter year. On October 1, 1896, he began his labors as pastor of St. John's German congregation at Tamaqua, Pa. He married Bertha E. Crone, Trevorton, Pa., August 27, 1896.

ZWEIER, CHARLES D., pastor of the Beavertown parish

since 1897, is a son of Adam and Clara Zweier, was born at Hosensack, Pa., April 12, 1866, was educated in Perkiomen Seminary, Pennsburg, Pa.; Keystone State Normal School, Kutztown, Pa.; Muhlenberg College, 1890-94; and the Philadelphia Seminary, 1894-97, and was ordained by our Ministerium in the latter year. Immediately after his ordination he entered upon the duties of the parish in which he is now laboring.

JUBILEE CONVENTION. MINISTERIUM OF PENNSYLVANIA, JUNE, 1898.

IV. Jubilee Celebration.

SESQUI-CENTENNIAL

OF THE

Evangelical Lutheran Ministerium

OF

Pennsylvania and Adjacent States.

The Sesqui-Centennial of the Evangelical Lutheran Ministerium of Pennsylvania and adjacent States was an occasion of more than ordinary importance in the long and interesting history of the body, and was celebrated with special services in Philadelphia, June 2-4, 1898, a complete report of which is presented in the following pages. It was proper that the celebration should take place in the city in which the Ministerium was organized one hundred and fifty years ago.

Already in the year 1893, the President of the Ministerium, in his official report, directed attention to this interesting event, in the following words: "We are now within five years of the one hundred and fiftieth anniversary of this venerable Ministerium, the Mother Synod of the Evangelical Lutheran Church on this continent. This anniversary will come about the close of the second century of the settlement of Pennsylvania, and the fourth since the discovery of America, and near the end of this nineteenth century itself. Would it not be advisable, even at this early time to take the necessary steps, in order to secure an accurate and reliable history of the Ministerium of Pennsylvania, so as to have it ready by the time of our one hundred and fiftieth anniversary in 1898?" In accordance with this suggestion, action was taken which resulted in making suitable arrangements for the proper observance of this event. The Officers of the Ministerium and the Faculty of the Theological Seminary were appointed a committee, charged with the duty of presenting a plan by which the suggestion of the President could be carried into effect. The following year this committee recommended the publication of a volume containing the Minutes of the Ministerium for the first century of its history, together with such historical matter as is now in the Archives of the Ministerium. After some discussion, the report was referred back to the committee with full power to act. The committee appointed the Rev. Drs. A. Spaeth, H. E. Jacobs and G. F. Spieker, as an Editorial Committee, the result of whose labors is the excellent Jubilee Memorial Volume of 600 pages, published during this year. The volume consists of two parts: The first part gives an account of the conventions from 1748 to 1780, as far as the material could be gathered from the correspondence and diaries of the fathers and other documents; the second part contains a full and exact reproduction of the written protocol from 1781 to 1821, the year with which the first volume of the written protocol closes.

Other literature called forth by the Jubilee may be mentioned, as follows: "Our Jubilee," a quarterly, presenting the history of the Ministerium and its Institutions; the "Jubilee Bulletin" of the Danville Conference, a monthly, presenting congregational histories; the Jubilee number of the "Lutheran Church Review," with important articles bearing on the history, position and activity of the Ministerium; the "History of the Wilkes-Barre Conference," an illustrated volume of 250 pages, presenting historical sketches of its congregations; and our own excellent "Danville Conference Memorial Volume" of more than 350 pages, presenting a history of the Conference, histories of its congregations, sketches of the lives of its pastors and pioneer missionaries, and the following report of the Sesqui-Centennial celebration.

The Jubilee Fund is an important part of our celebration. In 1895 the Danville Conference passed a resolution, recommending to the Ministerium the propriety of raising a fund of $100,000 for the purpose of liquidating the indebtedness of our Seminary and College. This suggestion was taken up by the Ministerium at its convention in 1895, and a committee was appointed, consisting of the Revs. Dr. A. Spaeth, C. J. Cooper and S. A. Ziegenfuss; E. Aug. Miller, Esq., and Thos. W. Saeger, charged with the duty of laying before the Ministerium, at its next annual convention, a well-prepared plan for the collection of a Jubilee Fund. In 1896 this committee recommended the raising of a Jubilee Fund of $150,000, apportioned among the Conferences, according to membership, wealth and general benevolence, of which amount the sum of $9,000 was assigned to our Conference. Of the whole amount to be raised, one-sixth was to be devoted to the Ministerium, and the balance to be equally divided between the Theological Seminary at Mt. Airy and Muhlenberg College at Allentown.

The arrangements for the Jubilee celebration were begun by the Executive Board, early in the year 1898. A sub-committee of the Board was appointed, consisting of the Rev. Drs. Theo. L. Seip, F. J. F. Schantz and S. E. Ochsenford, instructed in co-operation with the Central Jubilee Committee (already named) to make the necessary arrangements for the celebration. This joint committee reported the results of its labors to the Executive Board, which took final action on the same, directed the publication of the program as agreed upon, and invited all Lutheran Synods in this country and representatives of the institution at Halle to attend the Jubilee services

The program, as finally adopted, together with the addresses, is here reproduced in a form which we hope will prove both interesting and profitable to many of the members of our congregations.

GERMAN JUBILEE SERVICE.

The first service was held in St. John's German church, Fifteenth and Ogden streets, Philadelphia, on Thursday, June 2, 1898, at 8 p. m. The church was handsomely decorated with plants and flowers by the young people of the congregation, and was filled with an attentive audience. The full Vesper Service of the Kirchenbuch was conducted by the Rev. E. H. Pohle, German Secretary of the Ministerium. After the choir had rendered an anthem, the congregation sang the hymn, "Nun bitten wir den heiligen Geist." This was the hymn sung at the organization of the Ministerium in St. Michael's church, in 1748. Then followed, in regular order, the Versicle with the Gloria Patri; Psalm 46, with the Antiphon, "Out of Zion, the perfection of beauty: God hath shined;" the Scripture Lesson, Rev. 5:7-13; the Pentecost Responsory, sung by the choir; and the Festival Address by the Rev. Prof. Adolph Spaeth, D.D., LL.D., as follows:

JUBILEE ADDRESS.

It is a great pleasure to me to welcome the members and friends of our Ministerium on the joyous and solemn occasion of this Jubilee service, when we meet to remember what the Lord has done for us through a century and a half, how He blessed the self-denying and consecrated labors of our fathers, increasing that little band of devoted men, who, under the leadership of Henry Melchoir Muhlenberg, organized this Ministerium in August, 1748, to a large and influential body of more than 300 pastors and 125,000 communicants. But at the same time, it is with some embarrassment that I undertake to address you on this occasion. During the past months, in the preparation of

REV. A. SPAETH, D.D., LL.D.

the Memorial Volume, which contains the first installment of the Documentary History of our Ministerium, I had ample opportunity to realize, more than ever before, the labors, the difficulties, the perseverance, wisdom and faithfulness of the fathers. This work stands before me in such dimensions that I cannot think of attempting to present even an outline of the history of these 150 years. For this I refer you to the Memorial Volume itself. If I were to take up that history I would detain you till after midnight, and even then half would not be told. I therefore at once dismiss the idea of such a detailed historical account.

And yet, I propose to open and to read the book of history on this Jubilee occasion. I shall try to do so with two distinct points in view. In the first place I will endeavor to point out, in a short review of the historical surroundings, the great significance and importance of the organization of this first Lutheran Church body on this Western Continent, for the history of God's Kingdom and His Church in general. And in the second place, I shall attempt to draw some practical lessons from the work and experience of the fathers on some points which seem to me, at the present time, to claim our special attention and consideration.

I. One of the Church historians of the Missouri Synod calls the organization of the Pennsylvania Synod in 1748 the most important event in the history of our Church in this country, during the last century. No one will ever dispute the correctness of this statement. And yet, it is far from saying enough. When I had the privilege and honor to represent the General Council, eleven years ago, at the General Lutheran Conference in Hamburg, I ventured to make a statement which I will repeat this evening at this Jubilee service of our Ministerium. The organization of a Church body of the Augsburg Confession in America, I hold to be the greatest and most far-reaching event in the history of Protestantism since the Reformation Era. It means the transfer of Lutheranism, with all its peculiar gifts, its confession, its doctrine, its hymns and service, its devotional life and practical christianity, into this new World of the West. It means the organization of the Church of the Augsburg Confession, for the first time, not in the bonds of a State Church, with all its embarrassments and entanglements, but as a Free Church, unfettered by any political alliances, and in such a position that her own God-given powers and talents could be fully developed in new surroundings, on new ground, in a new language, the English, with all its providential destinies and opportunities—just two hundred years after the first English Lutheran movement, in England itself, had been thwarted through Reformed and Romanizing influences. In view of all this I hold that it is impossible to over-estimate the significance of the formal establishment of the Lutheran Church on this continent, which dates from the organization of our Ministerium in 1748.

The Church of the Augsburg Confession had to pass through a period of terrible struggles on its native German soil. There were first those bitter internal controversies which divided her theologians and pastors up to the time of the Formula of Concord. Then followed, in the first half of the seventeenth century the death struggle of the thirty years' war, in which the horrible threat of Alexander, the Papal Nuncio in Worms (1521) was realized, that, if the Germans would not submit to Rome they would be set against each other until the land would be filled with their blood. Just one hundred years before the beginning of our Synod the peace of Westphalia put an end to the terrible carnage. Germany, the Motherland of the Reformation, bleeding from a thousand wounds, began to breathe again. Pastors and congregations tried to gather the scattered sheep, to rebuild their broken altars, and to realize once more what a precious legacy had been committed to them through the Reformation. But another century had to pass before the Mother-Church of the Reformation was in proper condition to be transplanted to these Western shores. Those who have learned to read the books of history know the character of the period intervening between the peace of Westphalia and the year 1748, when our Ministerium was founded. The first section of that period may well be compared to that era in the history of Israel, when, after the seventy years of Babylonian Captivity the chosen people returned to their country and began to lay the foundation for religious and national reconstruction. What had been saved out of a terrible catastrophe was now guarded and preserved in a spirit of anxious, timid legalism. A scrupulous observance of the law and its rites and ceremonies was to prove their faithful adherence to the traditions of the fathers. Thus the Lutheran Church of Germany, after the great war, holding fast the doctrine of the fathers, anxiously restored the former orders, rites and ceremonies. It was, indeed, a period of reorganization for the Church of the pure Word and Sacrament. But, at the same time much of the spirit of the fathers was lacking. A new breath of life was needed, to enable those Lutherans to do the work which God in His providence had laid out for them. You know the impulses to which the Lutheran Church in Germany owed this quickening breath of life. It was the Pietistic movement which had established itself in Halle. There was the fountain from which sprang the organization of the Lutheran Church in America. In celebrating the 150th anniversary of the Mother Synod of Pennsylvania, we cannot and dare not shut our eyes to this historical fact. We must know how to appreciate, on our own ground, the great historic mission of German Pietism. What was the real aim and design of its author, Philip Jacob Spener? Did he look upon our Augsburg Confession as an antiquated document that had survived its usefulness? Did he intend to abolish it? Nothing of the kind. He was rather anxious to have it honored and appreciated as a living power in the Church of Christ. Whatever was therein testified, taught and confessed was to be, not a dead letter, but the very life of God animating the true Christian. His desire was not to establish a new theology, a new system of Dogmatics, but rather to quicken a life of true Christian Ethics, to plant and to nourish a thoroughly earnest, practical Christianity.

It is most interesting and instructive to notice in the Halle Pietism some of the very features which became of paramount importance for the successful planting of our Lutheran Church in this new world. It is well known how the good old Lutheran doctrine of the spiritual priesthood of all believers was emphasized in those circles. They wanted a church of the people, not of pastors and theologians alone. They were anxious to interest the lay-members of the Church in all her work, and to secure their hearty co-operation in the administration of her affairs, in her discipline, in her missionary enterprises. And it needs no word of explanation to show how indispensable these very features were for the successful planting of the Lutheran Church on American soil. Again, these fathers in Halle who are sometimes denounced and belittled as narrow men, who were inclined to shirk the Christian duty of bringing the power of the Gospel to bear upon the world at large, were in reality men of a wider horizon and a larger heart than most of the professors of Lutheran orthodoxy in their days. They had, if not a full consciousness, certainly a strong divination of the fact, that the Church of the pure Gospel, having been saved from the death-struggle of the thirty years' war, had still a great destiny to fulfill in the history of the world and of the kingdom of God. They understood that this Kingdom was not to be hemmed in within the four walls of a German village or town church, but that the seed of the Word had to be carried forward across the seas, and to be spread among foreign nations and tongues. There was a wide-awake missionary spirit in Halle, casting its eyes across oceans and continents, to the far East and the far West, always ready to take an active interest in every measure by which the extension of God's Kingdom might be advanced. It was through the fathers in Halle that Bartholomaeus Ziegenbalg, in 1705, was presented and recommended to King Frederick IV. of Denmark, as the most suitable man for his missionary enterprise on the coast of Trankebar. It was in Halle that the greatest missionary East India ever had, Christian Frederik Schwartz, was gained and prepared for the work of his life.

It was in Halle that Henry Melchoir Muhlenberg was engaged as a teacher, beginning his work with the smallest children, and gradually advancing to the higher classes, which he instructed in Greek, Hebrew, and some of the theological branches. Having thus had ample opportunity to form a judgment concerning his character and qualifications, the fathers in Halle first intended to send him to East India, to take charge of a new mission-field in Bengal. But untoward circumstances prevented the execution of this plan, and a few years afterwards Francke offered him a call to the "dispersed Lutherans in Pennsylvania." As he had been willing before to undertake the mission work in Bengal, so was he now to cross the Atlantic Ocean in the service of his Lord. Whether it was the East or the West, India or Pennsylvania, he was ever ready to follow the leadings of Divine Providence, and to give himself up wholly to the work of his Master. And surely the Lord Himself had chosen him for this field of labor among the German immigrants on this Western Continent. Muhlenberg came to this country fully equipped by his thorough Lutheran training, his living faith and trust in his God, his large-heartedness, his abundant pastoral experience and tact, his knowledge of the human heart which enabled him to deal with men of all classes of society as a true and conscientious "Seelsorger." In this new country he opened up new fields for the old Lutheran faith. He laid the foundation for a Church organization which was to be of the greatest importance and significance for a distant future.

Even at this present day we can hardly realize the full meaning of the work which the Lord accomplished through his labors. For with all its faults and shortcomings, this great land of the West has undeniably a great task assigned to it in the history of God's Kingdom. If it will once come to pass that this country learns to understand the voice of our fathers, their theology, their truly Evangelical conception of Christianity, their spirit of prayer and of work, their cheerful devotion to the cause of Christ, it will be seen that by the planting of the Lutheran Church in America the Lord God advanced the cause of His Kingdom in a manner that surpasses everything that has been done since the days of the Reformation.

The first period of the history of our Ministerium, that of the Patriarch Muhlenberg and his direct and personal influence, was followed by a second half century which we are accustomed to criticise and judge rather severely in many respects. It cannot be denied that the men of that period did not emphasize the confessional basis as clearly and consistently as the fathers had done. It is true, there is a decided falling off in sound Lutheran consciousness. It shows itself particularly in the spirit and language of the Agenda and Hymnbooks of that period. And yet I am ready to declare that since I had an opportunity to get a fuller and deeper insight into the details of the history of that time, I am constrained to confess that my judgment of that period of our history is considerably modified. In spite of all that must be justly condemned, there is still an undercurrent of positive faith which now and then comes to the surface in undeniable evidences of true christian life and activity. It must be affirmed of the majority of our fathers, even during that period of so-called "deterioration," that they preserved an unshaken faith in Christ, their Lord and Redeemer. The Ministerium of Pennsylvania, in those days, was certainly not below, but rather above the average Christianity of the time. If we examine into the state of religion, of Christian doctrine and life, at the end of the eighteenth and the beginning of the nineteenth century, in Germany, England, or any part of Europe, we look in vain for a clear direct confession of the Son of God, and the Word of the Cross. And yet in 1804 Dr. Christopher Kuntze, the son-in-law of H. M. Muhlenberg, could write as follows: "Of our men,—I know no one, God be praised, who denies the Lord who has redeemed him. But it is nothing less than this, that men are at present doing boldly in Germany, through pulpit, life and pen, who eat the bread of the Church. God preserve us, my dear brethren, in this sad time, from apostles coming from there.' (Documentary History, p. 343). And what was thus testified by Kuntze concerning the region of the Hudson, was equally true of Philadelphia and the whole of Pennsylvania, where men like Helmuth, Schmid and others preached the old Gospel of Christ crucified, with simple childlike faith. If we study the details of the Synodical Proceedings in our Documentary History, we will find numerous and strong evidences, during that very period, of great zeal and activity in the vineyard of the Lord. At that time when the Word of the Lord had become rare, our fathers made special and systematic efforts to spread the Gospel in distant parts of our country, and to gather the scattered and neglected members of their household of faith into permanent congregations. It was the time of the "Traveling Preachers" who were sent out to Virginia, Ohio, Tennessee, Kentucky, and North Carolina, to preach the Gospel, to baptize, teach and confirm, and to spread religious information through tracts, among them the Augsburg Confession. By these faithful and self-denying missionary labors the foundation was laid for the future establishment of Lutheran Synods on all these territories. At the same time also the first efforts were made to publish a Monthly, in the interest of the Mother Synod, "which shall especially contain extracts from Luther's writings" (Doc. Hist., p. 356). Again, there is no other time in the history of our Synod when we find such numbers of parochial schools entered in the Minutes under the names of the pastors, as the period from 1804 to 1820. In 1804 we have 26 congregations reporting 89 parochial schools. In 1820 there are 84 congregations reporting 206 parochial schools, a convincing testimony of the strong interest taken in those days in the religious training of the youth of the Church. Surely there are some things, even in this second period of the history of the Ministerium, that deserve to be appreciated and even imitated at the present day.

There is yet a third period in the history of our Mother Synod; the last half century that fills up the hundred and fifty years. Many of us that are celebrating this Jubilee have been members and workers in the Ministerium through a considerable part of this time. I myself, though not one of the oldest members of the Body, can count already 34 years of connection with the Ministerium of Pennsylvania. What a season of refreshment and revival, in the best sense of the word, these last 50 years have been! What Hutten said of the Era of the

Reformation, may be applied in some measure to this period of our own history: "It is a real pleasure and delight to live in it." There was indeed a springtime of new life breathing through our Synod and promising a rich harvest for the future when that far-reaching resolution was passed to establish our own Theological Seminary; when it was determined to break off a connection with a Body which was characterized by its indifference or even hostility to the confession of the fathers. Great efforts and sacrifices were needed to maintain consistently the position then taken. But a new life seemed to have been infused into the body of the old Mother Synod. All our institutions which are at present the great centres of our activity and of untold blessing for our Synodical life, came into existence during the last half century,—the Seminary, the College, the Orphans' Home. Look at the men whose portraits have found a place on our Jubilee Chart and remember how they labored with one heart and one mind for the restoration of the old faith and life of our dear Church, and let us take good care that we lose not the things which they have wrought.

II. And now let me add a few words of practical advice and admonition to these historical reminiscences which have been sketched so briefly. There are not a few points in the practice of our fathers and the historical development of our Ministerium, which appear to me as being peculiarly valuable and instructive for our own time and the church-work that is committed to our hands. First of all let me refer to a feature which strikes me as one of the most beautiful in the early history of our Ministerium. It is the relation of perfect trust and confidence between the congregations and the so-called Collegium Pastorum, that constituted the old Ministerium. I cannot prove or illustrate this point more forcibly than by quoting the very words of a letter sent in August, 1748, by the Tulpehocken and Nordkiel congregations to the Ministers assembled in Philadelphia. They make formal request to be taken under their pastoral care and supervision, giving the following reasons for their application: 1.—"Their true, regular, and, consequently, divine call. 2.—The good testimonies given by the spiritual fathers and public teachers of our Evangelical Lutheran Church in Europe—especially of those of the University of Halle, in Saxony, which is like a city set upon a hill. 3.—We are moved also by your steadfastness in the confession and doctrine of the Unaltered Augsburg Confession, which is violently attacked here, partly by false brethren, partly by fanatical sects, partly by Epicureans, as well as by others 4.—We are impressed by your faithful administration of your office whereby you have turned many from darkness to light. 5.—Your ministerial gifts and prudence and also your ability to accommodate yourselves to the peculiar circumstances of this country. 6.—This encourages us to hope that the blessings experienced in the foundation may be perpetuated for us and our posterity. 7.—The fidelity and carefulness you have shown in the administration of your office, not only in your own United Congregations, but also in others that have resorted to you . We hereby . recognize and declare all the pastors of the United Congregations of Pennsylvania as our pastors and shepherds Nor will we do, determine or change anything in church matters, without their previous knowledge and consent . We promise that whatever minister is sent by the Collegium Pastorum we will acknowledge and respect and obey as our regular and divinely called pastor . Nor will we object if, for important reasons, they agree to call him elsewhere, and supply his place with another pastor. We also promise that should any misunderstanding or division occur we will report the same to the Collegium Pastorum, await the result and acquiesce in their decision."*

The question may properly be raised whether such a declaration on the part of the Congregations was not going entirely too far, in disfranchising themselves and committing to the Ministerium a sort of hierarchical authority, in conflict with the true Lutheran idea of congregational rights and sound principles of Church government. Was not this rather an Episcopal form of government—and even High Church Episcopalianism at that? I admit that there was certainly no "Congregationalism" in it; but I prefer to call it an Apostolic, or rather patriarchal form of Church government—the very thing which the times and the circumstances required. It has often been claimed that only the so-called "Saxon" immigration under Walther had securely established the proper rights and privileges of the Lutheran local congregation in this country, and that not before the formation of the Missouri Synod the idea of the spiritual priesthood of believers had been consistently and practically applied to congregational and synodical constitutions. But it must not be

---

* Documentary History, p. 21, Halle'sche Nachrichten, New Edition, p. 139, seq. with a footnote from Dr. Mann's hand calling special attention to the significance of this application in the remark: "Of greatest importance in showing the relation of the local congregation and its pastor to the Collegium Pastorum."

forgotten that Walther brought his adherents with him from the Home Church in Germany. Muhlenberg had to gather the scattered and neglected Lutherans, and to train the laity into useful and reliable church members, who would be able, by and by, to take an active and intelligent part in the administration of general church affairs. And from the very beginning the representatives of the congregations were present at the synodical meetings, their number not unfrequently exceeding that of the pastors. They were invited to give an account of the condition of their congregations. They were questioned with reference to the life, the character and teaching of their pastor. They were expected, if there was any dissatisfaction or complaint, to lay it before the Collegium Pastorum. But during the first forty-four years of our synodical history the final decision on all points was altogether with the ministers. Not before 1792 did the delegates of the congregations receive the right of voting in the deliberations of Synod. We recognize in this feature also that divine providence and guidance by which the fathers were gradually led on from step to step. Their Church organization on this new ground was to be a steady, healthy growth, not a man-made fabric with shrewdly devised sets of laws, constitutions and paragraphs. It was *"Ecclesia Plantanda,"*—a Church to be planted, as Muhlenberg so happily defined the task of his life in America. And as a plant it was to have its own growth and development. There is a characteristic simplicity and informality in those beginnings. Not before 1781 is there a formal adoption of a constitution. Not before 1786 do we find a printed form of service, an "Agenda." Not even a president is regularly elected in the first meetings. Muhlenberg, as a matter of course, takes the place which Providence has assigned to him. But with all this there is so much of truly pastoral care, wisdom, and conscientiousness in things great and small, that we do not wonder that the people followed their leaders with implicit trust and unlimited confidence.

Things have changed considerably since those days. And, as far as our constitutional provisions are concerned, the change is undoubtedly in the right direction and for the better. The rights of our lay-delegates, representing our congregations, are fully and formally recognized. They stand on equal terms with the pastors in all our synodical meetings. We are happy to say that, as a rule, we have in all our congregations some earnest, devoted, gifted and intelligent men who are well qualified to assist the pastor in the administration of the affairs of the Church. The Lay-Element has been steadily and constantly coming to the front in our Church development. And we have every reason to be thankful for this and to do our very best to obtain and to preserve the hearty concord and co-operation between pastor and people. No one, at the present time, could justly complain that the people had no opportunity to be heard, or that there is an undue desire to rule or coerce the congregations, on the part of the pastors. All questions concerning the inner life or the administration of external affairs, points of doctrine, of order and discipline, of worship and cultus, are freely discussed on the floor of the Synod. And while we want full liberty for all our people to speak their mind on all these subjects, we do claim that those who have devoted their whole life to the study of these things should enjoy the full confidence of our people in the deliberation and decision of those questions. Take for instance things that belong to the sphere of Liturgy and Hymnology. Is it asking too much if we beg that the voice of men who have given years to a careful study of these departments be heard with respect and their advice be received with confidence? Or would it be wise and just to leave the decision as to the character of certain hymns or hymn-books to men who never had an opportunity, and, personally, have not the faculty, of judging on the real value of those collections which, next to the Bible itself, have the greatest influence on the formation and cultivation of the spirit of true devotion in the house of God and at the family altar?

Having thus freely spoken to our people, our vestries and congregations, pointing out what may be lacking here and there, at the present time, let me now address a few words to the pastors in particular—and those that are not directly concerned need not listen to what I am going to say to my clerical brethren. The relations between pastors and pastors, in the early history of our Ministerium, is also most instructive and exemplary. It was characterized by a thoroughly patriarchal spirit. It was a beautiful relation of perfect frankness and mutual confidence. There was on the one side a loving interest, a paternal oversight of the younger members, and on the other side, a filial reverence, modesty and submission to the advice and guidance of the older men. It is delightful to read how those fathers watched over their young theological fledgelings, and trained them and taught them how to become more and more efficient and successful preachers of the everlasting Gospel. Even when they first appeared as applicants for admission they were not, as is now the case, examined all by one large Examining Committee. They were assigned for examination to different groups of members, so that almost all the older members of the Ministerium took part in the actual examination of one or the other candidate. And after they had been formally received they were not left to themselves to struggle alone as best they could. They were kept under constant supervision. They were expected to keep full and regular "diaries," not of their own fanciful ideas and reflections, but recording what they had been reading and studying, and how they had attended to the duties of their ministerial office. They also had to submit their sermons, or sketches of sermons, for the criticism of their seniors, and in our Documentary History you will find the opinion of the fathers on the work of such young beginners as Charles Philip Krauth, Karl Rudolph Demme, and others, carefully and faithfully recorded. Such constant and paternal oversight could not but have the most beneficial results. The relations between the older and younger members of the Ministerium, were of a very intimate, personal and confidential character. There was true pastoral dealing between Brethren and Brethren, kind and forbearing, and yet strict and decisive wherever discipline was needed. It is worth while to read and to study the various cases of discipline recorded in our Documentary History. They are by no means rare. And whenever there was a convention when no complaints of any kind were brought up for adjustment, the Ministerium gave formal expression to its joy and gratification. But whenever a wrong was committed they did not shrink from investigating the case and rebuking the offender where such rebuke was justified by the facts. They would not allow one member of the Ministerium to attack another in the public press; and when once one of the younger men had sinned in this respect he was promptly rebuked and threatened with the revocation of his license, unless he would at once make the amende honorable. All honor is due to those men who carefully weighed right and wrong, punishing the offender and removing the offence that separated them, and then standing manfully and faithfully together, shoulder to shoulder, in joy and in sorrow.

I am well aware that such intimate and personal relations between ministerial Brethren are much more easily maintained in a comparatively little band of half a dozen, or even 50 or 60 pastors, than in a large body counting its members by the hundred. But even in the large body there are smaller local circles of pastoral and synodical Conferences. And why should it not be possible to continue, even under our present circumstances, the same paternal and fraternal spirit of mutual respect, affection and confidence, with all the frankness of Christian correction, discipline, admonition, and instruction? It will indeed be the most precious Jubilee gift to our Ministerium if God in His mercy grant us a rich share of the spirit of our fathers in this respect, that we may all learn to love each other, to bear with one another, to settle our difficulties openly and honestly eye to eye, man to man, and then stand together in sincere fraternal affection. This will indeed be a heavenly "Yea and Amen" to our celebration, the choicest blessing from on high upon this Jubilee.

After the address the congregation sang the hymn: "Sei Lob und Ehr dem hœchsten Gut." This hymn was sung at the dedication of St. Michael's church, August, 1748, and at the laying of the corner-stone of Zion church, May 16, 1766. After the singing of this hymn, the Rev. Geo. C. F. Haas, Delegate of the New York Ministerium, presented the greetings of his Synod, as follows:

JUBILEE GREETING OF THE DELEGATE OF THE NEW YORK MINISTERIUM.

When the mother of the house celebrates her seventieth, or, it may be, her eightieth, birthday, it is not only the children that are still at home who draw nigh to bring their wishes and congratulations and to help celebrate the festal day; nay, the sons and daughters too, who long since have left the maternal home and established their own households, feel constrained to come from near and far to the old home, in order to join with those at home in the expressions of joy and, like them, to bring their greetings. Thus to-day, when the Mother of Synods celebrates not only the seventieth or eightieth, but the one hundred and fiftieth anniversary of her birth, the daughters that have gone forth from her come to unite with her own sons in celebrating the jubilee. It is the first-born of her daughters, whom

REV. GEO. C. F. HAAS

I have the honor to represent, in whose name I bring the jubilee-greeting.

A venerable mother indeed is this Mother Synod with her 150 years of history to look back upon, venerable in her age and yet of youthful freshness and vigor with her 324 ministers and 500 congregations and her manifold activities. But her first-born daughter too, the New York Ministerium, is of by no means inconsiderable size and importance, having in the 125 years of her existence grown to number 150 ministers and about as many congregations, and covering a field that extends 500 miles from East to West and about half that distance from North to South.

In the name of this daughter it is my privilege to present *the Daughter's Jubilee Greeting*, borrowing thereunto from the words of St. Peter: *"The church elected together with you saluteth you."* (1. Peter 5:13). We salute you with the greetings of grateful recognition of God's grace, when looking back upon the past replete with blessings. We salute you again with the greeting of renewed assurance of brotherly love, when looking about in the present abounding in work. We salute you finally with the greeting of fervent invocation of God's blessing, when looking out into the future big with hope.

On an occasion like this, the past claims our first consideration, and looking back we have abundant reason to thank God that He blessed our Church in this Western land with such a Mother Synod. For we may remember with gratitude to God that her foundation was laid by men who not only held fast in faithfulness to the true evangelical faith as confessed by our Church, but who combined with their orthodoxy a true piety of heart and life, and bequeathed to their children this heritage of an orthodoxy conjoined with a genuine pietism. Then too we should remember with gratitude that the Mother Synod at all times strove for unity in the church and evinced this striving not only in her own foundation, but also by her activity in founding and fostering larger general church bodies, and yet she did not seek unity in mere external or official association and combination, but was so grounded in her faithfulness to the Confessions, that even in dark times she again cut loose from the body, which owes its existence to her, but which was not ready unreservedly to accept the doctrine of our Church, and that she valued the truth in love to such a degree as in protest against laxness of doctrine to become instrumental in founding another general body resting on the true foundation without reserve. Finally we may give thanks to God for the missionary and educational work accomplished by the Mother Synod. Of her constant readiness to extend the sway of the Gospel in our land, the many Synods that are more or less, directly children and grandchildren of the old Mother abundantly testify, as also her activity in providing for the education of ministers of the Gospel, which reached its culminating point in the founding of the Seminary at Mt. Airy. And, I venture to say, if the Mother Synod has done naught else to perpetuate and disseminate the teaching and faith of the fathers, she would deserve for this alone to be held in everlasting remembrance in our Church in this country. Therefore in remembrance of these things thank we all our God.

But it is meet and right also at this time to make expression of the thoughts and feelings of the heart with relation to our fraternal connection. Therefore I bring the greeting of renewed assurance of brotherly affection. The Mother Synod and her Daughter have at all times stood in friendly relationship. Founded by members of the Mother Synod, separate from it only owing to the distance separating them, the daughter has in the greater part of the course of her history had the same tasks set before her, the same conflicts to face, as the Mother Synod. Hence they were ever united by close bonds of friendship, as is shown even to this day in the official interchange of delegates between them. It is true, when the daughter has a household of her own, it may become necessary and expedient in minor matters to deviate from the way things were done in the mother's house, but this need not affect their relation. The New York Ministerium has indeed also had its special sphere of labor, and has it still. In her locally more extended field, she has not only in common with the Mother Synod passed through the conflicts against un-Lutheran laxness, but she has had to battle especially also against hyper-Lutheran orthodoxism. Again despite various changes the daughter synod is still prevailingly a German synod, having as such her special mission and requirements. Yet Mother and Daughter have in the end the same task and the same goal, in view of which I renewedly assure you of the still existing bond of fraternal love.

Finally let us turn our eyes to the future. In comparison with the small beginnings 150 years ago, great things have been attained. Yet this is but the beginning of things to be. The Mother Synod and her faithful daughters with her, have a future big with hopes. That these hopes may be realized, is to-day our

REV. JOS. A. SEISS, D. D., LL. D., L. H. D.

fervent prayer offered at the throne of Grace. God our Heavenly Father and our Lord Jesus Christ, the head of the Church, grant that the venerable Mother may continue to prosper and grow to the glory of His name and to the upbuilding of His Kingdom. Let us, however, stand fraternally united through the one faith in the work, praying as did the fathers at the founding of the Synod: "Now we beseech the Holy Ghost to grant us true faith uppermost." Then the Kingdom ours remaineth. Amen.

After the address the service closed according to the form of Vespers in the Kirchenbuch. Hymn: "Ein feste Burg ist unser Gott." Offering for the Jubilee Fund. Versicle. Nunc Dimittis. The Prayer. Hymn: "Nun danket alle Gott." Benediction.

ENGLISH JUBILEE SERVICE.

The second Jubilee Service was held in St. John's English church, Race, below Sixth street, on Friday, June 3, 1898, at 8 p. m. This historic church, the oldest English Lutheran church in America, was filled with an attentive audience. The Rev. S. Laird, D.D., President of the Ministerium, the Rev. S. E. Ochsenford, D.D., English Secretary, and the Rev. E. E. Sibole, D.D., pastor of the congregation, conducted the Vesper Service. The congregation sang the hymn of invocation: "O Holy Spirit Enter In;" the Versicle was intoned by students of the Seminary; Psalm 84; the Lesson; Responsory; and the Festival Address, delivered by the Rev. Joseph A. Seiss, D.D., LL.D., L.H.D., as follows:

JUBILEE ADDRESS.

DEARLY BELOVED,

Fathers, Brethren and Friends:

The oldest in office of the surviving members of our Ministerium, it has fallen to me to addres you on this occasion. Gladly do I respond to the appointment. My only regret·is, that I cannot meet it as satisfactorily as it would seem to demand.

So much has been written, spoken and published on the subject to be treated, and its various aspects have been so fully discussed, that it is hardly possible to find an untrodden path, or to avoid repetitions of what is already quite familiar. Yet, it is to be hoped, that interest has not departed with the novelty, and that the facts have not become too stale to be reproduced.

It is a common instinct of civilized man, and not without sanction of God, to recur to important events and beginnings, and to mark and emphasize particular times and seasons for their special commemoration. Our calendars, both secular and sacred, are dotted over with notations of such anniversaries; and the Church has never been without observances of this sort. From the days of Moses and Joshua, not only every seventh day, and certain weeks in every year, but every seventh year also, was held sacred by all faithful Israelites; while the seven times seventh ushered in the grand year of Jubilee. And while we are not under Law, but under Grace, there would seem to be no hindrance, but abundant divine sanction, for us, in the exercise of our Christian Liberty, to imitate some of these ancient observances, by setting apart certain times for devout jubilation over incidents and events in our own history; especially such as have tended to conserve our spiritual privileges, and our ecclesiastical life.

In the Providence of God, we have been favored with a goodly heritage. From Christ and His apostles, and through the labors of His confessors in more recent ages, possessions have come to us, for which we may well be joyously thankful. And for the effective planting of the same in this Western world, we have ample reason for mutual congratulations, exultant songs and gladsome demonstrations.

A century and a half has passed since our fathers came together, in this city, to form what has since become the ecclesiastical organization in which we rejoice to have membership. The beginnings were small, and against many hindrances; but God led the way, and attended those humble endeavors with His blessing. And so great and valuable have been the fruits thereof, that it has been justly described as "the most important event in the history of the American Lutheran Church of the eighteenth century."

Such an event surely deserves to be singled out for special commemoration by its beneficiaries, at least once in every fifty years. And as, in old times, every fiftieth year was a Jubilee, who will blame us for noting and celebrating this third fiftieth year of our Synod's existence, or for naming our observance of it a Jubilee?

A Synod, as we use the term, implies the presence of congregations; that is, local bodies of Christian people, organized for the maintenance and administration of Christ's Word and Sacraments. And only when these local bodies, through their chosen representatives, unite in a general organization, to which the charge of the common interests is assigned, do we have what we call a *Synod*.

Some congregations existed here and there in America, long before a Synod was formed; but they were few in number, and widely separated amid the wilds of a new country. They were mostly made up of fugitives, driven from their European homes by devastating persecution. They were largely destitute of proper ministerial service, often the prey of unprincipled adventurers, and frequently distracted with internal contentions; besides other troubles and disadvantages. And such was their condition, that little was to be hoped for them but ultimate extinction, which was indeed the fate of some of them.

The Lutheran congregations along the Hudson River, in 1735, moved to initiate the formation of a Synod. Perhaps providentially, all the facts considered, the movement failed. A meeting was held, consisting of three clergymen and nine laymen. It convened in the parish of one of these clergymen, whose attendance was not likely to be otherwise secured. The principal in the movement was zealous enough; but, in temper and egotistic claims to superior orthodoxy, he was a Missourian, "before the time." He considered it a compromise of his Lutheran faith to hear Muhlenberg preach! He was both President and Secretary of the meeting, and was the friend and shield of the miserable Wolf, in whose congregation the meeting was held, and who proved a scandal to his office, and the destroyer of the congregation he was called to serve. And the third of the trio was what might be called a shiftless ministerial weakling, nearly always in hot water, and a poor support to any cause. Of course, the proposed Synod amounted to nothing; and there never was another meeting. More than a dozen years passed thereafter before a Synod of Lutheran congregations in this country was successfully formed; and then it was by a different class of men, from quite another quarter.

On the banks of the Saale, in Saxon Prussia, there stands a small old city, described as one of the ugliest in Germany; full of antique and uncomfortable dwellings, and noted for its crooked streets, bad pavements and offensive smells from the peat bogs and salt springs of the neighborhood. Yet, it is a city distinguished in history for its Orphan House, its University and its Theological Faculty. It was long the literary stronghold of the Pietism of Spener and Francke, the latter being among its honored professors. In the after years, it became a nest of Neologians and Rationalists; but, in its palmier and purer days, it was a great conservator of the church, and fitted and sent forth thousands of devoted preachers in Germany, and a number of devout and able missionaries to heathen lands. And to the men of that city, in the days of the younger Francke, our Church in this country is indebted for the sending of him whom we fondly call our Patriarch, and the other devoted men who followed him.

Henry Melchoir Muhlenberg was not educated at Halle, as some have supposed and said. He studied at Goettingen and was one of the first graduates of that University. He lived one year in Halle as a teacher, and was for a short time a pastor in Northern Germany, before being called to this country. However, it was through the persuasion, and under the patronage of the authorities at Halle, that the suffering Lutherans, on this side of the sea, obtained their chief organizer and missionary bishop.

It is needless to rehearse the condition in which he found things here, the laborious self-denial with which he fulfilled the purpose of his appointment, or the toils and contentions by which he succeeded in establishing and defending the cause of our Church in America. The Swedes were here, they had built for themselves houses of worship and they joyously welcomed him as a co-laborer in the same Mother Church of the great Reformation.

Muhlenberg had been but a few years in this country, toiling in behalf of our Lutheran interests and congregations here, until the necessity of having those congregations united in a general body was deeply felt; and an attempt was soon made to accomplish that end. Two thoughtful, prominent and influential laymen, one of the Swedish congregation and the other from the German, succeeded in bringing together a conference of ministers and representatives in the Gloria Dei (Swedish) Church, May 1744, to consider and act in the case. The purpose of that convention was not then accomplished. It failed by reason of some disagreements on questions of usage, and particularly on the question of the admission of the Moravians into the contemplated union, which was insisted on by the pastor from Lancaster, who was a Moravian at heart, more sentimental than honorable, and came to an unfavorable end.

Nevertheless, that Conference was not fruitless in results. It did much to prepare the way for subsequent harmonious action. It hastened the preparation of a uniform Liturgy for the German churches. It tended to settle the questions between the Lutherans and the Moravians. And it emphasized the desirableness and need of some union of the Congregations, for mutual aid and protection, and the more effective furtherance of the common cause. Nor was it many years until the thing desired was realized.

An important event in the history of the German Congregation in this city was pending for August, 1748—an event which would itself have brought many of the clergy and representative laymen together. Other important matters were pressing for attention. A common Liturgical service was to be considered and adopted. A candidate for the Ministry was to be examined and ordained. And thus a combination of particulars created a sort of necessity for a co-operative Convention, which naturally resolved itself into a Synod.

The appointed time arrived. The clergy assembled. The candidate for orders was examined. St. Michael's church was solemnly consecrated. John Nicholas Kurtz was ordained. And on Monday morning, August 25, 1748, six ministers, with nineteen lay representatives, besides those of the Philadelphia Congregation assembled in the newly consecrated church to transact what further business had called them together. Two clergymen interested in the matter were unwillingly absent; one by reason of the infirmities of age, who sent his approval and fraternal greetings; and the other by reason of sickness, who sent his regrets that he could not participate in what he heartily favored.

Eight is the number of new life and new beginning; and eight was the number of clergymen concurring in the original formation of what is now the Evangelical Lutheran Ministerium of Pennsylvania and Adjacent States. The compact then formed did not at first have a written constitution; neither did it mean independence from the patrons and directors at Halle; but it did mean unity of action and advice, and the beginning of a regular organization for our Church in America.

And a healthful and sound beginning it was, well worthy of perpetual remembrance and honor.

The chief matter in Christianity is its doctrine. Without its distinctive Creed, there is no Christianity. It is divinely required of its ministers to be "nourished up in the words of the faith and of good doctrine,"—to "hold fast the form of sound words"—to eschew fellowship with those who "consent not to the doctrine which is according to godliness." And by the same authority, and for the same reason, all Christians are enjoined to "obey from the heart that form of doctrine" to which their Baptism obligates them,—to "earnestly contend for the faith which was once for all delivered unto the saints"—and not to fraternize with those who "bring not this doctrine;" seeing that "whosoever abideth not in the doctrine of Christ, hath not God." There can, therefore, be no right Christianity—no right Church—no right confederation of churches—without clear and unequivocal acknowledgment of the full Scriptural and historical Christian Creed, and the enthronement and pledged guardianship of the Faith. This has ever been the emphatic teaching of our Church from the beginning, wherever truly herself. And what that Faith is, she has grandly and most fully testified and proclaimed in her Symbolical Books.

To this Faith, founded on the Holy Scriptures, and thus set forth, the fathers and founders of our Ministerium, were all pledged; and this Faith they were all eager and zealous to teach, conserve and defend.

The Swedish pastors were here under willing obligation purely and clearly to teach and preach God's holy and saving Word, as briefly explained in the Symbolical Books accepted by the Evangelical Lutheran Church. The German pastors were the same. Muhlenberg was under pledge to preach and teach according to these same writings, and "never to depart from the sense they give." Brunholtz came charged "to teach the Word of God pure and uncorrupt, according to the Rule and guidance of the Holy Scriptures and the Symbolical Books of the Lutheran Church, and to remain steadfast in this faith until death." And the same is to be said of Handschuh and Hartwig.

And to these pledges and confessions these men were true. The congregations they found, formed and served, acknowledged and held to the same. The houses of worship they built were consecrated to the service of Almighty God, for the teaching and preaching of His Word according to the confessions of the Evangelical Lutheran Church. And the calls they gave for ministers to serve them with the Word and Sacraments, always implied, and more or less distinctly specified, that the ministrations they desired were to be conformed to the faith and usages of the Church of the Augsburg Confession.

And when these founders of our Ministerium came to the solemn act of ordaining men to the holy ministry, they exacted from candidates the same confessional pledges which they themselves had given. One such ordination occurred at their first meeting, and the candidate gave solemn promise that he would "teach nothing, either publicly or privately, save what is in accord with the Word of God, and the Confessional Books of the Evangelical Lutheran Church."

Others were subsequently received, but only upon solemn promise to conform all their ministrations to the Word of God, and the truth of that Word as set forth in our Symbols. When the constitution of the body was matured and signed, every clerical member, by his own sign manual, repeated his profession of adherence in doctrine and life to the Word of God and our Symbolical Books. When Muhlenberg was charged with departures from the pure faith of the Lutheran Church, he vigorously and indignantly challenged his accuser to produce a single instance in which his ministrations had not been in harmony with all our Confessional Books. And whatever any one may have to say to the contrary, the doctrinal foundation on which our Ministerium was originally built, was genuinely Lutheran, pure and soundly orthodox. It was an orthodoxy that embraced all our Symbols, and all that they contain; an orthodoxy, not satisfied with an indefinable *quatenus*, but demanding the definite *quia*, which accepts the Symbols *because* they truly set forth the saving doctrines of Holy Writ; an orthodoxy, not of mere name or frigid thesis, but of living faith; an orthodoxy which does not stop with the facts of Christ *for us*, but lays needed stress also upon Christ *in us*; an orthodoxy which does not kill out charity, or regard practical righteousness as a matter of indifference; but an orthodoxy, like that of John Arndt, John Gerhard, Philip Jacob Spener, the Franckes, of Halle, John Frantz Buddeus, and the like;—the purest, truest and most effective orthodoxy that has ever blessed the Church.

And what is said of the Creed, is equally true of the Liturgy. As there is no Christianity without the one, there is no proper Church without the other. A Creed means a Cult. With the faith delivered unto the saints, there was, and must be, a corresponding Ritual, as divine and essential as the faith itself. According to the New Testament, Confession is to be made; worship is to be celebrated; sacraments are to be administered; and various things are to be done which require time, forms and regulations, as indispensable as they are vital. And God has ever shown himself as strict and jealous with respect to the ceremonial part of right Religion, as to any other part. Cain, Nadab, Abihu, Korah, Dathan, Abiram and Uzziah, in their days, ventured to disregard or change the divine order, but they met with experiences at which we may well stand in awe. Some minor and indifferent things pertaining to sacred worship are necessarily left to human discretion and arrangement; but man might as well think to make a world, as to make an availing Ritual. God must speak, and His Word be consistently accepted, followed and maintained, before we can have assurance of His favor in anything. And to strip Christianity of its Sacraments and their right administration, of its Ministry, of its assemblies for worship, of its appointed times for sacred service, is to damage, mutilate and unmake it; and to that extent to install anti-Christ in the place of Christ. Ritual must go with Doctrine, and Doctrine with Ritual, or both are disabled in their purpose, and must end in blankness.

The founders of our Ministerium well understood this, or were so led by the Holy Ghost, that one of their chief anxieties and efforts was to secure a fixed Liturgical Order. From the beginning, Muhlenberg was deeply exercised on the subject, and gave his best wisdom and energies to it. Sundry consultations and two special conferences were had to mature common forms, true to the Lutheran spirit and traditions. The absence of the proper books to be consulted, was a disability seriously felt; and yet, the result was so close to the *consensus* of the best Lutheran Liturgies of the 16th century, and to what is now contained in our noble Church-Book, that we cannot but wonder and thank God that the work was so well performed and so unanimously accepted as the basis of Ritual Order for our Churches in America. It was a responsive service. And it substantially embodied the pure biblical parts of the Ritual of the Western Church for a thousand years before Luther's time, only purged of the impurities of the Middle Ages.

Yes, the founders of our Ministerium were soundly Liturgical, as all right Christians have need to be. They adopted a uniform and consistent Order of Service and Clerical Ministrations, to which the preachers and congregations alike pledged themselves as a matter of Christian duty, to adhere as closely as possible. Of the man ordained at their first meeting, and of the Catechists whom they appointed, they exacted promise "not to deviate in any way from the Order of Service prescribed by the Synod." And one of the last recorded utterances of Muhlenberg, was, to declare it "a most desirable and advantageous thing," for all the Lutheran congregations in North America to unite with one another in the use of "the same Order of Service, the same Hymn book, and in fraternal sympathy and correspondence in both good and evil days."

Another important thing to the Church is its Polity. It cannot live and reach its ends as a desultory mob. It must have organization. The Scriptures everywhere speak of it as a body —a sacred commonwealth—an organic unity—with offices, relations and activities which require definition and regulation. Order, oversight, and discipline are vital to it. Nothing can be of more importance to a family or a State than sound government. And so the Church must have a Polity, and fixed methods of administration, conformed to its nature and the Divine Word and intention.

But what is a true and proper Church Polity? That is a greatly mooted question on which antagonizing denominations have been built. On the one hand, we are met by a pretentious hierarchism, and on the other, by a lax and disorganizing liberalism, with various degrees of modification, from absolute tyranny to the completest anarchy—all claiming more or less of divine right. Evidently, the final decision on this question has not yet been reached, if indeed it ever can be. Yet, with this question, under many perplexities and disadvantages, the fathers of our Ministerium had to grapple. The people of their congregations were from different lands and nationalities, having brought with them different traditions and customs, some unable to distinguish liberty from lawlessness, and none of them familiarized with the principles of self-rule. And out of these inchoate and discordant elements, a consistent order had to be evolved and established. To accomplish this was no easy task. But, in the good providence of God, it was accomplished, and exactly in the lines with our "Fundamental Principles of Faith and Church Polity." Once for all, the original founders of our Ministerium inaugurated, in all its essential characteristics, the order of government for our Church in this country, which has never since been changed and is not likely ever to be.

The practical conclusions to which they were led, were distinct from what obtained in the old countries. What they inaugurated was not Episcopalianism, nor Congregationalism, nor Presbyterianism, nor Methodism; but Government *by Synods* in which congregations are represented and united, with equal voice and power, to advise and legislate for the general good; an order of government with ample recognition of popular and congregational rights, but without independency from general superintendence and oversight; an order of government in which all that is clearly divine is duly enthroned and guarded, while all else is subject to the best judgment of the Church as a whole. More than this, no one can rightfully demand; and less than this, no proper Christian can rightfully approve. And to abide by this order, with all due respect and obedience to the advice and directions of the Synod, both preachers and people stood solemnly pledged.

Such, then, was the mind and spirit of the men who founded this Ministerium. There have been attempts to give a different coloring to the facts; but they have been signal failures. Nor is it easy to see what better our fathers could then have done than they did in these particulars. And well it would have been, had the same mind and spirit more fully held and governed in the generation that followed. But trying times came, and mistakes were made, seriously interfering with growth and development on these wholesome and conservative foundations.

The long years of the war of Revolution swept some of the most prominent men out of the Synod's ministerial ranks, drove others for a time from their pulpits, depleted many congregations, deprived some of them of pastoral attention for years, and sadly lowered the moral and religious tone of the community in general.

French Infidelity, English Deism, and German Rationalism, insinuated their subtle influences, destroying the faith of some, weakening the zeal of others, fostering the spirit of independence from all creeds, casting out all constitutional mention of our doctrinal standards, and much enfeebling the voice of the Church's Evangelical testimony.

The inevitable change of language was attended with many and great disadvantages. The contentions for the preservation of the German, in a country prevailingly English, were damaging and disastrous. The Ministerium was made constitutionally and exclusively German, as it was not at the beginning. Many of our most advanced people were driven into other connections, or away from all church relations. The few congregations that worshiped in English were formed under great difficulties, and forced into conditions of practical independency. And proper care for the young and rising generation, throughout the length and breadth of the land, so far as respected our Church, was greatly disabled, and often shamefully neglected, either through incapacity, or resentfulness against the use of the English language.

Then came a wave of Puritanic and Methodistic emotionalism, which invaded and distracted many of our congregations, substituting "new measures" for the good old churchly ways, discounting proper and faithful religious instruction, subverting order in worship, and largely superseding the faith with a lawless subjectivism.

And while our Ministerium continued to be impressed with the need of a general union of all our Churches, and in the early part of the present century, even took the lead in a movement to bring about such a union, out of deference to certain jealousies and unreasonable fears of legislative oppression, it consented to withdraw from the whole proceeding, much to the disadvantage of itself, and the Church in general.

All these, with other adversities, combined to remand our Ministerium, and our Church in this country, far to the rear of what might and would have been, had the principles and policy of the fathers always remained in full practical force.

But, amid all these adverse experiences and trials, with Synod after Synod, North, South, East and West, formed out of her membership, the Mother Ministerium continued to live; for the Spirit of life was in her; and she lives to-day, in greater glory and power, than ever before. The salt of her beginning was never entirely lost, and never lost its savor. It still remains to preserve her in all generations to come. Her winter was long and severe, stripping away her foliage, and greatly disabling her fruitfulness; but her energies, though so dormant for a time, were meanwhile maturing for a new putting forth. The latter half of the century now closing, has brought her a new Easter and a blessed Pentecost. We point to the new Seminary, the new College, the new Orphans' Homes, the new General Council, the new Church Book, the restoration of the original name, principles and contemplations, and to manifold and plentiful fruits glowing as with prophetic promises, as the invincible proofs that we have come to the borders of a blessed summertime.

> O Plant of our Fathers! thy winter is past;
> The rose that lived through thee has blossomed at last.

New life, new courage, new activities, new hopes, now pulsate through all thy being. Extremists on the right, and extremists on the left, may criticise and condemn; but the reasonableness of thy position and the justness of thy testimony are being more and more acknowledged, thy conservatism more and more approved, and thy leadership more and more followed. Soundness in doctrine, order in worship, charity in spirit, consecration in work, and honesty in life, are the great Gospel principles to which thou standest pledged, and which, under the administration of thy God must triumph in the end.

Brethren of the Ministerium:—You are to be congratulated on your membership in this venerable Body. Built on the foundation of apostles and prophets, Christ himself being the chief Cornerstone, the world contains no ampler, truer, clearer faith, more unequivocally announced, than that which she confesses. There is no Order of Worship with higher sanctions of Scripture and pure tradition, or more soundly edifying in its use, than that which she accepts and recommends. And since the days of the primitive Church, history tells not of a more consistent evangelic piety than that with which this Synod first came into being. Great and precious, therefore, is the trust committed to our care; and devoutest fidelity to it should be our joy, as it surely is our duty.

For many of us, the time of service here is drawing toward its close. One by one, in brisk succession, our associates have been dropping into the grave. Who will be the next, none of us can tell. But, with heart and energies set to conserve the cause for which our Synod was created, we may be confident of being in the Master's service. And when the celestial curfew tolls the end of this our earthly day,

> Yon stars are but the shining dust of our divine abode,
> The pavement of those heavenly courts where we shall reign with God.

Brethren of other Synods:—Let me yet add a word to you. We welcome your presence with us in these jubilations. You are not without share in the subject of our joy. What we commemorate was a planting from which most of our Synods in America have directly or more remotely sprung. They have all had their part in developing a great Lutheran communion in this Western world. Six clergymen were present when the first Lutheran Synod in this country was formed; six thousand are now on the list, with ten thousand congregations, and a million and a half of confirmed members, supporting twenty-five Theological Seminaries, forty-four Colleges, and nearly a hundred Orphans' Homes, Asylums and Hospitals. You and we have a common share and gladness in what has been thus accomplished.

And yet, like our nation, we are only at the beginning of our mission and destiny on this continent—only getting into position for the work and possibilities that lie before us. And even these preliminaries are still somewhat incomplete. Could we "be perfectly joined together in the same mind, and in the same judgment," all speaking the same thing, as the apostle admonishes, what might we not expect by the time another three half centuries have run their course? With a common faith, a common service, a common spirit, and a common aim, even without regard to oneness of organization, it is doubtful whether the wildest calculations that now could be made would reach the sum of what the Mother Church of the Reformation would achieve under our national stars and stripes. So we all feel; and this we all would be delighted to see. And why, indeed, should it not be the goal for which to aim, labor, sacrifice and pray?

And in the quest for some common ground on which to meet and stand, what better, more natural, more reasonable can be suggested, than that on which this Synod, the Mother of us all, was originally founded? Why should not the principles and spirit which actuated and governed them, satisfy and govern now? Our fathers were careful to keep in full accord with the acknowledged Lutheran standards of doctrine, but without a harsh legalistic and polemic temper. Their orthodoxy was genuine and true to history, but warmed and pervaded with an active piety and the evangelic spirit of love—orthodoxy practically vitalized—which carried the old faith, the old forms, and all the established usages of our Church. This was the grand old ship launched by the saintly Muhlenberg and his faithful associates; and why should any of us wish to sail in any other?

Times came when many betook themselves to other crafts, to the sad disadvantage of the Church, and to their own discredit. But the unfavorable results, along with deeper study of the truth, have fortunately evoked a disposition toward return to the old ship. Gradually we are all coming to a deeper consciousness of who and what we are. There is, happily, a growing appreciation of the fathers, their convictions, and their ways. And as we all fondly cling to their name, why not let them decide for us wherein we still may differ? To what better arbitrators can we refer the case? And grand and blessed would be the gains of accepting and following their decision. The ship they launched 150 years ago, is strong enough for all emergencies, and able to outride all storms. Its Captain is Jesus. Its Chart is the unmutilated Bible. The star by which it steers is the star of Bethlehem. And millions and millions of souls has it safely landed on the blissful shores beyond the swelling floods.

This then is my suggestion, proposal and request, as the proper solution of the problems that hinder our unity: Let us all devoutly cling to the old ship. It is our best and safest dependence. And with honest heart, singleness of aim and fraternal sympathy embarked upon it, we may bid adieu to fear, and with every confidence commit ourselves to God, the lightnings, and the gales.

After the address the service closed according to the form of Vespers in the Church Book. Hymn: "See the Vineyard Thou Hast Planted." Offering for the Jubilee Fund. Versicle. Magnificat. The Prayer. Hymn: "Now Thank We All Our God." Benediction.

OPEN AIR SERVICE.

The third Jubilee Service was held on the Seminary grounds, in Mt. Airy, Philadelphia, on Saturday, June 4, 1898, at 3 p. m. The Rev. Prof. Jacob Fry, D.D., conducted the service. A platform had been erected under the shade trees on the rear campus and seats provided for more than a thousand people. Several thousand people were in attendance. The service was more informal than those previously held. It began with the hymn:

REV. PROF. J. FRY, D. D.

"Lord Jesus Christ be Present Now." Prayer was offered by the Rev. A. Phillippi, D.D., of Wytheville, Va., and the following address was delivered, in German, by the Rev. F. J. F. Schantz, D.D.:

THE MINISTERIUM—ITS CONGREGATIONS, ITS MISSIONS AND ITS INSTITUTIONS OF MERCY.

The observance of the Sesqui-Centennial of the Ministerium of Pennsylvania would be incomplete, if it were simply to commemorate the services of those, who were in these many years ministers of Christ and stewards of the mysteries of God.

At great family reunions, all honor is ever to be given to those, who were ancestors and parents. But who would think of ignoring children and grandchildren? On great festive occasions of institutions of learning, who would think of speaking only of learned and faithful instructors and say nothing of those who were benefited by their services?

Men would be dissatisfied in commemorating great events in the Commonwealth and Republic if only those, who held offices and were leaders in times of peace and times of war, would be remembered and no reference would be made to the citizens for whose benefit the State exists.

Men, who after the great war of 1861-65, visited Washington and witnessed the return of the soldiers, speak not only of the great officers, but also of the many veterans.

Those of us, who were able in the year 1889 to view on one day in New York 50,000 soldiers and on the following day 75,000 civilians in procession on the occasion of the Centennial of the Inauguration of the First President of the United States, received impressions that will never be forgotten. We felt proud that we are Americans.

On Friday, May 13th, of this year, I was with many Pennsylvanians at Mt. Gretna and witnessed the grand review of nearly 10,000 Pennsylvania troops. The Governor and his staff were honored by citizens. But the sight of the officers of regiments and of companies and of the strong men in the ranks, who had all become soldiers of our great Republic and were ready for active service in the present war, touched the heart of the true patriot and led him to pray: "God bless all the soldiers and sailors of our Republic in the present great conflict, the end of which no man knows."

How small a part of the Ministerium of Pennsylvania the Ministers and Lay-delegates constituted who attended meetings of the Synod in past years and who meet in this important year in the history of the Ministerium.

What a magnificent sight would be presented to us to-day, if in this year of Jubilee, the entire Ministerium of Pennsylvania had been brought to this city in which in August, 1748, the Ministerium was organized. Had arrangements been made for a review of the entire Ministerium, Pastors and Church Councils would lead the Congregations and Superintendents and Teachers their Sunday-Schools. To-day we have no such a review of the Synod and therefore it is fitting to speak of those, who are yearly represented at meetings of the Synod and particularly at the meeting in this Jubilee year.

I.—THE CONGREGATIONS OF THE MINISTERIUM.

On this festive occasion we are to remember the congregations of the Ministerium. Before the formation of our National Government there were colonies with varied forms of government and the National Government was formed to meet the wants of the different parts of the Republic. Before the organization of the Ministerium in 1748, congregations existed already for many years and the Ministerium was formed to meet the wants of the congregations. Not all of the congregations then existing participated in the formation of the Ministerium and yet a large territory was represented: Philadelphia and Germantown, New Providence (Trappe) and New Hanover (Faulkner's Swamp), Saucona and Upper Milford, Lancaster and Earltown (New Holland), Tulpehocken and Nordkiel (Bernville). At all of these places congregations existed. The congregations at Macungie, at the Jordan and in Salsburg in Lehigh County, at Mosilim, in Alsace, Schwartzwald and Allemangel in Berks County, at the Swatara, the Quitapahila and Bindnagel's in Lebanon County, in Warwick (Brickerville) and at Moden Creek in Lancaster County, and the congregations in York County, and in other parts west of the Susquehanna and congregations in other parts of Pennsylvania and New Jersey were not represented. To-day we should remember the congregations of 1748. They had plain church-buildings and school-houses. Their meetings in the churches were precious to them. They often

REV. F. J. F. SCHANTZ, D D

came great distances to the churches. Their participation in the services was fervent. Their souls were refreshed by the means of grace. To-day we also think of the congregations of 1898 with their fine church-buildings, their regular services on each Lord's Day and the services of the Sunday-school. God's Day, God's House, God's means of grace are to be highly prized, thus also the services of the congregation. To-day we think of worshipers who meet in great cities and towns, we think also of the congregations in villages and rural districts, in agricultural, manufacturing and mining regions. Whilst the city congregation has its magnificent church-building, worshipers in rural districts have the same means of grace and the same opportunity to join in the worship of the Triune God. God is no respecter of persons, the Lord knoweth not only those who are his in the great cities, the Lord knoweth also those who are his in rural districts. All who are in true fellowship with the Head of the Church, are His people, and He delighteth in those who are truly His children. The greatest riches of the Ministerium of Pennsylvania are the precious souls in true fellowship with the Triune God. To-day we think then of the great number of baptized children, the many children in the Sunday-schools and the great number of the confirmed members of the congregations, precious as they have been purchased by Christ, precious as they are also individually temples of the Holy Ghost. Our greatest joy should thus be this day "in the Holy Christian Church, the communion of saints" to whom not only "the forgiveness of sin" is secured, but also the "resurrection of the body and life everlasting" are promised. Our joy is on this day in the great number of the Saints on earth. But shall we forget those, who in the past 150 years were also part of the congregations on earth, but who are now in the church triumphant? The congregation on earth has a House of Worship, but also its God's acre, and when the congregation observes its Jubilee, Centennial and Sesqui-Centennial, it does not forget those, who have already attained the precious gift of God—eternal life through Jesus Christ our Lord.

Congregations have many reasons to thank God for the services rendered them by the Ministerium. The Ministerium has been the conservator and teacher of the true Faith, confessed by the Apostolic Church, and also by the Church of the Reformation; the Ministerium has given the congregations the proper formula of the Constitution of the congregation; it has prepared the Hymn-Book and Agenda of earlier years, and in recent years secured the Kirchenbuch and the Church-Book for the congregations, and the excellent Sunday-School Books for the Sunday-Schools; it approved and favored the supply of Sunday Schools with superior books for teachers and scholars for instruction; it recommended good Church papers for adult members of the congregations, and instructive papers for the Sunday-Schools; it cared for the founding of a good College and a good Theological Seminary; it aided poor young men in their preparation for the ministry; it examined candidates for the holy ministry and provided for their ordination; it watched over pastors of congregations and assisted congregations in the division of large pastoral charges and the formation of new pastoral charges; it has always wisely counseled congregations when strife occurred in the congregations; it protected congregations from the wicked assault of a hostile world, and the intrusion of sects, which endeavored to lead congregations astray. For all these services the congregations owe thanks to the Ministerium. But we must not forget on this festive occasion, that without a proper appreciation of the actions of the Ministerium on part of the congregations and the constant willingness of the congregations to aid in the execution of the resolutions of the Ministerium, the Ministerium could not rejoice in the congregations as it does in this Jubilee year. The future prosperity and the proper care of the congregations depend upon the loyalty of the congregation to the Ministerium and constant willingness by proper approval of the actions of the Synod and aid by prayer, offerings and services, to advance the interests of the united congregations.

There were times, in which some congregations were not loyal to the Synod, and did not follow the Counsel, and wished to be independent. Other congregations yielded to fanatical influences and suffered much. Some congregations had sad experiences occasioned by strife among members. We have reason to rejoice that our congregations are generally true to the Ministerium. We rejoice in the number of congregations and the great number of souls in the gracious Covenant with the Triune God.

II.—THE MISSIONS OF THE MINISTERIUM.

On this festive occasion we must not forget to refer to the Missions of the Ministerium. Patriarch Muhlenberg had but for a short time entered upon the regular ministrations to the congregations, which had called him, when appeal after appeal came from Christian people in other regions, that he might help them, as they were as sheep without a shepherd. To meet such wants, it became necessary to have co-laborers, who came from the Fatherland. The Church on the Continent did not only send men to this country, but also material aid as is evident from old Church Records containing acknowledgments of the aid received from the Fathers of Europe.

The labors of Muhlenberg and his co-laborers were to a great extent Missionary work. Congregations which in time grew stronger and richer were appealed to for aid of the poor congregations in the new world. In the year 1770, Patriarch Muhlenberg visited pastors and congregations in the Eastern part of the Kittatinny Valley and was appealed to by a congregation, that he would care that the richer congregations would aid it. The younger Muhlenberg (Frederick Augustus Conrad) in the beginning of the seventies of the last century visited Shamokin, preached from a porch, the people had assembled before the house, and were protected from the rays of the sun by saplings that had been brought for the purpose. He baptized children, conducted the service of confession and absolution and administered the Holy Communion. This also was Mission work.

Later, traveling preachers were sent out to supply the spiritual wants of the people, who had settled in the western part of Pennsylvania, in the South, and in regions further west. Aid extended to our new Synods was also Missionary work. Shortly before the middle of the present century there was an increased interest in Home Missions, and this interest grew from year to year so that for a number of years the Ministerium has yearly aided from 50 to 60 missions within its own bounds. A careful examination of the minutes of the Ministerium, proves that from 100 to 200 congregations received aid in our own time. Congregations which were at one time small mission congregations, aided by the Ministerium or directly by congregations, have become large and rich congregations, and are now able to contribute much to missions. The Mother Synod has however often extended aid beyond its geographical limits. Western Synods—also the Synod in Canada and the Synod in Texas have often acknowledged aid extended to them. How could the General Council have carried on its German Home Mission Work and its English Home Mission Work without the aid extended by the

Ministerium? It was the Mother Synod, which first furnished the means for Father Heyer's work in India, and to-day the interest in Foreign Missions increases and the offerings grow larger from year to year. Mission work will not cease as long as there are souls that need the means of grace, and as long as the Church still heeds the last command of the blessed Lord and continues to pray to the Lord of the Harvest to send laborers into the Harvest.

III.—THE INSTITUTIONS OF MERCY OF THE MINISTERIUM.

We must acknowledge that we have not in this line, what we ought to have. But we have reason to thank God for the Orphans' Home and the Asylum for the Aged and Infirm at Germantown. The gradual growth of the Institution at Germantown to its present condition is one of great interest. The blessings which orphans and the aged have received and are still receiving will never be fully known in this world. We have also reasons to rejoice that a New Orphans' Home has been established at Topton, and will be soon opened for the reception of orphans who have no Christian home. Although the Ministerium has no organic connection with the Emmaus Orphans' House, of Middletown, Dauphin Co., and the institution is not aided by the congregations, we must not forget that the Orphan House which now cares for 30 orphans, does so by means of the bequest of George Frey, and that Mr. Frey in his will provided that the children be taught daily God's Word and Luther's Catechism. So much the more ought we to rejoice since the institution exists by the bequest of one man, and is a Lutheran Orphans' Home. The orphans in the Home at Germantown number nearly 100, the Asylum numbers nearly 40 aged persons. Emmaus Orphans' Home has 30 orphans, may the Topton Home also soon number 100 orphans. We also have reason to rejoice in view of the increased interest in Deaconess Work, which increases yearly and bestows rich blessings by its services rendered to the sick and suffering in hospitals, congregations, and in private residences. The services of ministers, who minister to the poor and suffering in various institutions, to meet their spiritual wants bestow great blessings.

But, I would ask, should we not have some special provision for aged and infirm ministers of the Gospel, who after long and faithful services find the evening of their life full of cares in view of the want of means to meet their daily necessities. An aged minister wrote to me some time ago and stated that he desired to serve a small congregation with the ability which he still possessed. I replied that I did not know of such a congregation and added that in our day many congregations did not wish to have aged ministers. He wrote again and said that he knew that many congregations did not wish to have ministers advanced in years, and that this reminded him of the action of men, who in former days crossed the Alleghenies with their freight wagons. An aged horse would be unhitched and turned into the forest to die from want. A young horse would be put in the place of the old one and the driver would be delighted. But the young horse would often be given to such ugly pranks that the driver sincerely wished he had kept the old horse longer. Some of us saw not long ago in a paper a picture of a church building with a representation of people entering a church; on the left column of the church door a placard showed the following: "Our new preacher will preach to-day." The new preacher approaches the church on a bicycle. The old minister is seen on the burial ground near the church. He is seated on a stone. His carpet bag is by his side. He is looking at the grave of a beloved one. The minister's old horse is also seen on the burial ground, trying to find a little grass. No X-rays would be required to find his ribs! No comments are neccessary.

I would, however, say the Church ought not to forget its aged and infirm ministers and make the necessary provision that the evening of their life may be full of peace and hope. At the place where I reside, the Reformed Church has a beautiful Home for aged and feeble ministers. The large house and the grounds were presented by a lady, a member of the Reformed Church. The Church pays the expenses of the Home. I have often wished that our Church had such an institution. Possibly some one here to-day may say, "thus shall it be soon."

For the growth of the congregations, for the prosperity of the Missions, for the increase and liberal support of Institutions of Mercy, for the full endowment of our College and our Theological Seminary, for the aid of young men preparing for the holy ministry, our pastors and congregations should show a sincere interest and constantly labor, and with the blessing of God our beloved Zion will grow and increase in power and blessings.

Let us not forget that the Ministerium resolved to raise $150,000 as a thank-offering in this Jubilee year. May the love of our blessed Saviour, who gave himself for us, the labors and trials of the reformers of the sixteenth century, the self-denying services of Muhlenberg, and his co-laborers and their successors, the blessings which our ancestors, our parents and we have enjoyed to this day, and the desire to perpetuate rich spiritual blessings to future generations, incline us to liberal offerings in this Jubilee year. The Lord loveth a cheerful giver, and may the Lord find us willing to contribute according to our ability. Many here to-day may participate in the Bi-Centennial of the organization of the Ministerium of Pennsylvania, but many of us will then be no longer here. May God grant us grace and lead all of us—that we then may have part in the glory of the Church Triumphant.

This was followed by the hymn: "Come, Thou Almighty King," after which the Rev. Edward F. Moldehnke, D.D., President of the General Council, presented

GREETINGS FROM THE GENERAL COUNCIL.

It behooves the General Council to participate in the celebration of the Jubilee which in these days is held by the Pennsylvania Synod. For as the State of Pennsylvania is the Keystone State of the Union, even so the Pennsylvania Synod is the Keystone Synod of the General Council. Not only was she instrumental in laying the foundation of the General Council, but by her untiring labors in the various fields of church work, viz: in missionary enterprises, doctrinal discussions, forms of worship, education and literature, she has in a marked degree contributed to its development and consolidation. I consider it as a very happy coincidence that on the Seminary grounds the congratulations of the General Council are offered; for the fraternal address, ordered by the Pennsylvania Synod and sent out to the various Lutheran Synods in 1866, and which eventually led to the organization of the General Council, was composed by the professors of the Seminary (Revs. Dr. G. F. Krotel, Charles P. Krauth, J. W. Mann, C. W. Schaeffer) and Dr. J. A. Seiss, the President of the Board of Directors; and it is to the Seminary that the General Council owes so much of its power and influence.

To me personally it is a great pleasure to be present on this festive occasion, for since my arrival in this country in 1861, I conceived a predilection for the Pennsylvania Synod. When I saw the many large boxes sent from Pennsylvania to Wisconsin,

REV. EDW. F. MOLDEHNKE, D. D.

though myself not amongst the favored ones who received the gifts, yet I was heartily thankful for the sympathy shown the poor Wisconsin brethren by the Pennsylvania Synod, and when as a traveling preacher I followed the missionary footsteps of the sainted Father Heyer in the wilderness of Minnesota, or when I occasionally preached in the stately church built by him opposite the Capitol at St. Paul, I was reminded of the love and liberality of the Pennsylvania Synod. Thus it was quite natural that, when I was about to return to the old country in 1866, one of my last acts was an effort to prevail upon the Wisconsin Synod to accept the invitation of the Pennsylvania Synod and participate in the formation of the General Council.

We congratulate the Pennsylvania Synod not only on its great age, although even this, especially in the new and restless country of ours, certainly is a sign of a strong vitality and the gracious preservation by the Lord, but also on account of the many rich blessings which she has received and bestowed upon others. A good inheritance has come down to her from her fathers and founders, viz., the true Lutheran faith according to the confessions of our Church; and although, our country being the echo of Europe, afterwards Rationalism and Unionism, indifference concerning true Lutheran docrine and practice for a time hindered her development more or less, yet all these evils as well as the hurtful excitement of the so-called new measures of revivalism had to make way for a sober and healthful Lutheranism. It is the sobriety and circumspection, the steadfastness of purpose and perseverance, inherited from the German ancestors, it is the moderation without bitterness, animosity or fanaticism, it is the steady, zealous activity in the sphere of doctrine and in all good works, it is all these virtues of the Pennsylvania Synod which merit our praise and admiration. Many have most willingly adopted and vehemently employed the "horns and teeth" which Luther disdained at the Diet of Worms, but the Pennsylvania Synod has chosen the way of peace and faithfully kept it. In spite of the ungrateful conduct of many and in spite of the defection of some daughter synods she has proved herself as a devoted, faithful, homely, patient mother. As a true mother she never sought the vainglory of ostentatious fashionableness, nor has she aspired to the new-fangled behavior of the "new woman," but in all simplicity and candor she is following the example of the old fathers and clinging to the faith once delivered to the saints. Being indeed the "Mother Synod," she always was and is even now the leading Synod of our Church in the East and has therefore to meet the great issues and to shoulder the vast responsibilities that are implied in such a leadership. In her development we see what by the Lord's blessing may become of small beginnings in this country of far-reaching possibilities and great successes. Well may the Synod apply to herself the cheerful declaration of the Apostle: "Having obtained help of God, I continue unto this day" (Acts xxvi:22.) And we having her welfare at heart, say with the Psalmist: "Pray for the peace of Jerusalem; they shall prosper that love Thee. Peace be within thy walls and prosperity within thy palaces!" (Ps. cxxii.)

The large assembly sang the hymn: "Glorious Things of Thee Are Spoken," and then the Rev. Prof. Theodore L. Seip, D.D., President of Muhlenberg College, delivered the following address in English:

THE COLLEGE OF THE MINISTERIUM.

The Ministerium of Pennsylvania, in arranging to celebrate its sesqui-centennial Jubilee, wisely provided a place on the program for the presentation of its educational work in the college and theological seminary. The Synod's growth and development, nay, its ability to maintain its very existence, are due largely to the work done for our Church by these institutions of learning during the past three decades. It would have been impossibe, as far as we can see, to have procured from other sources the kind of ministers needed to provide for the vacancies caused by death, to say nothing of the many laborers required for the reaping of new fields within the bounds of the Mother Synod, that were ripe for the harvest. Under God, the educational work lies at the foundation of the Church's growth in every direction.

It is, therefore, eminently appropriate that these important interests of the Ministerium, the College and the Seminary, should be represented at this Jubilee celebration.

The duty and privilege of speaking for Muhlenberg College has been assigned to me. I therefore ask your attention and indulgence during the brief time allotted to me.

Muhlenberg College bears the name of the illustrious founder of our Ministerium—Henry Melchoir Muhlenberg.

REV. THEODORE L. SEIP, D. D.

It is well known to the historians and scholars of our Church that the Patriarch Muhlenberg had already felt, in his day, the necessity of having our own institutions in this country for the education of young men for our ministry, but, it is not so well known that, in his wise foresight, he had purchased the ground for the Ministerium, with the view of locating such institutions on it. The war of the Revolution came on and frustrated his plans so that he did not live to see them realized.

The dark ages of our Church followed, when indifferentism, rationalism and unionism had their sway, and for a long time, very little thought was given to this most important matter, although there were always those in the Ministerium who felt the need of such institutions, and put forth efforts to secure them. This is not the time or the place to enter into a detailed narrative of the efforts made by members of this Ministerium, themselves and jointly with others, notably the work of Muhlenberg's distinguished son, Henry Ernst, at Lancaster. It is sufficient to say that they all failed to meet the real wants of our Ministerium. The first successful effort in this direction was made by the men of faith and heroic courage of a generation ago, when this Ministerium, under their leadership, founded the seminary in 1864, and made it possible to establish the college in 1867. When the seminary had opened its doors, it soon became apparent that the Ministerium needed a college on its own territory, inculcating the same faith and cherishing the same spirit; in its religious services, worshiping the Lord in the beauty of holiness, by using the same Scriptural forms as the seminary and the Synod itself. It needed a college to prepare its young men for the seminary, so that there might be a steady supply of liberally-educated students for it from the territory of the Ministerium itself.

Whilst this was the prime need, a college was necessary also to develop the educational interests of our Synod among the lay element so that our youth might be educated in an institution of our own Church, in accordance with its faith, spirit and usages, and thus be saved to our Church, instead of being educated away from it, and lost to it with all their influence and power for usefulness, as has often been the case. The college, therefore, being needed, under the providence of God, was called into existence, and Muhlenberg College was founded and consecrated in the name of the Triune God, to the cause of Christian education in our Church.

Allentown, beautiful for situation, in the picturesque Lehigh

Valley of our State, became its site. This flourishing inland city was then already a strong Lutheran centre and has been the seat of institutions of learning for nearly a century. Academies of high grade had been founded here, one as early as 1813. In the providence of God the location of the college was provided for by one of these institutions, which may be regarded, in a certain sense, as the historical origin of Muhlenberg College. The Allentown Seminary, whose grounds and buildings became the property of the college, was founded in 1848, and the college will for this reason, celebrate a semi-centennial in connection with its annual commencement, on June 23 of this year.

It may be of interest to state in this connection, that the grounds on which the college stands, as well as those occupied by our thelogical seminary were formerly the property of the same owner, Chief Justice William Allen, of colonial fame, whose son, James, was the founder of Allentown. The institution retained the name of the Allentown Seminary until March, 1864, when it was regularly chartered by the Legislature of Pennsylvania, under the name, style and title of the "Allentown Collegiate Institute and Military Academy." Under this charter it possessed full collegiate powers and privileges. Notwithstanding this fact, it remained in reality merely a private school.

Many of the pastors and laymen of the Lutheran Church in Allentown and vicinity were warm friends and patrons of the institution through all the years of its existence, and they repeatedly directed the attention of the Ministerium of Pennsylvania, to which they belonged, to the importance of securing it for the Synod. Committees, who were charged with the duty of looking after the educational interests of the Chruch in the institution at Allentown, were appointed by the Synod, and reported annually from 1860 to 1867, and as early as 1862, the Synod recommended the institution to young men who desired to prepare for the ministry, Many of the public-spirited citizens of Allentown, anxious to secure the benefit of a higher institution of learning for their young city, co-operated earnestly and efficiently with the Lutheran pastors and laymen in the effort to enlist the interest of the Ministerium, and to establish a college. The agitation and labors of seven years, from 1860 to 1867, resulted in the formation of a joint stock company for the purchase of the propery and the management of the institution by a Board of Trustees, two-thirds of whom were to be elected by the stockholders, and one-third by the Synod from among such of its members as were stockholders. The charter was amended in 1867 to meet the new requirements.

The new board elected under this charter took charge of the institution April 4, 1867, and unanimously elected the Rev. Professor F. A. Muhlenberg to the presidency of the college. The friends of the new enterprise were exceedingly encouraged by his final acceptance of the position, after he had at first declined it. It gave prominence and standing to the college from the start. At a meeting of the board, held May 21, 1867, the institution was named Muhlenberg College, in honor of the distinguished patriarch of the Lutheran Church in this country.

At the meeting of the Synod, at Lebanon, June, 1867, the following was reported: "The committee appointed in 1860, charged with the duty of securing an institution at Allentown for our Church, has the pleasure of reporting that with the help of God, its labors of seven years have resulted in the attainment of the chief objects in view of its appointment, namely, to secure the continuation and advancement of the school established nineteen years ago, for the promotion of Christian education, to bring this institution under the supervision of our Church, and to raise it to the full-grade of a college. Muhlenberg College can and will soon be formally opened with very fair prospects of success."

The Synod, at this meeting, elected its representatives on the board, very heartily approved the election of the Rev. Dr. Muhlenberg as president of the college, and earnestly commended the institution to the patronage of the Church.

It is not my purpose to attempt a review of the history of the college or the administrations of its presidents. For a full history up to 1892, we refer all interested to Dr. Ochsenford's Quarter-centennnial Memorial Volume. I desire briefly to show the origin of the institution and its relation to the Ministerium. At the meeting of the Synod at Allentown, May, 1877, the full control and responsibility for the maintenance of the college were assumed by the Ministerium by its election of the entire board of trustees. This right had been vested in the Synod by a change in the charter, which had been secured for that purpose by the stockholders. Within the last decade, the Synod has become the absolute owner of nearly all the shares of the capital stock of the corporation by the free gift and transfer of them to the Ministerium by the original stockholders or their heirs.

The Synod, therefore, and not the corporation, has the virtual ownership as well as the control of Muhlenberg College.

The few moments allotted to me forbids more than a mere allusion to the changes that time has brought with it in the personnel and officials of the institution; the addition of new instructors to the faculty; the death of the lamented Professor Davis Garber, and the appointment of Professor Philip Dowell to the chair of scientific department; the celebration in 1892 of its quarter-centennial; the reduction of the debt and the increase of the endowment fund; the repairs and recent improvements to the property; the laboratories and equipments of the institution; the faithful labors of the trustees, especially of its Central Executive committee and its officers; the fidelity of the faculty, and other matters of recent years, that well deserve fuller mention.

Where so many have faithfully served the college, it would be invidious to mention any by name.

Our past history has been one of alternate struggle and relief, the Lord sending help when the need was the greatest.

It remains for me to state briefly what the college has accomplished under all its disabling conditions.

It has continued, without interruption, from the beginning until now, the beneficent work for which it was founded. It has educated and graduated four hundred and sixteen men, who, with comparatively few exceptions, have been a blessing to the Church and the world as men of character and worth, useful in their several occupations. Hundreds of others, not graduates, have been helped to a better education than they would otherwise have received, from the fact that the college brought the needed facilities within their reach.

Over half the number of the graduates, and many non-graduates who received their education in the college have devoted themselves to the ministry of the Gospel. Over one hundred and twenty-five of the ministers, now in connection with our own Ministerium, received their college training in Muhlenberg College, a number itself larger than the membership of many respectable Synods.

We may well ask whence we could have obtained so large a number of ministers for our own pulpits to say nothing of others that have been supplied by us, if the college and the seminary had not been founded when they were.

Although the college is only thirty-one years old, and most of her graduates are young men, yet a goodly number have

MUHLENBERG COLLEGE, ALLENTOWN, PA.

already distinguished themselves as professors in our theological and literary institutions, as pastors of most important charges and congregations, as missionaries of the cross; as superintendents and officers of public instruction; as authors, editors and writers for the religious and secular press; as laymen prominent in the professions of their choice, some having won honorable names and titles in public life.

Who can measure the influence for good upon our fellow men, which so large a body of educated Christian gentlemen has already exerted, and will exert in the course of their lives? Many a struggling soul has been cheered on its way, many a death-bed has been made easier by the kindly ministration of these men.

Eternity alone will reveal the extent of the beneficent influences which have emanated from this institution. We think we remain within the bounds of modesty, when we claim that Muhlenberg College has done a great work for the Church and the world during the brief period of its existence, in comparison with the limited means which have been placed at its command. Much more, doubtless, would have been accomplished, if the educational work of the Church had received from our people the attention and support which it deserved. But we thank God for the good which the college has been permitted to do in the past, and we trust Him for the future. When we look back over the history of the college, and consider the difficulties in the way of its successful establishment and maintenance, the completion of older and munificently endowed and equipped institutions on the same territory; the various claims pressing on the congregations and the Synod, and the indifference and dense ignorance of many in regard to the importance and needs of such an institution, we are filled with wonder and gratitude to God that it has successfully passed through these trials, and still lives to bless the Church.

The year of its founding, 1867, was a year of Jubilee in the Church of the Reformation. It was the three hundred and fiftieth anniversary of the nailing of the "Ninety-five Theses" by Luther on the church door at Wittenberg. Our Ministerium proposed to celebrate the event by raising one hundred thousand dollars, one-half of which was to be given to the college to assist in defraying the debt which the trustees were obliged to make in order to procure its property and buildings. Very nearly one hundred thousand dollars were raised, but the share which should have gone to the college, was largely used by the congregations for local objects such as church buildings, repairs and the like. A comparatively small sum, about eleven thousand dollars was given to the college. Thus a heavy debt rested upon the institution from the beginning, in every way impeding its progress and limiting its usefulness.

The present year, 1898, marks another Jubilee in our Church on this territory, the one hundred and fiftieth anniversary of the organiation of the "Mother Synod," the Evangelical Lutheran Ministerium of Pennsylvania and adjacent States, to which we belong. The Synod has solemnly resolved, in the fear of the Lord and in reliance on His help, to signalize this Jubilee by raising one hundred and fifty thousand dollars, to enable it to remove the debts still resting on its college and seminary, and to promote the Synod's educational and missionary work. The college is pressed for room to accommodate its students and departments of instruction. It needs new and additional buildings to successfully meet the demands of the present, to say nothing of the future. These cannot be supplied unless our good people furnish the means. May we not, therefore, hope that our pastors and congregations, heeding the lesson of disappointment arising from the diverting of funds from the general to local congregational objects in the Jubilee of 1867, will unite their efforts, and strive earnestly to secure the offerings for which the Synod justly asks in commemoration of the Jubilee of 1898?

May we not hope that in addition to the contributions of the congregations, those to whom the Lord has entrusted large wealth, may be moved by His spirit to devise liberal things, to give their thousands to the cause of Christian education in Muhlenberg College?

There is wealth enough and to spare in the hands of our people, and there is no object to which it could be devoted where it would be more good to our fellowmen in Church and State than the cause of the Christian education of the young; for upon this, under God, depends the perpetuity of both. Unless the youth are brought up in the nature and admonition of the Lord, we cannot expect them, when old, to walk in His ways.

In order to secure faithful members of the Church and upright citizens of the State, we must look to the Christian training of the young, and the maintenance of Christian institutions of learning.

May God grant that, as a result of this Jubilee celebration, the

REV. HENRY E. JACOBS, D. D., LL. D.

institutions of the Synod may be richly blessed with the earnest prayers and liberal gifts of His people. Amen.

After the address, the audience sang the hymn, "A Mighty Fortress is Our God," and then the Rev. Prof. Henry E. Jacobs, D.D., LL.D., Dean of the Theological Seminary, delivered the following address in English:

THE THEOLOGICAL SEMINARY OF THE MINISTERIUM.

Before proceeding to the theme assigned me, I have a message of an unusual character to deliver. The words of congratulation from distant synods, were read this morning. But the word entrusted me comes from one who has passed from these earthly scenes, and has entered into the full realization of his heavenly citizenship. A father in Israel who tarried among us, until this Jubilee was already in prospect; a child of this Ministerium, the son and grandson of honored pastors; an active participant in fifty-nine annual conventions; its President for an unusual, if not unprecedented number of terms, the ex-President of both the General Bodies of which this Ministerium is the mother; for fifteen years the Chairman of the Faculty of the institution upon whose grounds we have assembled, the late Dr. C. W. Schaeffer looked forward towards this occasion with most earnest expectancy. But fearing lest, before this day would dawn, his strength would fail he asked me, and repeatedly reminded me of my promise, that, should God remove him, I should assure the assembly of his interest and blessing; and "tell the brethren," were his pathetic words, "to remember me."

Assuredly no such message is needed to remind us of those into whose labors we have entered; but the assurance of their abiding interest, until the very moment they entered within the vale, encourages us amidst the frequent trials of the way, and inspires us with enthusiasm in continuing the work they have begun.

The wonderful foresight of the fathers who planted this Ministerium and the general outline which they framed for the organization of the Church, can be ascribed to nothing less than a clearly discernible Providential guidance. Planning far beyond their times and opportunities, or even those of their children, their schemes must have seemed to the men of the next two generations as the dreams of mere visionaries. Among these schemes was that of the seminary. To such a degree of confidence in its necessity and possibility had Muhlenberg advanced, that, according to an indenture in our Archives, in October, 1749, the very next year after this Ministerium was organized, he purchased the ground for its future home, and transferred it to Dr. Ziegenhagen, of London, and Dr. Francke, of Halle, in trust forever for this purpose, with several others therein mentioned. The history of that purchase is yet to be traced. Like many other pious wishes of the fathers, it lay dormant for over a century. Muhlenberg never abandoned it, but, until life's end, continued to urge its importance.

John Christopher Hartwig, one of the six pastors present at the founding of the Ministerium, and the preacher of the ordination sermon, one hundred and fifty years ago, acquired a large estate in the State of New York; and, on his death, in 1796, left it all for the establishment of an institution for the training of Lutheran missionaries and pastors, with Dr. John C. Kunze, President of the New York Ministerium; Dr. J. H. Helmuth, President of the Ministerium of Pennsylvania, and Hon. Frederick Augustus Muhlenberg, active both in Church and State, as its directors. Mr. Muhlenberg soon died; Dr. Helmuth felt his parochial duties too urgent to admit of his acceptance of the trust, and thus lost for our Ministerium its representation; while the bulk of the estate in the hands of its trustee—not its surviving director—dwindled to a small fraction of what had been bequeathed. Dr. Kunze alone remained alive to the importance of the trust. In most eloquent and just words, he plead for the education upon American soil of German-American pastors and insisted that the very face of the will showed that Pastor Hartwig meant that in this work the two Ministeriums should unite. But in vain. Providential hindrances deferred the plan once more. Roused probably by Dr. Kunze's appeal, the Ministerium of Pennsylvania adopted in 1805 another plan to reach the same result. A "Tract" was widely circulated through its congregations in behalf of "an institution for the training of young ministers." But the title is misleading; as the "institution" was only a beneficiary fund, while several of the more scholarly pastors were appointed theological preceptors, and rudimentary seminaries were established in several parsonages. All honor to the men, who struggled hard to meet, with insufficient resources, the crying want of their times; and who constantly discharged the duty under protest, and with the declaration that nothing but a regular organized seminary could meet the demand. A time came when an elaborate scheme was proposed for co-operation with the Reformed in the establishment of a Union Seminary; but the Ministerium never approved it. Then, for awhile, it seemed as though all wants could be met by co-operation with institutions, which some of the children of the Ministerium had founded but entirely beyond its control, and for whose course and the character of whose training it could have no, or, at most, very small responsibility. The dream of Muhlenberg gradually forced itself upon the attention of the Church, as it returned to a heartier appreciation of the faith taught by Muhlenberg. It became necessary to provide for the training of students both in the German and English language, in the doctrines, for whose teaching this Ministerium was founded, and according to the pledge required by the Ministerium at its first ordination.

The name of every man who responded to this call thirty-four years ago deserves, at this convention, reverent recognition. Of one, the Rev. Benjamin Keller, who departed this life, after the Ministerium had resolved upon this movement, but before it could be executed, the President reported at the next meeting: "The project for the establishment of a Theological Seminary in the genuine spirit of the Lutheran Church, appeared to have such a quickening and reviving power upon him, that for a while it arrested the progress of his disease, and seemed even to whisper the promise of recovery." Never did an institution of this kind begin with a stronger corps of professors. The Church realized the fact that, in order to properly meet the demands of the hour, it could be satisfied with nothing less than the very best at its disposal. It placed its recognized scholars and leaders at the front as the leaders of the generations of ministers who were to be trained, as they were of those already in the office. Charles Frederick Schaeffer, a veteran theologian, who had proved his gifts, as a teacher, by distinguished services in two theological seminaries; Charles Porterfield Krauth, universally conceded to be the most scholarly product of the Lutheran Church of America; William Julius Mann, whose thorough university training, brilliant genius and stupendous industry, would have made him eminent in any land or calling; Charles William Schaeffer, whose message you have just heard, and Gottlob F. Krotel, whom we had hoped to greet to-day, and who will receive in due time the credit which his unwearied efforts by voice, and pen and private influence have contributed to the fruits enjoyed at this hour—such was the body of devoted men in whose hands the most important work of the new seminary was placed. At that critical hour, among the important acquisitions made by the Ministerium was the eloquent preacher and distinguished author, Joseph Augustus Seiss, who at once threw all the weight of his influence into the movement, and who, through all these years, has, amidst all the trials through which the seminary has grown into power, been its most active and staunchest friend, and excepting one year, the President of its Board of Directors. With them, among the departed, stood Samuel K. Brobst, who for years had been agitating the necessity of the seminary, in order to satisfy the needs of the German and Pennsylvania-German elements of the Synod; and Beale M. Schmucker, whose clear and systematic methods and wide information were always at its service; the Geissenhainers, Frederick W., the first President of the Board; and August T., for a time its Treasurer; Christian F. Welden, its first agent, and John Kohler, whose loss is recent, and to whose modest, quiet, unobtrusive influence, probably is due the securement of the largest amount ever given towards the endowment. Nor must we forget the devoted laymen, who placed their wealth at the service of this cause—Charles F. Norton, whose example in endowing the first chair assured the beginning of the enterprise, and Hiester H. Muhlenberg, who provided the beginning of the library; Mrs. Burkhalter, of New York, who endowed the chair of Church History; Henry Singmaster and wife, whose bequests came just when the Seminary most needed them, and Miss Elizabeth Schaeffer, to whose means this campus owes so many of its improvements. Others have contributed no less in proportion to their means, but these stand forth as brilliant examples of the good that may be accomplished by the judicious use of gifts.

The work was not of man; it was of God. He raised up friends. He has led us from the very beginning by a way we knew not. The best-formed plans, to accomplish important results, have been repeatedly defeated; and then, by the wonderful working of His Providence, a greater result has been attained without any plan whatever. When the seminary was a matter of synodical resolution, at the meeting of 1864, it was not seriously believed that the end would be reached for some years to come; and yet, to the astonishment all, the classes were organized the very first week of the succeeding October. So,

THEOLOGICAL SEMINARY, MT. AIRY, PHILADELPHIA.

in every crisis, as the signal has been given to move forward, the way has unexpectedly opened as we advanced. Providence has often led the Seminary beyond what was intended. If it has been retarded at any time, it has been so only because of our fears and unwillingness to assume responsibilities.

Forty years ago, a corps of two, or at most, three professors, was deemed sufficient for any of our seminaries. The founders of this seminary had in mind the fact that, for efficiency, professors must devote themselves to particular branches, and be devoted and aggressive students in their own departments, instead of having their attention distracted by a multiplicity of interests. True, it must be conceded, that the scheme projected could not be immediately carried out, because of a mistaken economy that suggested that, as a temporary expedient, a Professorship could be a mere sidework to the pastoral office, upon which a professor could be supported, while the Seminary received his services as a gratuity, or what was scarcely more. But the plan was outlined, and placed before the mind of the Church, to be realized hereafter. A faculty of five members was none too many, then, with less than a score of students. Nor is a smaller number to-day adequate, with an attendance six times as large.

Before the seminary was opened, the theological course had been shortened from the three years prescribed by the Ministerium for its private students, to two years. When this seminary recurred to the standard, it was generally adopted. Thirty was the maximum number in attendance on any of our institutions in the East, before 1864. When, as the number gradually rose, one of the Faculty expressed his opinion that, in the remote future, the seminary might reach the extraordinary high number of 60 students, he was wildly rebuked by one of his colleagues for allowing his imagination to run ahead of his sober judgment. For two years, we have exceeded 90. Crowded out of the center of the city, we have come hither for ampler space to a choice spot, upon which the eyes of Muhlenberg often rested, as he rode to and from his Barren Hill congregation, with mind absorbed in the perplexities of that church, for which he risked so much, and in his projects for the secure establishment of the Lutheran Church in America. Dreamer as he was, little did he imagine that this resort of the highest social circles of the city, adorned lavishly with what wealth can bring, would be consecrated to the work for which he spent his life. Here our home was prepared by those who knew not for what they were toiling. Of us, as of

Israel, it may be said: "I have given you a land for which ye did not labor; of the vineyards and olive-yards which ye planted not, do ye eat." Many of these trees have been thriving here for considerably more than a century, and have even been shrouded in the smoke of battle in the struggle which gave to our country its place among the nations of the world. But the ampler space here provided, is already more than filled; and were it not for the opening of other institutions, manned by our own graduates, on the territory from which we formerly drew students, we would be compelled to appeal for a new dormitory.

If the contributions of those who have been connected with this seminary as directors, students and professors, were to be expunged from the literature of the Church a computation might be made as to what this would imply. The "Church Book," in English and German; the "Common Service;" the annotated edition of the "Halle Reports;" the "Conservative Reformation;" the "Life of Muhlenberg;" the "Lectures on Gospels and Epistles;" the "Ecclesia Lutherana," and the long list of publications in Dr. Seiss' "Bibliography;" the "Saatkoerner" and the "Life of Krauth;" the translations of "Tholuck on John;" "Lechler on Acts," and that once widely used text-book in many seminaries and colleges, Kurtz's "Sacred History;" the translation of Ledderhose's "Life of Melanchthon;" the "Church Year;" "Evangelical Pastor, and Liturgics;" the "Way of Salvation in the Lutheran Church;" the "Elementary Homiletics;" the "Way of the Cross;" the numerous manuals of Dr. Weidner; the "Negative Criticism;" the "Life of Melanchthon;" and the "Parish Hymnal;" the historical researches of Dr. Nicum, the popular books of Dr. Trabert, the solid Swedish-American "Dogmatik" of Dr. Lindberg, are some of the volumes, to say nothing of the extensive literature of Reviews, and the wide influence of editors of Church papers, German, English, Swedish, Norwegian and Icelandic, represents a portion of the loss that would be sustained. The Revised English translation of the Bible would vanish. The best of American Cyclopædias (Johnson's), the valuable additions of our historiographer, Dr. Ochsenford, to the Annual Supplement to "Appleton's Cyclopædia," and his contributions to the Dictionary of American Biography, Dr. Krauth's contributions to McClintock and Strong's Cyclopædia, and Dr. Mann's to Herzog's "Real Encyclopædia," should be added. Julian's "Dictionary of Hymnology" bears many traces of the industrious aid of Dr. B. M. Schmucker. In "The Lutheran Commentary," with its twelve volumes, eight of the contributors would be excluded. In the Memorial Volume, commemorating this Jubilee, a result has been attained that would have been impossible, but for the facilities afforded by the present arrangements whereby professors and students are brought together within one enclosure, and enabled to work harmoniously and efficiently upon one common literary undertaking, with material that the past history of this synod has brought to our hands. The editors of the Sunday-school literature of both General Synod and General Council, are among our alumni.

In the theological faculties of Salem (Va.), now discontinued, Newberry, S. C., Rock Island, and Chicago, Ill., and Minneapolis, Minn., it has had representatives, all the professors at Chicago having been trained here.

With the class graduated this week, the seminary enrolls among its alumni 533 names. Thirty-three have been called from us; 456 have left the seminary, able to preach in the English, and 301 in the German language. Over 200 other students have taken only a partial course. They have come hither, from all parts of the United States, except the Pacific Coast and the Rocky Mountain and Gulf regions; from Canada, Manitoba, Nova Scotia, Sweden, Norway, Denmark, Switzerland, Austria, Russia, Holland, Iceland, Brazil, East India, Persia and Japan. Former students are preaching the Gospel from the extreme northwestern portion of this country in the German Home Mission fields of Assiniboia, on the borders of the Arctic zone, and the English work in Oregon and Washington, to the Foreign Mission fields among the Telugus, in India. They are laboring in all parts of the Lutheran Church of this country. The General Synod and United Synod of the South have honored our Alumni with the office of President, and the United Norwegian Synod has made one of these professors in its theological seminary. It has its representatives in the ranks of the Missourians, and a very few in other denominations, partially because the seminary opens its doors to all without regard to denominational origin, and partly because once in every ten years, some student is induced to change his ecclesiastical connection—a proportion so small that it only shows the loyalty of the entire spirit of the seminary to the Lutheran Church.

Nor are those trained here mere theorizers. They are active in every sphere of the Church's work. Missionaries, superintendents of missions, directors of orphanages, hospitals and deaconesses' homes are among them. It has its roll of martyrs who have laid down their lives in the mission field (Carlson, Artman, Dietrich), and of others who by their no less self-sacrificing devotion in posts of hardship at home have shown themselves worthy of their calling. The spirit of the sainted Heyer, the great pioneer of Lutheran missions in the West and among the heathen, the "cosmopolite," as he used to call himself, born in Europe, a pastor in America and a missionary in Asia—a prominent figure already in the proceedings of the Synod recorded in the volume just issued, and, for fifteen months, having his home within our seminary, beginning to write the chronicles of its history, and consecrating it to the cause of missions by his intercourse with the students and his death within our halls, still lives among us, and we pray may never be forgotten.

Of the 324 ministers enrolled at the last meeting of the Ministerium, 232, i. e., 72 per cent., had been students of this institution. As successive classes have gone forth, the Synod has gained even more than was immediately anticipated. Many new congregations have been established and old parishes divided, a work that otherwise would have been impossible. During these thirty-four years, the synod has grown from 121 to 324 ministers, and from 192 to 500 congregations; the missions sustained within the synod, from 9 to 52; and the number of students for the ministry aided from 8 to 45. A majority of the pastors of the New York Ministerium and the Pittsburg Synod were trained here. The founding of the seminary carried with it, as a necessary result the founding of Muhlenberg College, and of the General Council, with all the influences proceeding from these centres. Other seminaries and colleges profited by the example given by the liberality displayed at the founding of this seminary. From the time of the bequest of Hartwig, such munificence as that which endowed the Norton Professorship had not been known in the Lutheran Church; and its indirect results in the emulation that enabled others to expand their courses and facilities are such that in them all should rejoice.

Far from the purpose of the founders of this seminary, however, was the ambition to create an institution that should administer to their own personal renown. Alike in simplicity and purity of character, they were men of prayer, who had left the impress of their character upon the congregations they had served, and the various circles in which they moved. Through severe conflicts, they had learned the preciousness of the Lutheran faith, and deemed no sacrifice to maintain it too great. What they believed from the heart they were ready to confess; and in this, lay their greatness. Their firmness and positiveness were not bigotry and narrowness. Depth of conviction was united with sympathy with every form of truly Christian life. Appreciation of the past of the Church, did not prevent them from realizing the importance of the present. They were not romanticists whose great aim it was to simply reproduce the conditions and methods of an idealized past; nor were they swept away by the intoxication of an imagined progress, that regarded all the lessons of their predecessors unworthy of attention.

The seminary stands to-day firmly grounded upon the entire body of the Lutheran Confessions. It has receded in no respect from the testimony of its founders. Current discussions, instead of in any way undermining our faith, in the old Confessions, the old Bible, the old Christ, only render them all the more necessary and precious. The most lauded assumptions of those who boast of their scientific acquisitions, for which they demand a revision of the old faith we recognize as chiefly the reiterations of long ago refuted and long ago forgotten heresies. The Lutheran Church of America has been saved from much of the rationalism that has done sad work in certain influential communions only because it was fortified and armed for the contest by the discussions connected with the founding of this seminary.

Its growth has been probably more and more in the direction of a deeper reverence for the Confessions, and back of them, for the fresh and living theology of Luther himself, in preference to the scholastic methods and somewhat legalistic spirit of the later period of the dogmaticians, even though we insist upon the thorough study and discriminating use of her treatment. It is the aim of the seminary to go back of the Confessions to the Holy Scriptures themselves, and to follow a Luther, a Melanchthon, a Chemnitz, in renewed attention to Biblical and particularly Pauline theology. It gratefully uses modern methods. It aims to discriminatingly study every system and tendency that occupies wide attention, and to seek for the underlying truth that gives every error its charm. It realizes that every age and place and language must have its own peculiar way of confessing the one truth in Christ; and that the definitions of the XVI Century, after being thoroughly learned and their relations understood, must be recast into the language of the XIX Century. We are practical only when we adjust what is accidental in Christianity to the peculiar calling of each day and hour.

The Language Question must be decided according to the principles that the Lutheran Church has laid down concerning adiaphora in her Confessions. On this subject, there has never been a division within the Faculty. The English-speaking professors have never been hostile to the use of the German, and have prized it not only for its practical necessity, with so many of our congregations requiring German pastors, but, even beyond this, because the German is the language of the theology, and the devotional literature, and the very life of our Church in the past. They would, if possible, have every Lutheran pastor and student of theology thoroughly infused with the spirit of the German Church life of his fathers, and entirely at home in its expression in words. If possible, they would have the classics of the Lutheran religion, particularly the principal writings of Luther, thoroughly studied and assimilated. The German professors have, in no way, been lacking in loyalty to the interests they were called to serve, because they have, in like manner, appreciated the importance of the English language for the needs of our Church in this country. Apart from all personal preferences, and any attempts to regulate it by synodical legislation, the language question is solved by the life of the Church, as water ever seeks its level, without regard to our efforts to turn it into another channel.

Important as the Seminary deems a thoroughly scientific course, this never so absorbs the attention that the great aim of the ministry is forgotten, which is not that of becoming erudite doctors, or prominent leaders, or pastors of congregations, whose prosperity evokes the admiration of the world, but of humble service, even to the humblest of the people, and of seeking the approval of God, rather than the admiration and favor of men.

"Ask, and ye shall receive" is a title that may be written over every page of its history. "Ye have not, because ye ask not," may also be true in regard to certain necessities. If the bolt of lightning that only a few nights ago, rent the bark of yonder pine had been diverted a few feet to the south, we would probably be lamenting the loss of a library that no amount of insurance could replace. When it is remembered that the students who have been in attendance this year, will, in three years, be the pastors of no less than 25,000 communicants, and the spiritual guides of 100,000 people, and that, for their efficiency, so much depends upon their reading, and habits of study while here; when we remember also that the seminary is not only for the instruction of students in the rudiments of theology, but the arsenal where the weapons are to be found to repel attacks and the store-house whence seed is to be drawn for future harvests; when we appreciate the fact that to the library not only the students must resort for the gathering of information, but that the professors must have no excuse for ceasing to be growing scholars as long as they teach and should be furnished every appliance to keep pace with current discussions and methods; when we reflect upon the fact that we will be judged by others to a great extent, according to the attention which we pay to our library, which they correctly regard an index of our scholarly resources and tastes—we are certainly not overstating the case when we declare that no stately Church building erected, at any important center, at thrice the cost, could compare in influence, as a witness to our faith, to that which the erection and equipment of such a building would afford. The most valuable apparatus, for our purposes, has been gathered. Our library of over 23,000 volumes has been solidly built from the foundations. Scholars of other churches who visit it, are astonished that it should be left so long in such peril. If it should perish, its loss is not simply that of the Seminary, but of the entire Church, of theological science in general, of all liturgical scholars, and historical investigators, and the country at large. If what single congregations can do for their local interests, without any very great difficulty, a synod of 500 congregations hesitates to undertake, the individual or group of individuals, may be found to respond to this clear call.

For the past, we are thankful. For the present, we gird ourselves for still more earnest and abundant work, and ask your sympathy and prayers that we may not fall beneath the standard that has been set us. The future is God's, to Whom belongs this Seminary, as one of His instrumentalities for saving souls, and hastening the coming of His kingdom. He who has safely conducted it through all perplexities unto the present, will continue to aid it far above all we can ask or think.

The assembly sang the Doxology, "Praise God From Whom All Blessings Flow," and the Rev. J. B. Remensnyder, D.D., of New York City, pronounced the benediction.

INDEX.

Biographical sketches and histories of congregations are indicated in heavy-faced characters.

For alphabetical list of portraits see page 7.

Abele, J. F. 25, **203**.
Albert, J. J., 26, 70, 180, 186, 189, **203**.
Alleman, M. J., 66, 191, **205**.
Altpeter, P., 52, **205**.
Anspach, J. G., 81, 159.
Anspach, J. M., 26, 63, 70, 81, **206**.
Anstadt, P., 109, 144, 156, 160, **206**.
Arbogast's, Zion, **134**.
Armstrong Valley, St. Jacob (Miller's), **105**.
Augusta, Lower, Twp., North'd Co., Elias, **186**.
Augustaville, see Cross Roads.

Babb, Isaiah, 26, 39, 42, 45, 47, 49, 68, 69, 74, 76, 122, 124, **207**.
Barnitz, F. A., 122, **207**.
Barr, W. P., **207**.
Bartholomew, O. D., 120, 124.
Bayer, J. F., 109, 116, 117, 144, 187, **208**.
Beach Haven, St. Paul, **46**.
Beavertown, St. Paul, 27, 28, **31**.
Beaver Twp., Columbia Co., St. Peter, 118, **122**.
Beaver, West, Twp., Snyder Co., see Lowell.
Bellharz, J. J., **208**.
Bell, J. W., 123.
Berg, A., 181, 185, **208**.
Berwick, St. John, **50**.
Bergner, J. G. C. A., 99, 100, 108, 109, 113, 114, 144, **209**.
Binninger, J. J., 45, 48, 73, 120, 124, 125, **209**.
Bloomsburg, 25.
Bockstahler, 89, **211**.
Botschaft's (Grubb) Church, **82**.
Boyer, S. R., 25, 188, 189, 190, 191, **211**.
Braunwarth, W., **209**.
Breinig, A. J. L., 181, 182, 185, **210**.
Breininger, H., 36, 150, **210**.
Brenninger, see Breininger.
Briar Creek, 25, **41**.

Bruning, H. H., 27, 36, 156, 160, **210**.
Bucher, J. C., (Ref'd), 150.

Casper, A. B., (Ref'd), 31, 36, 150.
Catawissa, St. John, 25, 26, 27, 28, **52**.
Cherry Twp., Sullivan Co., 26.
Clymer, H. T., 181, 182, 185, 187, **211**.
Coal Twp., North'd Co., 26.
Cogan Station, St. Michael, 26, 27, **57**.
Conyngham, 25.
Cooper, C. J., 75, 100.
Cornman, W. O., 26, 63, **212**.
Cross Roads, (Augustaville), Emanuel, 26, 28, **183**.

Danville Conference, 21, 22, 23.
Danville, St. John, 60, **65**.
Danville, Trinity, 25, 26, 27, **60**.
Darmstetter, J., **212**.
Derr, J. H., (Ref'd), 31.
Dewart, 26.
Diefenbach, J., (Ref'd), 47.
Dietsch, L., **212**.
Dimm, J. R., 69, **213**.
Dormantown, St. Mark, **32**.
Druckenmiller, G. D., 82, 85, 88, **213**.
Drumheller, C. K., 27, 63, 64, 105, 120, 171, 173, **214**.
Dry, C. F., 120, 122, 124, **214**.
Duenger, R., (Ref'd), 31.
Dushore, Peace, 28, **72**.
Dushore, Zion, 28, **75**.

Early, J. W., 19, 21, 26, 27, 51, 67, 68, 69, 70, 75, 77, 81, 88, 90, 92, 116, 121, 127, 153, 156, 159, 160, 171, 181, 184, 185, **214**.
Eberts, E. H., 183, **215**.
Edmonds, L. C., (Ref'd), 36.
Eggers, H., 68, 89, **219**.
Eggers, L. G., 180, 185, **216**.
Ehrhard, C. J., 161.
Eister, G., **219**.
Elizabethville, Salem, 28, **100**.
Engel, J. F., 39, 42, 68, 188, 189, **219**.

369

Engel, W. G., (Ref'd), 146.
Enterline, J. M., 36, 78, 82, 83, 85, 107, 136, 137, 141, 143. **220.**
Erie, C. L., 73, 74, 75, 76, **220.**
Erlenmeyer, C. G., 19, 21, 36, 37, 80, 81, 82, 85, 87, 133, 134, 150, 156, 159, 160, **223.**
Espig, C., 107, 156, **225.**
Eyer, W. J., 19, 25, 26, 27, 62, 63, 62, 65, 66, 67, 68, 69, 120, 125, 127, **225.**

Fahs, J. F., 193, **228.**
Felix, John, 111.
Felty, J., **228.**
Fifth Conference, 18.
Fogelman, D. L., 67, 69, 123, **228.**
Fox, W. B., 26, 39, 43, 46, 47, 49, 122, **229.**
Freeburg, St. Peter, 26, 27, **78.**
Freemont, St. John, (Schnee's), **85.**
Fridrici, M. C. S., 39, 41, 42, **229.**
Fries, Y. Henry, (Ref'd), 37, 79, 190.
Fritzinger, J., (Ref'd), 144.
Fry, Jacob, 148.
Fuchs, A., **229.**

Gearhart, Isaac, (Ref'd), 79, 81, 83, 146.
Geiger, W. H., 100, 102, 103, 124, 146, 171, 176, 179, **230.**
Geisenhainer, A. L., 127.
Georgetown, Trinity, 27, **173.**
German, J. P., 43, 47, 120, 122, 124, **230.**
German, W., 36, 37, 82, 83, 85, 87, 189, **230.**
Getz, Carl C., 107.
Globe Mills, St. Peter, 27, **149.**
Gratz, Simeon, 27, **98.**
Greenwald, E., 62.
Greymiller, Geo., 36, **231.**
Groff, J. R., 27, 63, 67, 68, 69, 71, 186, **231.**
Grotbe, Edward, **232.**
Grovania, St. Peter, 28, **69.**
Grubb's Church, see Botschaft.
Grubler, J., **123.**
Guensch, G. F. W., 89, **232.**
Guensel, M., 35, 85, 143, 156, 160, **232.**

Haal, Peter, (Hall), 42, 62, **232.**
Haas, G. C. F., Jubilee Address, 310.
Haas, J. W., (Ref'd), 88.
Hassinger's, see Paxtonville.
Hasskarl, W. R. C., 25, 69, 100, 109, 114, 144, 180, **233.**

Hazleton, 25.
Hebe, David, **113.**
Heim, Geo., 37, 156, 158, 160, **233.**
Hemping, J. N., 97, 98, 103, 105, 108, 111, 114, 139, 141, 144, 170, 173, **234.**
Henkel, D. M., 25, 36, 51, 56, 61, 62, 68, 69, 120, **235.**
Hennicke, F. F., 89, **238.**
Henry, S. S., 27, 43, 47, 90, 122, 173, 181, 185, **238.**
Herbst, John, 31, 35, 78, 82, 85, 138, 141, 143, 156, **238.**
Herndon, Zion, **115.**
Hill, Reuben, 161.
Hillpot, Jos., 58, 98, 102, 103, 104, 105, 142, 146, 173, **239.**
Himmel's Church, **109**, 138.
Hintze, Fred., **239.**
Hinze, E., 85, 141, **239.**
Hoffman, C. F., (Ref'd), 81.
Horine, M. C., 27, 63, 70, 71, 93, 115, 118, **239.**
Hornberger, J. F., 68, 69, 113, 180, 185, **240.**
Horne, A. R., 194, 196, **240.**
Hottenstein, A. R., (Ref'd), 146.
Hursh, Stephen, **241.**

Ilgen, L. A. W., **242.**

Jacobs, H. E., Jubilee Address, 357.
Jasinsky, F. W., 82, 156, **243.**
Jaeger, Nathan, 91, 97, 141, 170, **243.**
Jersey Shore, Zion, 21, 26, 27, 28, **89.**

Keiser's, St. Paul, **88.**
Keller, I. B., 161.
Kempfer, D. O., 32, 36, 38, **243.**
Kerschner, C. A., 100.
Kerschner, J. B., (Ref'd), 105.
Kessler, J. P., 39, 42, 44, 47, 52, 65, 68, 190, **243.**
Kline, S. S., 19, 26, 124, **244.**
Klingler, J. W., 59, 74, 77, **244.**
Kohler, John, **244.**
Kopenhaver, W. M., **245.**
Kramer, J. P. F., 67, 107, 141, **245.**
Kratzerville, Zion, 27, **157.**
Kuhn, S., (Ref'd), 106.
Kunkle, G. G., 43, 47, 61, 183, 185, 196, **245.**
Kuntz, W. H., 58, 89, **246.**

Laitzle, W. G., 52, 106, 118, 120, 127, **246.**

Lampe, F. C. H., 193, **246.**
Lancaster, 27.
Lazarus, R., 36, 150, **247.**
Lebanon, 28.
Lenker, M. B., 85, 92, 94, 102, 103, 104, 139, 173, 181, 184, **247.**
Lentz, A. P., 133, **247.**
Leopold, O., 103.
Lewisburg, 26.
Lindenstruth, L., 52, 120, 127, 129, 185, **247.**
Line Mountain, 23.
Linsz, Aug., 89, **248.**
Lochman, Geo., 138.
Lock Haven, First Church, 27.
Lowell, West Beaver Twp., Snyder Co., St. John, 27, **33.**
Lykens, St. John, 23, 27, 28, **91.**
Lykens Valley, St. John, 27, **136.**

Mahanoy, Little, Immanuel, **112.**
Mahanoy, St. Peter, **143.**
Mahanoy, Upper, St. John, 27, **116.**
Mahoning, see Ridgeville.
Mainville, Emanuel, 53, **118.**
Martin, C., 174.
Mayne, J. W., 77.
McClure, St. Matthew, **34.**
Mening, George, 111.
Meyer, Hans, 200, **248.**
Middlecreek Twp., Snyder Co., St. Paul, **150.**
Mifflinville, St. John, 25, 26, 27, 28, 118, **120.**
Miller, C. P., 189, **248.**
Miller, H. P., 157, **249.**
Milton, 25.
Moeller, H., 141, 143, **249.**
Moldehnke, E. F., Jubilee Address, 442.
Montana, St. Peter, **131.**
Moyer, Philip, 111.
Mt. Carmel, Zion, **165.**
Myers, U., 120.

Neiman, J. H., 27, 28, 52, 53, 120, 121, 127, 129, **250.**
Nescopeck Twp., Columbia Co., Mt. Zion, **43.**
Nescopeck Twp., Columbia Co., St. James, **48.**
Neuman, E. J., 106, 113, 114, **250.**
Neumann, C. J. M., 180, 185, 186.
Numidia, St. Paul, 53, **125.**

Oak Grove, Trinity, 28, **70.**
Ochsenford, S. E., 27, 28, 32, 34, 77, 88, 94, 129, 130, 131, 156, 160, 178, 185, 199, **250.**
Oefinger, C., 26, **252.**
Oriental, St. Paul, **133.**
Orwig, S. P., 32, 150, **251.**

Paxtonville, Christ, **35.**
Perry Twp., Lycoming Co., 25.
Pillow (Uniontown), Zion, 26, 27, **171.**
Pflueger, A. P., 27, 28, 103, 120, 185, 189, **252.**
Pflueger, O. E., 28, 32, 33, 34, 37, 38, 36, 98, 142, 179, 200, **252.**
Philadelphia, 26.
Plitt, J. F., 39, 41, 52, **253.**
Pomp, Thos., 44.

Raker, J. H., 182, **253.**
Reading, 26.
Reber, O., 57, 59, **253.**
Reed, D. E., 58, 90, 193, 134, 150, 174, **254.**
Reed, E. L., 52, 85, 156, 160, **254.**
Renninger, J. S., 124, **254.**
Repas, J., 189, 190, **255.**
Richfield Church, **133.**
Rick, W. F., 196, 197, **255.**
Rickert, W. H., 27, 196, **255.**
Ridgeville (Mahoning), St. James, 27, **67.**
Rife, Zion, **103.**
Ringtown, 23.
Ritter, I. B., 106.
Ritter, J. H., 142, **256.**
Rizer, Peter, 149, **256.**
Roney, W. E., 64, 118, 120, 122, **256.**
Rosenberg, L., 59, 90, 199, **256.**
Ruthrauff, F., 66, 68, 149, **257.**

Salem, Snyder Co., Salem, 14, **146.**
Sailman, C. F. F., 25, 49, **257.**
Sander, John, **257.**
Sanner, D., 93.
Schaeffer, C. F., 62.
Schaeffer, C. W., 155.
Schaeffer, G. J., 133, 134, **258.**
Schaeffer, Wm. Ashmead, 178, 179.
Schantz, F. J. F., 139, 173, Jubilee Address, 333.
Scheffer, N., 39, 43, **258.**
Scheirer, O. S., 32, 33, 34, 37, 38, **259.**
Schindel, Jer., 52, 65, 68, 97, 100, 101, 120, 122, 125, 141, 171, 172, **259.**

Schindel, J. P., Jr., 31, 36, 37, 113, 149, 160, **263**.
Schindel, J. P., Sr., 25, 31, 36, 37, 47, 79, 82, 85, 87, 98, 108, 112, 113, 129, 141, 156, 159, 160, 170, 171, **265**.
Schmidt, J. C., 109, 113, 114, 144, 145, **268**.
Schmidt, J. H., 162, 180, 185.
Schnee's Church, see Freemont.
Schontz, Jacob, 142.
Schuetz, Jared, **269**.
Schultze, G., 25, 26, 57, **269**.
Schwartz, Elias, 65, 66, 68, **269**.
Scranton, 26.
Seip, T. L., Jubilee Address, 346.
Seiple, T. J., 36.
Seiss, J. A., Jubilee Address, 217.
Selinsgrove, First Church, 25, 27, 28, **151**.
Sell, D., 61, **270**.
Shade, J. S., 81.
Shamokin, Grace, 28, **161**.
Sixth Conference, 15.
Smith, J. W., 31, 36, 37, 66, 68, 82, 85, 87, **270**.
Smith, Lewis, 63, 74, 89, 129, **270**.
Snable, H. G., 82, 85, 88, 146, 148, 150, **270**.
Spaeth, A., Jubilee Address, 296.
Spieker, G. F., 34, 94, 148.
Sprecher, S., 62.
Steck, Thos., 26, 27, 43, 47, 96, 97, 122, 140, 142, **271**.
Steinhagen, E. F., 90, 199, 200, **271**.
Steinmetz, J. W., 68, 144.
Stetler, D. M., 28, 32, 33, 34, 36, 38, 107, 109, 150, 182, **271**.
Stetler, Eugene, **272**.
Stetler, I. H., **272**.
Stock, V. G. C., 39, **272**.
Stoever, C. F., 52, 99, 174, 189, **273**.
Stone Valley, Zion, 27, 139, **169**.
Stover, M. J., 68, **273**.
Strauss, A. M., 59, **273**.
Strodach, H. B., 74, 75, 77, **273**.
Stupp, S. B., 40, 43, 47, 51, **274**.
Sunbury, St. Luke, **176**.

Tower City, 23, 27.
Treverton, Zion, 26, 27, 28, **180**.
Troxelville, St. James, 37.
Turbotville, Zion, 25, 26, 27, 28, **188**.

Uhrich, John M., 27, 93, 139, 171, **274**.
Ulrich, Daniel, 85, 107, 143, 170, **275**.
Ulrich, L. Domer, **274**.
Ulrich, S. J., 157, **275**.
Ulrich, Wm. S., **275**.
Umbenhen, J. H., 77.
Ungerer, J. J., 68, **275**.
Uniontown, see Pillow.
Unkerer, August, 100.
Urban, St. Paul, **114**.

Vera Cruz, St. Luke, 27, **175**.
Voss, J. H., **276**.

Waage, Frederick, 189, **276**.
Wagner, R. S., 26, 27, 45, 49, 74, 92, 93, 97, 124, 138, 142, **277**.
Wahrmann, H. E. C., 91, 94, **277**.
Walter, Isaac, (Ref'd), 37.
Walter, J. C., 31, 35, 36, 37, 78, 79, 82, 85, 86, 107, 141, 143, 146, 156, 157, 170, **277**.
Walz, F., 91, 92, 93, 97, 114, 140, 141, 144, 171, 175, **279**.
Wampole, J. F., 19, 26, 27, 28, 70, 81, 82, 85, 87, 145, 150, 156, 160, 161, 164, 166, 178, 179, 185, 189, **282**.
Washingtonville Church, 25, 26, 27, **190**.
Weber, Carl, 89, **282**.
Weland, W. H., 38, **283**.
Weicksel, F. A., 129, 131, **283**.
Weicksel, H., 124, 130, 162, 164, **283**.
Weicksel, W., 162, 165, 166, **286**.
Weiser, Reuben, 150.
Welden, C. F., 89, 97, 141, 170, **286**.
Welker, Jos., 193, **286**.
Wenrich, S., 74, 75, 76, 77, **286**.
Wetzler, J. N., 28, 32, 33, 34, 37, 38, 104, 142, 176, 177, **287**.
Wilkesbarre, 26.
Willard, Peter, 66, 67, 191, **287**.
Williamsport, St. Mark, 25, 26, 27, 28, **193**.
Williamsport, South, Christ, **199**.
Wilmot Twp., Bradford Co., St. John, **74**.
Witmer, Chas., **287**.
Woerner, G. F., **288**.
Wott, W., 47.

Yeager, N., see Jaeger.
Yount, A. L., 28, 77, 196, **288**.

Zeiser, J. N., 47.
Zeller, **289**.
Zeigler, Henry, 191, 193, **289**.
Zizleman, P. F., 26.
Zuber, T., 164, 176, 182, 183, 185, **289**.
Zweier, C. D., 32, 33, 34, 37, 38, **289**.

www.ingramcontent.com/pod-product-compliance
Lightning Source LLC
Chambersburg PA
CBHW051243300426
44114CB00011B/872